The Many Faces of the Southern Baptist Convention

Copyright © 2018, *Revised*
The Southern Baptist Convention Executive Committee

All rights reserved. Passages from this book may be reproduced and distributed by cooperating churches with the Southern Baptist Convention or other Southern Baptist entities for informational purposes only. Non-SBC entities may not reproduce or transmit any part of this book in any form or by any means whatsoever without express written permission from the publisher.

Scripture quotations marked NIV are from The Holy Bible, *New International Version*® NIV® Copyright © 1973, 1978, 1984, 2011 by Biblica, Inc.® Used by permission of Biblica, Inc.® All rights reserved worldwide.

Scripture quotations marked KJV are from The Holy Bible, *King James Version*.

Scripture quotations marked HCSB are taken from the *Holman Christian Standard Bible*, Copyright © 1999, 2000, 2002, 2003 by Holman Bible Publishers. Used by permission.

Scripture quotations marked NKJV are from the *New King James Version*®. Copyright © 1982 by Thomas Nelson. Used by permission. All rights reserved.

Unmarked Scripture quotations are taken from the *Holy Bible*, King James Version, or are the contributing writer's personal paraphrase.

ISBN: 978-0-9980183-2-4

Published by the Southern Baptist Convention Executive Committee
901 Commerce Street
Nashville, Tennessee 37201
www.sbcec.org

About this Project

The Southern Baptist Convention (SBC) adopted twelve action steps in 2011 to encourage increased participation of ethnic minority churches and pastors in the overall fabric of Southern Baptist life. That same year, Frank S. Page, president and CEO of the SBC Executive Committee, appointed the first of numerous ethnic advisory councils to assist the Executive Committee and the Convention's entity leaders to understand and appreciate perspectives ethnic minority churches bring to the Convention's task of reaching our nation and the nations with the Gospel of our Lord Jesus Christ.

The chapters in this book set a contemporary context for the Convention's progress in racial reconciliation, summarize the ethnic advisory councils' reports, and highlight their recommendations to strengthen the Convention's effectiveness in reaching people from every race and language group with the Gospel of Jesus Christ. The writers inform the larger Southern Baptist family on the state of ethnic work within the SBC, reflecting on the Convention's past efforts to reach and include ethnic churches and leaders, assessing the present reality of ethnic church participation in Southern Baptist life, identifying what needs to be done to increase effectiveness of reaching people from every ethno-linguistic group with the Gospel, and suggesting specific action steps for prayer, collaboration, and unity for a Great Commission Advance.

Contents

About this Project iii
Foreword vii
Acknowledgments x
Introduction 11
The Biblical Mandate: *Ta Ethnē* 16
A Demographics Review 26
A Progress Overview 36
African Americans in the SBC 54
Asian Americans in the SBC 83
Hispanics in the SBC 120
Native Americans in the SBC 144
Multi-Ethnic Ministries in the SBC 160
Women in the SBC 171
What the SBC Looked Like 185
Bivocational and Smaller Church Ministry 202
Where do we go from here? 214
Synergy, Cooperation, and Autonomy 218
Endnotes 226
Contributors 243
Index 250

Foreword

Kenneth Weathersby

For many decades, the Southern Baptist Convention has been known as the most culturally diverse evangelical denomination in the United States. This has not happened by chance; for from its inception in 1845, the Southern Baptist Convention expressed a commitment to reach lost souls in America and around the world with the saving message of Jesus Christ.

The task of reaching every ethnic/racial group in America with the Gospel has not been easy because, throughout the years, each of these groups has continued to grow, thus continually changing the cultural face of America. For example, between 2000 and 2015, the African-American population expanded by 23 percent; the Hispanic population by 60.3 percent; the Native American population increased by 62 percent; and the Asian American population grew by 76.1 percent.[1]

From the perspective of percentage population growth, the picture that emerges is that while in 1950 the ethnic/racial groups comprised less than one-fifth of the American population, by 2010 they comprised one-third of the population. By 2050, ethnic/racial groups are projected to comprise more than half of the US population.[2]

These demographic realities clearly illustrate that the cultural face of America is constantly shifting. This leads to the question, "How is the face of the Southern Baptist Convention changing?"

The answer is that in 2017, more than 20 percent of the churches and church-type missions that cooperate with and contribute to the Southern Baptist Convention were predominantly-ethnic/racial congregations. This is supported by the fact that between 2000 and 2015, SBC-related Native American congregations grew by 24 percent; Asian congregations by 52.3 percent; Hispanic congregations by 56.2 percent; African-American congregations by 61.4 percent; and "all other" congregations (including Haitian and multiethnic) grew by 71 percent.[3]

In light of these changing demographics, it is indeed encouraging that in 2015 the Southern Baptist Convention approved a Resolution on Racial Reconciliation that called for Southern Baptists to be more proactive in enlisting participation and representation from ethnic/cultural groups in its boards and entities.

We are indebted to Dr. Frank Page, former president of the SBC Executive Committee, for his passion to lay the foundation and carry forward the recommendations adopted by the SBC in 2011, which concluded the Ethnic Study Committee Report. The report called for greater participation of ethnic churches and church leaders at all levels of Southern Baptist life.

As a response to this 2011 report, and in an effort to seek greater involvement from the ethnic/racial groups participating in SBC life, the SBC Executive Committee was instrumental in appointing numerous advisory councils representing African Americans, Asians, Hispanics, Native Americans, multi-ethnic, and bi-vocational church leaders. The Executive Committee also appointed a Women's Advisory Council and a Young Leaders Advisory Council.[4]

In order to provide leadership and coordination among these groups, I was appointed vice president of convention advancement for the SBC Executive Committee. In turn, I enlisted Paul Kim to serve as Asian relations consultant and Bobby Sena to serve as Hispanic relations consultant in the Office of Convention Advancement.

This collective work contains a number of essays written by representatives from many of these advisory councils. The introduction was written by Roger S. (Sing) Oldham, SBC Executive Committee vice president for convention communications and relations, who was instrumental in crafting the Ethnic Study Committee report and worked closely with each advisory council in its work.

Daniel Sanchez wrote the foundational chapter on "The Biblical Mandate: The *Ta Ethne*," and Richard (Richie) Stanley prepared a "Demographic Review of the Convention." These chapters provide an excellent underpinning for the chapters which follow.

Robert Wilson compiled the chapter on African Americans, and Peter Yanes, Paul Kim, and Minh Ha Nguyen wrote the chapter on Asians. The chapter on Hispanic Americans was written by Daniel Sanchez and Bob Sena, while the information on Native Americans was contributed by Gary Hawkins. The Multi-Ethnic ministries chapter was penned by Lennox Zamore, and Rodney Webb wrote about Anglo church planting. The chapter on bi-vocational and smaller church ministry was scripted by Ray Gilder, and the chapter on women in the SBC was compiled by Rhonda Kelly and Candi Finch.

These chapters provide valuable information on the history of each ethnic/racial group or subset in this country, the establishment and development of Southern Baptist work among them, and the vision that they have for spreading the Gospel and expanding collaboration between them and the SBC.

The book concludes with a review of the progress made in racial reconciliation from 1995 to 2015 in the Southern Baptist Convention. This progress report, adopted by the Executive Committee in 2015 and commended by messengers to the 2015 SBC annual meeting, is truly informative of the positive collaborative steps that Anglo and ethnic/racial leaders have taken to bring about genuine inclusion and participation within the SBC family. At the same time, this report presents a realistic picture of the task that is still before us to demolish walls of partition that remain.

The conclusion, "Where Do We Go from Here?", offers seven points to consider. It is a powerful challenge to the entire SBC family to commit our lives and our ministries to fully implementing the Great Commission.

In closing, I remain very grateful for the work of the Convention Advancement Advisory Council, which works closely with me to continue to actualize the recommendations passed by the Southern Baptist Convention.

Acknowledgments

Kenneth Weathersby

This book has not been the work or achievement of any one person; but rather, it reflects the collective contributions and experiences of many. We salute and express special appreciation to all who have contributed to the undertaking and achievement of this project.

I wish to extend special thanks to Frank S. Page, former president and CEO of the SBC Executive Committee, for his vision and encouragement regarding this venture. From its inception, he gave his full support in allowing this project to proceed.

We also gratefully acknowledge the Virginia Sugg Furrow Foundation, a fund of the Community Foundation for Southern Arizona. This resource is made possible in part by a generous grant from this Foundation.

There are many details needed in completing a project of this size, and I am very grateful to Bobby S. Sena, Hispanic relations consultant with the SBC Executive Committee, for serving as the project facilitator. He provided invaluable assistance and was the moving force in working with the writers to completion. Special thanks, also, to Roger S. (Sing) Oldham, vice president for Convention communications and relations, for his leadership and oversight to the project's completion; Olivia M. Cloud, who edited manuscript and prepared the book for publication; and then, to Andy Beachum, production manager with the SBC Executive Committee, who designed the book cover by adapting artwork created by the North American Mission Board.

I'm grateful for Bobby Sena, Paul Kim, and Betty Sue James who serve faithfully alongside me on the Executive Committee Convention Advancement team.

Above all, we thank our Lord and Savior, Jesus Christ. It is our hope and prayer that the Holy Spirit will utilize this book to change how we see and serve the changing face of our communities, nation, and world. May the Lord give us wisdom, strength, and passion to take the His message to all nations.

Introduction

Roger S. ("Sing") Oldham

Partition. Participation. Partnership. Though these three words begin with the same set of letters, they point to very different outcomes.

Walls of Partition

God's redemptive plan is that people of every nation, tribe, people, and language—equally indwelt by the Holy Spirit and equipped to fill every needed role—will be ushered into His Church. His redemptive plan also pointed to the incarnation of the Messiah, whose sinless shoulders would bear the iniquities of the world.

Jesus was born to Jewish parents, yet He consistently pointed beyond the racial identity of Israel's chosenness as the line of the Messiah to herald God's love for all humanity. Whether it was the cleansing of the temple ("my house shall be called a house of prayer for all nations," Mark 11:17, referencing Isaiah 56:7), or His pointed illustrations about Elijah's ministry to a Gentile widow and Elisha's healing of a Gentile general (Luke 4), or His foray into Samaria where He proclaimed His Messianic identity to a Samaritan woman (John 4), Jesus repeatedly pointed to a time when the "middle wall of partition" between the races would be dismantled and the church would find unity in Christ alone (Ephesians 2:14, KJV; "dividing wall of hostility" in CSB and ESV).

The gathered Church—the collection of saints spanning multiple times and places, all of whom will be assembled in heaven for eternity—is His Bride. The expansion of the early church, as recorded in the book of Acts and beyond, reveals this often overlooked social dimension of the Gospel: namely, that God has made every nation of humankind from one (Acts 17:26). In Christ, we are one (1 Corinthians 12:13; Galatians 3:27–29).

Throughout the book of Acts, the dividing wall of hostility between culturally-distinct groups crumbled in successive layers. The dissolution began with the cultural challenge of ministry to the Hellenistic Jewish widows in Acts 6. The Samaritan revival, recorded in Acts 8, continued the trajectory toward collapse of hostility's divisive wall. Then, the conversion of Cornelius and his household, the first Gentile converts (Acts 10), challenged the tacit assumption that Jesus was singularly the Messiah for the Jews.

Coupled with Barnabas and Paul's successful first missionary journey (Acts 13–14), the early church leaders called a conference to discuss this new phenomenon and all of its implications. Recognizing the unmistakable activity of the Holy Spirit, the Apostles at the Jerusalem Conference formally declared the wall of racial separation between Jew and Gentile should cease (Acts 15), setting the precedent for eradicating division among all races in Christ.

Debris from the collapsing wall, however, often impeded full partnership of the races in worship and service even among the Apostles (Galatians 2). Each successive generation of Christ-followers has had to navigate the rubble of this ever-crumbling wall in their efforts live out this social dimension of the Gospel amid a fallen world.

In the last third of the twentieth century, Southern Baptists adopted numerous resolutions that addressed the sin of partition that largely segmented the American Baptist movement along racial lines. In its historic 1995 Resolution on Racial Reconciliation, the SBC formally "apologize[d] to all African Americans for condoning and/or perpetuating individual and systemic racism in our lifetime" and "genuinely repent[ed] of racism of which we have been guilty, whether consciously or unconsciously."

Five years later, the Convention adopted a revised statement of faith that specifically addressed the biblical truths that every person of every race possesses full dignity and worth (Article III); that heaven will be populated by believers from every tribe, and tongue, and people, and nation (Article VI); and that "[i]n the spirit of Christ, Christians should oppose racism" (Article XV).

Greater Participation

Between 1961 and 1995, the Southern Baptist Convention adopted ten resolutions expressing its desire to see "greater ethnic participation" in SBC life. During those three and one-half decades, the Convention experienced significant growth in the number of non-Anglo congregations cooperating with the SBC, along with an increase in the number of ethnic-minority seminary students trained through the six SBC seminaries.

The Home Mission Board (now North American Mission Board) implemented specific church planting and evangelism strategies to reach and engage multiple ethnic and language groups with the Gospel. By the mid-1990s, the HMB reported that on any given Sunday the Lord was worshiped in more than one hundred languages across the United States through churches that cooperated with the SBC.

In 1994, African American pastor Gary Frost was elected as second vice president of the SBC. Re-elected in 1995, he was one of the principal participants in helping frame the historic 1995 Resolution on Racial Reconciliation. After the resolution was adopted, Frost responded to the resolution and led the Convention in a prayer of forgiveness and reconciliation.

Over the next fifteen years, incremental changes at various leadership levels occurred, as African American, Hispanic, and Asian pastors were elected SBC second vice president and selected to serve as senior staff at several SBC entities. At the state level, one-half of the forty-two cooperating state conventions elected one or more individuals from ethnic minorities to serve one- or two-year terms as president of their conventions. A small number of individuals were also elected to serve on SBC boards and committees.

Steps Toward Partnership

Despite these small steps, by 2009 it was apparent that full participation of ethnic minorities in elected and appointed roles in SBC life lagged behind the growth in the number of ethnic congregations and church members that cooperated with the Convention. That year, Korean pastor Paul Kim asked the Convention to study ways to increase participation of ethnic churches and church leaders in the total fabric of Convention life. His motion resulted in a two-year SBC Executive Committee study that called for intentional, measurable steps toward greater inclusion of all Southern Baptists in Convention processes.

In 2011, twelve recommendations contained in the report were adopted by the SBC. That same year the first of numerous ethnic minority advisory councils was appointed by Frank Page, elected in 2010 as president and CEO of the SBC Executive Committee.

Reports of these advisory councils consistently revealed a glaring void in the life of the SBC. Though SBC entity ministries and ministries at state convention and local levels engaged in numerous ministries to people of various racial and ethnic minority groups, these ministries frequently failed to yield full partnership from the targeted groups. A common refrain across the Convention's ethnic minority churches—and echoed during the councils' deliberations—was that ethnic minority church leaders want to be viewed as more than a *mission field* of the SBC (the objects of mission and ministry); they want to be part of the Convention's *mission force*, valued and respected for their contributions as equal partners in reaching the peoples of our nation and the world with the Gospel.

Southern Baptists of every ethnicity embrace the doctrinal positions espoused by the Convention: personal conversion from sin through faith in Jesus Christ alone; the inerrancy of Scripture; baptism as an external sign of the inner working of God's grace; regenerate church membership; fidelity to a biblical world view in matters of ethics and morality; and commitment to the Great Commission—to proclaim the Gospel, making disciples of all the people and peoples of the world (*mathēteusate panta ta ethnē*, Matthew 28:19).

And yet . . . too often these brothers and sisters in Christ feel marginalized from Convention processes. For generations, white Southern Baptists have largely shaped the culture of the Convention. They have made the decisions about how Cooperative Program funds are distributed through state Baptist convention and SBC ministries. They have stood before SBC messengers as the visible leaders of the Convention. They have filled the vast majority of executive and administrative leadership positions. They have promoted the ministries they believe best represent the biblical mandates outlined in Scripture.

Our work is not done, and we will continue striving for a Southern Baptist Convention that reflects the diversity of God's kingdom. This book is a brief summary of the findings of six advisory councils appointed by Dr. Page. Members of the various councils represent more than two dozen ethnic groups and cultural subsets within those groups that identify as Southern Baptist. Their reports face two directions. First, they challenge members within their ethnic minority fellowships to take the lead in proclaiming the Gospel and making disciples of the nations residing in the United States and abroad. Second, their reports call on current Southern Baptist leaders to recognize that the Holy Spirit has called, gifted, and equipped leaders from every racial and ethnic group in the SBC to serve as full partners in leading our Convention to achieve its Kingdom-focused objectives—to the praise of the glory of His grace!

PART ONE
Many Faces, One Convention

- *Ta Ethnē*: The Biblical Mandate —Daniel Sanchez
- A Demographics Review — Richard Stanley
- A Progress Overview: Report of the SBC Executive Committee

The Biblical Mandate: Ta Ethnē

Daniel Sanchez

The teachings of Scripture are essential and foundational to anything we do in the Lord's name. In this book, we endeavor to challenge and encourage Southern Baptists to reach every ethnic group and population segment with the Gospel of Jesus Christ.

While there are ethical and social reasons why we would be motivated to share the Good News of salvation with all the world, we must ensure that we have a strong biblical foundation in this endeavor. In the Word of God we find a clear and compelling mandate to lead everyone in every nation to Jesus Christ. In order to accomplish this, in this chapter we will focus on understanding the biblical mandate and implementing that command.

Understanding the Biblical Mandate

If we ask Christians whether they know what the Great Commission says, most of them will answer: "Yes, of course." However, if we probe, most of them will give evidence that they do not fully understand it and sadly enough, the vast majority of them are not putting it into practice in their daily lives. Considering that these were the last instructions Jesus gave His followers, it is extremely important that we understand precisely what He said and then make the commitment to obey it.

Before His ascension, Jesus gave His final instructions to His followers: "All authority has been given to Me in heaven and on earth. Go therefore and make disciples of all the nations, baptizing them in the name of the Father and of the Son and of the Holy Spirit, teaching them to observe all things that I have commanded you; and lo, I am with you always, even to the end of the age" (Matthew 28:18–20, NKJV).

In order for us to fully understand Jesus' mandate and be motivated to put it into practice daily, it is important for us to have a clear understanding of the authority of the One who sends, the command that He gives, the scope of His command, and the promise that He gives.

The Authority of the One Who Sends

The post-resurrection account of the Gospels helps us to understand the events that unfolded immediately thereafter. Verses 16 and 17 of Matthew 28 reads: "Then the eleven disciples went away into Galilee, into a mountain where Jesus had appointed them. And when they saw him, they worshipped him: but some doubted" (KJV). To dispel any doubts, Jesus appeared to them once more. He had appeared to the women who had gone to the tomb (Matthew 28:9–10). He had appeared to the disciples while Thomas was absent (see John 20). When the apostles told Thomas they had seen the Lord, Thomas replied: "Unless I see the nail marks in His hands and put my finger where the nails were, and put my hand into His side, I will not believe" (John 20:25, NIV). When Jesus appeared to the disciples with Thomas present, He said: "Reach your finger, here, and look at my hands, and reach your hand here, and put it on My side. Do not be unbelieving, but believing" (v. 27, NKJV). Thomas responded: "My Lord, and my God!" (v. 28).

By the time of Jesus' final appearance to the disciples, they were fully convinced that their Teacher had risen from the dead. It is very likely that the ones who doubted were others that were present at the ascension of the Lord. Paul indicated that over five hundred were present at the ascension, most of whom were still alive when he wrote to the Corinthians (1 Corinthians 15:6). There is clear evidence that the vast majority who gathered to hear Christ's last instructions were convinced that they were listening to the risen Lord and Savior.

Believers often begin their recitation of the Great Commission with the words "go and make disciples." While it is true that Jesus did say this, it is extremely important to know what He said before giving this command. The apostles had seen the evidence of Jesus' power over nature (when He calmed the storm in Mark 6); over demons (when He liberated the Gadarene demoniac in Mark 5); over sickness (when He restored the sight to the blind man in Mark 8); over death (when He raised Lazarus, (see John 11); and when He rose from the dead (John 20). They also had seen Jesus teach with authority, which came only from God (Matthew 7:29). At His ascension, Jesus assured His followers that "all authority" (*pasa exousia*), "has been given to me" (*edothe*), which means that there is no limit to the time (it has been given to Him forever) and no limit to the expanse (for it is "in heaven and on earth"). This means that no area, no people, no culture lies beyond the domain of His power and authority. Having risen, He now has exalted authority over the whole world.

It is important to note that authority precedes mandate. The mandate does not come from someone who wishfully hopes that somehow we might be able to fulfill it. Rather, it comes from the resurrected, exalted, empowered Christ who is able to provide all of the resources needed to fulfill His command. If we have any doubts about being able to fulfill the mandate, we must remember that the one who sends is the one who has all of the power to equip us to fulfill it.

Are there times when you feel that someone is simply "too resistant" to the Gospel message? Perhaps you have already tried to witness to someone who just hasn't shown any interest. Do you sometimes wonder whether certain cultural groups are simply too committed to their religious traditions, and no matter what you say or do they have already determined that they are not going to be receptive? While it is only human to feel this way, we need to remind ourselves that Jesus has all the power in every single location of the earth to empower us to share the message of salvation and to bring people to faith in him. We are not witnessing in our power or through our intelligence, but rather, through the power of the resurrected Savior. We need to remember that Saul of Tarsus was a persecutor of the Church and was even an accomplice in the murder of Stephen. However, when he had an encounter with the resurrected Christ, he responded, "Lord, what do You want me to do" (Acts 9:6, NKJV). The power of the ascended Christ was so real in the Apostle Paul's life that he became an instrument for spreading the Gospel throughout the known world. So convinced was he of Christ's power that he said: "I can do all things through Christ who strengthens me" (Philippians 4:13, NKJV).

His Command

After making it clear that He has all authority, Jesus gave the missionary mandate in Matthew 28:19–20: "As you are going, make disciples, of all nations, baptizing them in the name of the Father and of the Son and of the Holy Ghost, and lo I am with you always, even to the end of the world" (personal translation).

In the Greek, the words going, baptizing, and teaching are all participles. In a sense, they explain how the Great Commission is to be carried out. The mandate is "make disciples" (*mathēteusate*). The imperative of the command of Christ involves more than exposing people to the Gospel message or even guiding them to make decisions (which is the starting point). Making disciples involves leading people to receive Jesus as Savior and Lord, and to become an integral part of His church as lifelong followers, learners, and ministers working toward the expansion of His kingdom. That is why we emphasize evangelism (leading people to make a decision for Christ), as well as discipleship (assembling in congregations of faith where new believers can grow in their knowledge of Jesus Christ and become evangelists and disciple makers).

The Scope of His Command: "...all nations"

The Greek word for "nations" is *ta ethnē*, which is where we get the word "ethnic." This means that all people groups need to be reached with the Gospel and discipled. In order to implement the command, Christ followers must cross linguistic, sociological, racial, cultural, religious, ideological, generational, and geographical boundaries. Another way of stating this is that churches need to be planted among all segments of all societies around the world. Every barrier to the Gospel needs to be bridged by establishing churches that are as near to the unchurched as possible, not only geographically, but also socially, speaking their language and reflecting their culture.

As we seek to carry out Jesus' command to make disciples of all people groups, we need to ask ourselves: What cultural groups and population segments in this country and around the world are not being witnessed to? The answer to this question should motivate us to do everything within our means—personally and through the use of our resources—to make it possible for unreached people groups to hear and respond to the Good News of salvation.

To obey the *ta ethnē* focus of the Great Commission, we must commit to reach every people group and population segment in America for Christ. Simultaneously, we must go to unreached people groups around world, thus reaching our "Jerusalem, Judea, Samaria and to the ends of the world" (Acts 1:8).

The Promise that He Gives

Chapters 16 and 18 of Matthew's Gospel reveal two powerful and reassuring promises. In Matthew 16:18, Jesus promises: "I will build my church and the gates of hell shall not prevail against it." It is clear from this passage that the establishment and expansion of the Church is first and foremost a divine endeavor. Jesus has promised to build His church and He never made a promise that He could not keep.

The picture Jesus gives of His Church is not one that defensively survives the onslaught of the enemy, but one that aggressively tears down the enemy's strongholds and rescues people with the Gospel of salvation.

Second, in Matthew 28:20, Jesus promises always to be with His followers as they obey His command: "and lo, I am with you always, even to the end of the age."

In the Greek, *ego meta humon* means that the resurrected Christ promises His spiritual presence will be with His followers in every life situation as they continue to obey His command to "make disciples." Jesus promises to be with His disciples and His Church until He brings human history to the conclusion He has determined. There will not be a time when He will not be with followers who are doing His will and obeying His command.

The expression, "to the end of the age" assures us that He will not rescind His command until He has accomplished His purpose. His church has gone through many trying times throughout her long and arduous history, but true followers have never been without His presence.

Let's look for a moment at the ways in which the word "all" is used in the Great Commission—all power, all peoples, all the commands, and all of the time. In other words, the one who has all power sends us to make disciples of all people groups, teaching them all of the things He has commanded. He will be with us all of that time. As A. T. Robertson so aptly states: "The blessed hope is not designed as a sedative to an inactive mind and complacent conscience, but an incentive to further endeavor to pass on to the farthest limits of the world that all the nations may know Christ and the power of His Risen life."[1]

Implementation of the Biblical Mandate

A clear understanding of the biblical mandate will motivate us to do everything within our power to put it into practice daily. Today there are many opinions on how the Great Commission can be fulfilled. Some have such a broad definition that almost everything they do is considered Great Commission activity. But how did Jesus' early followers put the mandate into practice? To answer this question definitively, we can go to God's Word and examine what two churches did to obey Jesus' mandate—the Jerusalem Church and the Antioch Church.

The Jerusalem Church Initiated the Mandate

In Acts 2:40–47 we find a description of how Jesus' followers put His mandate into practice. Here, Peter witnessed (*diemartúrato*) to the crowd that had gathered at Pentecost (v. 40). Then, among those who heard, many "gladly received" the word, "were baptized" (*ebaptísthesan*), and "the same day there were added unto them about three thousand souls." The apostles followed Jesus' command to baptize in the name of the Father and of the Son and of the Holy Spirit. Then, the new believers were not abandoned to fend for themselves. Through the ordinance of baptism they were incorporated into the Church, but that was not the end of their experience.

After baptism, "they continued steadfastly in the apostles' doctrine and fellowship" (v. 42). This means that there was ongoing discipleship. The apostles did not forget that Jesus had instructed them to continue in the discipling process: "Teaching them to observe all things (*pánta ósa*) whatever I commanded you." They continued in fellowship (*koinonía*) as they added believers. There was genuine camaraderie in which they rejoiced as members of the Body of Christ. In this spirit of fellowship they celebrated by bread breaking, following the ordinance that Jesus had given them in the upper room prior to His death.

We also find that the newly-formed church engaged in prayer. Through Jesus, they were in communication with God as they prayed. As they continued in prayer, another promise of the Great Commission became vividly evident: "and behold I am with you." The expression in Greek (*ego eimi*) communicates that Jesus would be personally present with His followers. Verse 43 gives evidence of God's presence and power, as "many wonders and signs were done by the apostles."

Verses 44 and 45 describe the marvelous unity of the newly formed church at Jerusalem, and the inspiring way they ministered to various needs among their fellowship. Verse 46 describes the manner in which the new Christians went outside their own place of worship and into homes to fellowship and celebrate the presence of God with joy and genuine adoration. The devotion and generosity of the believers impacted the outsiders, for they were "having favor (*xárin*) with all the people." As a result, "The Lord added to the church daily those who were being saved" (v. 47, NKJV) Undoubtedly, seeing this, the apostles were reminded of Jesus' promise: "I build my church and the gates of hell shall not prevail against it" (Matthew 16:18).

From this brief study of Scripture we can obtain a clear understanding of how Jesus' disciples put the Great Commission into practice. They communicated the message of salvation, baptized the believers, spent time discipling them, and then further engaged them in worship, prayer, and celebration of the Lord's Supper. New disciples were encouraged to participate in caring fellowship and to accept ministry and leadership roles to the body of Christ as well as to unbelievers.

Based on these teachings we can reasonably assert that the disciples worked toward the implementation of the Great Commission by sharing the Good News of salvation and gathering believers into local congregations that contributed toward the spreading of the Gospel.

The Antioch Church Expanded the Mandate

While it is inspiring to read how the church in Jerusalem grew, we might ask, Why did it take so long for the Church to expand beyond its borders? Could it be that even though they had heard the Great Commission, Jesus' disciples still had not captured the vision about expanding the Gospel? We find one of the clues to this in the apostles' last question to Jesus before His ascension: "Will you at this time restore the kingdom to Israel?" (Acts 1:6).

The disciples had heard Jesus speak repeatedly about proclaiming the Gospel throughout the world. In Mark 16:15 He told them: "Go into all the world and preach the gospel to every creature." In Matthew 24:14 He told them: "And this gospel of the Kingdom shall be preached in all of the world for a witness unto all nations; and then the end will come." Despite their Master's instructions to branch out, however, the disciples focused primarily on their own cultural group.

In response to the disciples' question, the resurrected Christ reiterated the Great Commission: "But you shall receive power when the Holy Spirit has come upon you; and you shall be witnesses to Me in Jerusalem, and in all Judea and Samaria, and to the end of the earth," (Acts 1:8, NKJV).

The first seven chapters of Acts detail the expansion of the Jerusalem church. It almost seems as if the disciples heard Jesus say, "And you shall be witnesses unto me in Jerusalem and in Jerusalem and in Jerusalem," because that is where they stayed. Included in these chapters is an introduction to Saul and the stoning of Stephen, the first Christian martyr (Acts 7).

Acts 8 opens by painting a picture of the tumultuous conditions to which the early believers were subjected: "At that time a great persecution arose against the church which was at Jerusalem; and they were all scattered throughout regions of Judea and Samaria, except the apostle." (NKJV). It is interesting to note that it took Acts 8:1 to start implementing Acts 1:8! This leads us to ask the vital question: What will it take on a personal, congregational, and denominational level for us to implement the Great Commission today?

In Acts 11:19, the biblical narrative explains how the Gospel was spread to broader regions: "Now they which were scattered abroad upon the persecution that arose about Stephen travelled as far as Phoenicia, and Cyprus, and Antioch, preaching the word to none but unto the Jews only." These were refugees fleeing religious persecution, but they are to be greatly commended for preaching the Word unceasingly, even while they were displaced in foreign lands. It is inspiring to see their zeal for the Lord and their commitment to be witnesses unto the

Lord. It is also understandable that they spoke primarily to their own cultural group, for it is estimated that there were at least 50,000 Jews in Antioch. They certainly understood their language and their customs, so it made perfect sense for them to start by evangelizing their own cultural and linguistic group. But there is a question that we cannot avoid: "What would have happened to the implementation of the Great Commission if they had confined themselves to their own cultural group?"

In connection with this, there is another question we cannot escape: How many Acts 11:19 churches do we have today? While it makes sense to start with the people whose language and culture we understand, it goes directly against the spirit of the Great Commission to focus exclusively on our own group. Christ did not intend for His disciples to ignore all of the other ethnic and cultural groups that desperately need the message of salvation. Is there reason for us to stop here and pray a prayer of repentance and seek the Lord's guidance in obeying His Great Commission?

Thank God for Acts 11:20, which reads: "And some of them were men of Cyprus and Cyrene, which, when they were come to Antioch, spake unto the Greeks, preaching the Lord Jesus." These were Jewish Christians who had been born outside of Israel. Their contact with Gentiles equipped them to understand their culture and language and to feel so much compassion for them that they wanted to share the Gospel message. We need Christians who are so committed to obey the command of Jesus that they are willing to cross all barriers to share the Good News of the Savior. We need churches that are willing to look at their communities and make a conscious decision to reach all surrounding cultural groups with the message of salvation.

The emphasis of this book is to reach all of the ethnic groups and population segments with the Gospel. This means that majority churches, as well as minority churches, must be willing to emulate the men of Cyprus and Cyrene and stretch beyond their own cultural group to reach America for Christ.

The task is not easy, and often may seem overwhelming; however, we have the promise of Christ's presence. It is indeed inspiring to read in verse 21, "And the hand of the Lord was with them: and a great number believed and turned to the Lord." We could paraphrase this verse and say: "And the Jesus who promised to be with them as He gave the Great Commission was right there with them when they were implementing it; and a great number believed and turned unto the Lord." O how we yearn for the hand of the Lord to be upon us and upon our churches! We can safely say that when we are going into the world and making disciples, the presence of the Lord will be with us in a tangible way.

The remainder of chapter 11 tells us that when the Jerusalem church received the news of how the Gospel spread in Antioch, they sent Barnabas to investigate what had happened. When he got there, he saw the "grace of God" (v. 23).

Barnabas then went to Tarsus and got Saul and together they ministered at this missionary church. We cannot overlook that it was at Antioch that Christ followers were first called Christians (v. 26). It was also this church, comprised of Jews and Gentiles, that collected an offering for the Jewish Christians who were experiencing famine in Jerusalem (vv. 27–30). A church that is willing to fulfill the Great Commission is also willing to break down the walls of partition that this world erects between the cultural groups (Ephesians 2:14, 15).

Acts 13 gives further detail of the Antioch church's trailblazing efforts to implement the Great Commission. Verse 1 reveals the cultural and socio-economic diversity among the church's leadership. Manaen was the half-brother of Herod. Saul was highly educated. Some scholars believe that Simeon, called Niger, was of African heritage, and some speculate that he may have been the one who carried Jesus' cross. We have no way of knowing, but we can conclude that this church was open to diversity among its leaders.

A clear example of the missionary spirit at Antioch is that "As they ministered to the Lord and fasted, the Holy Spirit said, 'Now separate me Barnabas and Saul for the work to which I have called them'" (v. 2, NKJV). Now, this church could have said, "No, Lord, these are our best leaders, how can we give them up?" Aside from that they could have said, "Saul is a tent maker and he tithes to our church. If he leaves, this will affect our budget." It is good for us to reflect on the excuses we use before the Lord for not investing ourselves and our resources in the Lord's work.

It is truly inspiring to read: "And when they had fasted and prayed, and laid their hands on them, they sent them away" (v.3, KJV). Can this be said of our churches as we focus on the dire need to reach the people groups and population segments in our nation for Christ?

G. Campbell Morgan addressed how the Church at Antioch was constituted:

> Certain men of Cyprus and Cyrene had preached in Antioch to these Greek men the Gospel of the Lord Christ; and these men hearing the Gospel of the Lord Christ had believed and been baptized by the Holy Ghost, constituted the Church. There had been no consecration of a building. There had been

no apostolic visitation. The Church was not the result of official action, but of proclamation of the Lord and belief in Him and baptism into His life, by the overruling God.. In that church in Antioch were gifts bestowed by the Spirit: prophets and teachers. Whence came these gifts? From the Lord himself. How? By the bestowment of the Holy Spirit.[2]

Conclusion

The Great Commission is clear and compelling. Matthew 28:19–20 offers an explanation of the authority of the One who sends, the command that He gives, the scope of His command, and the promise that He gives. The fact that Jesus promises to be with us "to the end of the age" assures us that His commission has not been rescinded or modified. We are still under the mandate to make disciples of all people groups.

The ministry of the Jerusalem church reveals the manner in which the disciples implemented the Great Commission. Preaching the Gospel message, incorporating the believers into the church through baptism, and enabling the believers to worship the Lord in a fellowship of love and ministry made it possible for the message of salvation to spread rapidly and reach unbelievers.

The Antioch Church is an inspiring example of a congregation that understood the Great Commission and was willing to make any sacrifices necessary for the Gospel message to spread to the ends of the earth.

The contributing writers of this book have a deep burden to reach all of America for Christ. Each of the cultural groups represented is an important segment of the population of this country. May the Lord give us a vision to be His instruments in fulfilling the Great Commission so that it can truly be said of us personally and as congregations: "And the hand of the Lord was with them" (Acts 11:21, KJV).

A Demographics Review

Richard (Richie) Stanley

The landscape of the United States has changed in many ways since the year 2000, not the least of which is demographically. This chapter will compare population shifts among ethnic and racial groups of the population with comparable changes in the makeup of congregations (churches and church-type missions) that cooperate with the Southern Baptist Convention (SBC).

Population Trends

Table 1 shows the change in the ethnic and racial makeup of the population during the past fifteen years. White non-Hispanic (also referred to as Anglo) population had modest growth of less than 2 percent. Hispanics experienced the greatest numeric growth (21.3 million persons), while Asians had the fastest rate of growth, 76 percent.

Table 1
Population[1] by Racial and Ethnic Groups

Racial/Ethnic[2] Group	Population 2000	Population 2015	Change Numeric	Percent
White Not Hispanic	194,552,774	197,970,812	3,418,038	1.8%
Hispanic	35,305,818	56,592,793	21,286,975	60.3%
African American	34,658,190	42,632,530	7,974,340	23.0%
Native American	2,475,956	4,010,885	1,534,929	62.0%
Asian[3]	10,641,833	18,742,385	8,100,552	76.1%
Total Population	281,421,906	321,418,820	39,996,914	14.2%

Table 2
Percent of the Total Population in Each Major Racial/Ethnic Category

Racial/Ethnic Group	Percent of the Population 2000	2015	Percent of Total Growth
White Not Hispanic	69.1%	61.6%	8.5%
Hispanic	12.5%	17.6%	53.2%
African American	12.3%	13.3%	19.9%
Native American	0.9%	1.2%	3.8%
Asian	3.8%	5.8%	20.3%

Further evidence of demographic shifting is found in Table 2. During the 15 years between 2000 and 2015, the Anglo percentage of the US population decreased from 69.1 to 61.6 percent. Each of the other ethnic and racial groups increased its share of the population, led by Hispanics with 17.6 percent in 2015, compared to only 12.5 percent in 2000. Also, the numeric growth of 21.3 million Hispanics accounted for more than half (53.2 percent) of the total growth of 40 million during the period.

The growth of 8.1 million Asians resulted in a substantial increase of their proportion of the population, from 3.8 to 5.8 percent. And although the numeric growth of African Americans was also about 8 million, their share of the population remained relatively constant, increasing from 12.3 to 13.3 percent.

Increasing Diversity within the Southern Baptist Convention

In many ways, the SBC has mirrored population trends in the United States. Table 3 shows changes in the number of congregations for six racial and ethnic groups from 2000 to 2015. As was true with the population, the slowest growing group in the SBC is the Anglo (White non-Hispanic) group. The change among Anglo congregations was only 3.4 percent, compared to 11.4 percent overall growth in SBC congregations (the phrase, "SBC congregations," is used in this chapter to refer to churches and church-type missions that cooperate with the SBC).

There is a misconception among some Southern Baptists that the Convention would be in decline except for non-Anglo growth. Although this statement is false, it is certainly true that growth among other racial and ethnic groups has greatly impacted the Convention's congregational growth.

The largest numerical growth occurred among the African American racial group, with a net gain of 1,425 congregations. The Hispanic ethnic group also fared well, gaining 1,234 congregations.

Asian congregations also experienced a healthy numeric growth of 665, a growth rate of more than 50 percent. While it is beyond the scope of this chapter to provide details for all Asian subgroups, there is strong and significant SBC work among Koreans (872 congregations in 2015), Chinese (245), Filipinos (192), Vietnamese (151), and others.

The Native American growth rate of 24 percent was more modest, but still exceeded the Anglo rate of 3.4 percent.

Another interesting phenomenon is the growing number of churches that describe themselves as multi-ethnic or multi-racial. Included in the Other category, the number of multi-ethnic congregations grew from 148 in 2000 to 288 in 2015, an increase of 95 percent.

The Convention also has very strong work among Haitians, numbering 503 congregations in 2015. Haitian congregations are included in the Other category.

Table 3
Southern Baptist Congregations[4] by Racial and Ethnic Groups

Racial/Ethnic Group[5]	Congregations 2000	Congregations 2015	Change Numeric	Change Percent
White Not Hispanic	39,268	40,597	1,329	3.4%
Hispanic	2,195	3,429	1,234	56.2%
African American	2,322	3,747	1,425	61.4%
Native American	354	440	86	24.3%
Asian	1,271	1,936	665	52.3%
Other[7]	755	1,295	540	71.5%
Totals	46,165	51,444	5,279	11.4%

A closer comparison of the percentage growth of population and SBC congregations makes it possible to determine if Convention growth has matched population growth. For example, the Anglo population growth rate from Table 1 was 1.8 percent, and the corresponding growth rate in congregations from Table 3 was 3.4 percent. This implies that the modest growth among Anglo congregations slightly outpaced

Table 4
Ratio of Population per SBC Congregation by Racial and Ethnic Groups

Racial/Ethnic Group	Ratio 2000	Ratio 2015
White Not Hispanic	4,954	4,876
Hispanic	16,085	16,504
African American	14,926	11,378
Native American	6,994	9,116
Asian	8,373	9,681
Overall	6,096	6,248

the corresponding population growth. Another way to make a similar comparison is to calculate and compare the ratio of population per SBC congregation in 2000 and 2015. Table 4 shows these ratios by racial/ethnic group.

Focus again on the white non-Hispanic (Anglo) comparison. Since the congregational growth rate outpaced the population growth rate, one would expect an improvement in the ratio of population per congregation from 2000 to 2015. Indeed, Table 4 shows that the ratio of Anglo population per Anglo congregation decreased from 4,954 in 2000 to 4,876 in 2015.

Conversely, population growth was faster than growth in congregations for both Native Americans (63 percent versus 24 percent) and Asians (76 percent versus 52 percent). This resulted in increases in the ratio of population per SBC congregation for these two groups in Table 4.

African American Population and Growth Trends: A Closer Look

African Americans comprise the third largest population segment in the United States and have the second largest number of SBC congregations. Furthermore, Table 5 shows that the share of SBC congregations classified as having an African American majority increased from 5 percent in 2000 to more than 7 percent in 2015.

The increase of 1,425 congregations from 2000 to 2015 was more than any group, including Anglos. (Refer to Table 3.)

Table 5
Percent of SBC Congregations by Racial and Ethnic Groups

Racial/Ethnic Group	Percent of Congregations 2000	2015	Percent of Total Growth
White Not Hispanic	85.1%	78.9%	25.2%
Hispanic	4.8%	6.7%	23.4%
African American	5.0%	7.3%	27.0%
Native American	0.8%	0.9%	1.6%
Asian	2.8%	3.8%	12.6%
Other	1.6%	2.5%	10.2%

The momentum of Southern Baptist work among African Americans is impressive. Table 4 reveals that the growth rate of African American congregations of 61 percent far outpaced the population growth of 23 percent for this group. As a result, the ratio of African Americans per SBC congregation improved dramatically, from 14,926 in 2000 to 11,378 in 2015.

Table 6 gives an even more dramatic view of the strengthening work among African Americans. Back in 1990, only 568 African American SBC congregations existed, in comparison to a US population of nearly 30 million African Americans. That equated to a ratio of more than 50,000 persons per congregation. Each five-year period from 1990 to 2010 saw a significant increase in African American congregations relative to the corresponding population increase.

It is a concern, however, that the increase in African American congregations since 2010 has become stagnant, with a net gain of only 213. Future projections for growth in the African American population are given in the bottom portion of Table 6. For the ratio of population per congregation to reach the levels suggested, a new emphasis on planting and conserving African American congregations is needed.

Because African American population growth is less rapid than some minorities, projecting just modest net growth of 686 congregations from 2015 to 2030, 991 from 2030 to 2045, and 1,208 from 2045 to 2060 would result in lowering the ratio to 9,000 by 2060. More robust growth of churches would lower the ratio even more.

Table 6
African American Population per SBC African-American Congregation, 1990 to 2015

Year	African-American Population	African-American SBC Congregations	Population per Congregation
1990	29,986,060	568	52,792
1995	33,144,000	1,665	19,906
2000	34,658,190	2,322	14,926
2005	37,909,341	3,038	12,478
2010	40,250,635	3,534	11,390
2015	42,632,530	3,747	11,378
Future	**Projections**	**Needed Congregations for This Ratio**	
2030	48,768,000	4,433	11,000
2045	54,244,000	5,424	10,000
2060	59,693,000	6,633	9,000

Church planters and others often ask where the greatest needs are among population segments. Seven counties in the US have African American population per SBC congregation ratios of more than 100,000. They are listed in Table 7.

Table 7
Counties with Largest African-American Population per SBC Congregation, 2015

County	State	Population per Congregation
Nassau County	New York	172,360
Queens County	New York	160,617
King County	Washington	143,352
Kings County	New York	114,562
Essex County	New Jersey	111,050

Each February, the Census Bureau publishes factoids for use during African American History Month. Following are some recent figures published:

- New York State had an estimated 3.8 million African American residents in 2015.
- The District of Columbia had the highest percentage (50.0 percent) followed by Mississippi (38.3 percent).

- In 2014, there were 108,473 businesses owned by African Americans, of which, 31,216 were healthcare and social assistance firms.
- There were 2.2 million African American military veterans in the US in 2015.
- One in five African Americans age 25 and over had a bachelor's degree or higher in 2015. In 2015, 1.9 million attained an advanced degree.
- The median income of African American households was $36,544 in 2015, compared to a national median of $55,775.
- There were 9.8 million African American family households in 2016. Of those families, 45.1 percent were married couples living together.

Hispanics: A Closer Look

Hispanics comprise the second largest population segment in the United Sates and are third in the number of SBC congregations (see Table 1 and Table 3). From 2000 to 2015, the proportion of SBC congregations classified as Hispanic rose from 4.8 percent to 7.3 percent. Hispanic congregations also accounted for 1,234 (23.4 percent) of the net growth of 5,279 of SBC congregations during those fifteen years.

The net gain of 1,234 Hispanic SBC congregations yielded a growth rate of 56 percent. Since the US Hispanic population growth has exploded by 60 percent during the past fifteen years, not even the notable efforts of Southern Baptists have kept pace. Table 8 shows that the population per congregation ratio among Hispanics increased from 16,085 in 2000 to 16,504 in 2015.

The SBC added 500 to 600 Hispanic congregations every five years from 1995 to 2010. A net gain of only 68 congregations was realized between 2010 and 2015. Thus, the population per congregation ratio improved steadily from 1990 to 2010, then worsened (increased) from 2010 to 2015.

Hispanic population projections present a challenging opportunity for Southern Baptists. Improving the population per congregation ratio to an arbitrarily selected 15,000 will require the addition of 808 congregations between 2015 to 2020 and roughly 1,500 congregations every fifteen years through 2060.

Keeping pace with projected population growth will require Southern Baptist to return to the results achieved from 1995 to 2010.

Each of the ten counties listed in Table 9 had a Hispanic population per Hispanic SBC congregation ratio of more than 100,000. Every area of the country is important, yet these counties seem to be key areas for planting Hispanic congregations.

Table 8
Hispanic Population per SBC Hispanic Congregation, 1990 to 2015

Year	Hispanic Population	Hispanic SBC Congregations	Population per Congregation
1990	22,379,000	649	34,482
1995	27,107,000	1,685	16,087
2000	35,306,376	2,195	16,085
2005	43,023,614	2,827	15,219
2010	50,477,594	3,361	15,019
2015	56,592,793	3,429	16,504
Future	**Projections**	**Needed Congregations for This Ratio**	
2020	63,551,000	4,237	15,000
2030	77,463,000	5,164	15,000
2045	98,644,000	6,576	15,000
2060	119,044,000	7,936	15,000

Table 9
Counties with Largest Hispanic Population per SBC Congregation, 2015

County	State	Population per Congregation
Bronx County	New York	401,111
Kings County	New York	256,621
Essex County	New Jersey	178,837
Middlesex County	New Jersey	170,536
New Haven County	Connecticut	148,257
Tulare County	California	146,202
Suffolk County	New York	139,932
Milwaukee County	Wisconsin	138,888
El Paso County	Colorado	111,671
Wayne County	Michigan	101,015

Hispanic Heritage Month is celebrated each year in the United States from mid-September to mid-October. The dates for this celebration were chosen because seven Latin American countries celebrate their independence during these thirty days, including Chile, Costa Rica, El Salvador, Guatemala, Honduras, Nicaragua, and Mexico. Interesting facts shared by the Census Bureau for the 2016 observance are listed below.

- An estimated 119 million Hispanics will live in the United States by the year 2060; Hispanics would then constitute 29 percent of the nation's population.
- The origins of Hispanics in the US were distributed among these countries in 2015.

Country	Percentage
Mexico	63.4%
Puerto Rico	9.5%
El Salvador	3.8%
Cuba	3.7%
Dominican Republic	3.3%
Guatemala	2.4%
Another Country	13.9%

- Nine states have more than one million Hispanic residents: Arizona, California, Colorado, Florida, Illinois, New Jersey, New Mexico, New York, and Texas.
- More than half of all Hispanics reside in the states of California, Florida, and Texas.
- There were 16.2 million Hispanic households in the US in 2015. Of that number, 48 percent were married couples with children.
- The number of US residents age five and over speaking Spanish at home was forty million.
- The median income of Hispanic households was $45,150 in 2015.
- Among Hispanics, 4.7 million (14.8 percent) age 25 and over had at least a Bachelor's degree.
- Foreign-born Hispanic residents totaled 35 percent.
- The number of Hispanic military veterans in 2015 was 1.2 million.
- There were 3.3 million Hispanic-owned companies as of 2012.
- The majority of Hispanic-owned businesses (91 percent) had no paid employees.

Concluding Thought

The United States has been impacted by the realities of world globalization. By 2044, it is estimated there will be no majority population group in the US, as the White non-Hispanic population dips below 50 percent of the total population.

Southern Baptists have a heart for all people and desire to share the Gospel with them. As the United States becomes more diverse in the years ahead, Southern Baptists must continue to diversify and adapt methods to share the truth that Christ died for all people.

A Progress Overview

Executive Committee of the Southern Baptist Convention

At the 1995 annual meeting in Atlanta, Georgia, the Resolutions Committee voted unanimously to present a resolution, "On Racial Reconciliation," for consideration by the Convention. The Resolutions Committee felt that on the historic occasion of the Southern Baptist Convention's 150th anniversary, it was appropriate for the Convention to address aspects of its past that needed to be acknowledged.

The resolution acknowledged that relations with African Americans had been damaged by the role slavery played in the formation of the SBC, lamenting and repudiating "historic acts of evil such as slavery from which we continue to reap a bitter harvest." It repented of racism past and present, saying, "We apologize to all African Americans for condoning and/or perpetuating individual and systemic racism in our lifetime; and we genuinely repent of racism of which we have been guilty, whether consciously or unconsciously." The resolution concluded by committing to pursue "racial reconciliation in all our relationships" for the glory of God.[1]

Gary Frost, then the second vice president of the Convention, spoke in favor of the resolution, calling on messengers from the churches to lead the reconciliation process based on the unifying power of Christ. After the resolution was overwhelmingly adopted by the messengers, Frost, on behalf of African American Christians, accepted the apology and extended forgiveness. He closed by praying for forgiveness for racism in all forms and thanking God for the grace He extends to all people.[2]

Nineteen years later, at the 2014 SBC annual meeting, Alan Cross moved that, in light of the resolution's twentieth anniversary at the 2015 SBC annual meeting, the SBC president assign a task force to assess the progress Southern Baptists have made in racial reconciliation since 1995 and offer recommendations to the

2015 SBC annual meeting regarding "how Southern Baptists, facilitated by the Convention's entities and seminaries, may better reach, make disciples, and raise up leadership from and among diverse racial and ethnic groups in North America." Upon recommendation by the Convention's Committee on Order of Business, messengers referred the motion to the Executive Committee.[3]

Measuring Reconciliation

The Executive Committee determined that the Alan Cross motion largely paralleled a motion made by Paul Kim at the 2009 SBC annual meeting in Louisville, Kentucky, asking the Executive Committee to examine ways in which ethnic churches and church leaders could be more involved in SBC life and leadership.[4] Following a two-year review, the report, *A Review of Ethnic Church and Ethnic Church Leader Participation in SBC Life*, was presented to the messengers at the 2011 annual meeting.[5]

The 2011 report included ten recommendations to the SBC and offered two suggestions to outside groups—ethnic and racial church leaders and the Southern Baptist Pastors' Conference leadership—about ways to expand intercultural diversity in Convention life (see APPENDIX at the conclusion of this report).

The recommendations sought to provide a consistent mechanism for enlisting racial and ethnic church leaders for elected leadership positions in Southern Baptist life, including service on SBC committees and boards; to encourage SBC entities to give special attention to employment and involvement of ethnic church leaders through their ministries; and to increase visibility of diverse Southern Baptists through Convention communications and selection of platform personalities at the SBC's annual meetings. The recommendations were adopted by the messengers, with the requests forwarded to the groups specified in the report.[6]

During deliberations for this present report, members of the Executive Committee considered how racial reconciliation can be measured. Suggestions included (a) whether potential "barriers to participation" in Convention life have been identified and removed; (b) what "markers of inclusion" serve as sign-posts that greater participation is taking place; (c) where "proportional representation" of qualified individuals to positions of leadership and service in Convention processes falls on the continuum of visible and strategic leadership roles; and (d) how or whether the "conversation" about intercultural engagement has changed, especially since the 2011 report was adopted.

This report provides a brief chronological overview of significant events in Convention life from 1995 through 2015 and reviews specific action steps taken since the 2011 recommendations were adopted by the Convention.

A BRIEF CHRONOLOGICAL REVIEW, 1995–2015

Racial Reconciliation Task Force, 1996–1999

Following adoption of the 1995 Resolution on Racial Reconciliation, the SBC Inter-Agency Council (IAC; renamed the Great Commission Council in 1997) named a task force "charged to work toward a strategy and implementation of full racial and ethnic reconciliation."[7] It named Richard Land, president of the Christian Life Commission (now the Ethics and Religious Liberty Commission), as chairman of the task force. In establishing the task force, the IAC called for SBC entity heads "to strive for representation on our boards of trustees, our staffs and faculties, and all other bodies, based on biblical qualifications and embracing the ethnic diversity of the Southern Baptist Convention."[8]

Then-IAC Secretary Paige Patterson told *SBC LIFE* at the time that the IAC had an obligation and an opportunity to profoundly influence progress toward racial reconciliation in the SBC. "As the IAC reflected on the resolution made last year on racial reconciliation," he said at the time, "and as we listened to the thoughts and the counsel of a number of our fellow Southern Baptists of African American ethnic background, we decided it was essential that we take a direct leadership role in putting actual feet to the resolution."[9]

The task force was comprised of representatives of each SBC entity and agency and included African American, Hispanic, and Native American consultants.[10] The Task Force met several times from 1996 through 1998, with its last meeting on January 27, 1999.

Some of the major accomplishments of the Racial Reconciliation Task Force included the following: (a) advised the Executive Committee how to administer funds raised through an "Arson Fund" established during the 1996 SBC annual meeting in New Orleans to assist ninety-five African American churches victimized by arsonists;[11] (b) encouraged the SBC Implementation Task Force, charged to oversee the restructure of the SBC in 1997, to maintain a strong focus on "African American and ethnic ministries";[12] (c) affirmed redirecting the unspent Arson Fund to the SBC seminaries for theological training for African American pastors;[13] (d) urged ethnic fellowship leaders to develop a pool of eligible candidates to serve as SBC trustees "so the SBC

Committee on Nominations can consider these individuals in their selection process";[14] and (e) heard reports about the "unabated" growth in the number of ethnic and language churches being planted and/or choosing to align with Southern Baptists.[15]

SBC and State Baptist Convention Officers

In 1994, the Convention elected a Chinese pastor and an African American pastor as two of its top three officers—Simon Tsoi, pastor of First Chinese Baptist Church in Phoenix, Arizona, was elected as first vice president, while Gary Frost, pastor of Rising Star Baptist Church in Youngstown, Ohio, was elected second vice president.[16] The following year, in 1995, Frost was reelected to serve a second term as second vice president[17] and subsequently served as a consultant to the Racial Reconciliation Task Force.[18]

The year after the resolution was adopted (1996), African American pastor Fred Luter, of Franklin Avenue Baptist Church in New Orleans, was elected as second vice president of the Convention.[19] Luter would later be elected as first vice president of the Convention (2011),[20] and then, in 2012, he was elected by acclamation as the first African American president of the Southern Baptist Convention.[21] He was reelected in 2013, also by acclamation.[22]

In the nineteen SBC officer elections since 1995, the Convention has elected ten presidents to first-year terms (each was also elected to a second term) and thirty-eight first and second vice presidents to one-year terms. Of the ten presidents, one was Native American (Johnny Hunt, elected in 2008 and 2009)[23] and one was African American (Fred Luter, elected in 2012 and 2013).[24]

Of the thirty-eight first and second vice presidents elected since 1995, four have been African American, one Hispanic, and one Korean, representing 15.8 percent of those elected to serve in these roles. Others have been nominated to serve as president, first vice president, or second vice president without being elected,[25] most recently when Korean pastor Dennis Manpoong Kim received 40.7 percent of the vote as the runner-up in the 2014 SBC presidential election.[26]

Numerous African Americans and Chinese Americans, as well as Filipinos, Hispanics, and Japanese Americans, had been elected as state Baptist convention presidents prior to 1995 (in Alaska, California, Hawaii Pacific, Illinois, Michigan, New Mexico, New York, Ohio, Pennsylvania/South Jersey, and Utah/Idaho).[27] The number of state Baptist conventions to elect non-Anglo presidents continued to grow following the 1995 SBC resolution. From 1996 to 2013, twelve additional state conventions joined the ten above in electing almost forty African Americans or individuals from other racial or ethnic groups as state convention presidents.[28] In 2014, Nevada and Tennessee became the twenty-third and twenty-fourth state conventions to have elected African American or other non-Anglo state Baptist convention presidents.[29]

The Baptist Faith and Message, 2000

Building upon the theological framework of the 1995 Resolution, members of *The Baptist Faith and Message* revision committee addressed the sin of racism with both explicit and implicit wording in their proposal to the 2000 SBC annual meeting. Both the 1925 and 1963 versions of *The Baptist Faith and Message (BF&M)* urged Christians to oppose "every form of greed, selfishness, and vice."[30] Among other changes, the 2000 *BF&M* committee added the words "should oppose racism," placing them in the lead position in the sentence, "In the Spirit of Christ, Christians *should oppose racism*, every form of greed, selfishness, and vice..." (emphasis supplied),[31] which was adopted by the messengers at the annual meeting.

More subtly, the committee highlighted the biblical doctrine of the unity of the human race in Article III ("every person of every race possesses full dignity and is worthy of respect and Christian love") and Article VI ("the redeemed of all the ages, believers from every tribe, and tongue, and people, and nation").[32]

Growth in Membership and Numbers of Churches

Under both the Home Mission Board and its successor, the North American Mission Board, church planting initiatives have targeted the underserved urban centers of the United States and Canada. For example, in March 2015, NAMB President Kevin Ezell reported that "more than 58 percent of the churches Southern Baptists started in 2014 were non-Anglo."[33]

This NAMB report reflects a multi-year trend. The growth of racial and ethnic congregations and congregants that voluntarily cooperate with the Southern Baptist Convention has significantly outpaced that of Anglo churches. Between 1998 and 2013, growth in membership of the 40,371 predominantly Anglo churches declined by 2.33 percent (from 14,700,709 in 1998 to 14,658,060 in 2013) while total membership in predominantly non-Anglo churches increased by 115.78 percent (from 637,934 in 1998 to 1,376,504 in 2013). Church membership in predominantly non-Anglo churches now accounts for almost 10 percent of total membership of cooperating Southern Baptist churches, with almost 6 percent being African

American.³⁴ Given that membership in predominantly Anglo congregations reflects varying numbers of other racial and ethnic populations, it is likely that the total percentage of non-Anglo involvement is slightly higher.³⁵

The total number of non-Anglo congregations (churches and church-type missions) also outpaced the percentage growth of Anglo congregations during the same period. In 1998, the Convention reported 44,949 congregations, of which 6,048 were non-Anglo (or 13.45 percent of congregations). By 2013, the number of congregations had grown to 50,474, of which 10,103 were non-Anglo, or 20.02 percent of total congregations.³⁶ The 2014 Annual Church Profile report, which will serve as the basis for NAMB's Center for Missional Research to update these statistics, had not been released at the time this report was prepared.

Fellowships and Networks

Following an organizational meeting in 1993, the National African American Fellowship (NAAF) was formally established in 1994 and celebrated its twentieth anniversary during the 2014 SBC annual meeting in Baltimore. NAAF provides an affinity fellowship for churches and pastors who desire to identify with the doctrinal and missiological vision of the Southern Baptist Convention. Throughout NAAF's twenty-year history, it has been on the front lines of encouraging church planting, enlisting existing churches to become part of the Southern Baptist Convention, and helping African American churches, many of which are new to the Convention, Navigate through SBC culture; Affect individual lives and churches; Actively influence society; and Fulfill the Great Commission.³⁷

The Black Southern Baptist Denominational Servants Network (BSBDSN), chartered in 1997, was designed to connect African American employees of SBC entities for scholarly fellowship and mutual encouragement. The BSBDSN produced six issues of *The Journal of Black Southern Baptist History* between 2003 and 2008;³⁸ honored several key Southern Baptist leaders for their contributions to the advancement of African American participation in Convention causes (for example, during its 2004 annual meeting, the Network honored The Southern Baptist Theological Seminary President R. Albert Mohler Jr. for his commitment to provide black church and intercultural studies at the seminary and his commitment to employ African American faculty and staff);³⁹ and hosted two Southern Baptist African American History Project seminars in conjunction with the 2003 SBC annual meeting in Phoenix, Arizona, and the 2004 SBC annual meeting in Indianapolis, Indiana.⁴⁰

In the inaugural issue of the *Journal*, executive editor-in-chief Sid Smith listed a timeline containing twenty-five milestones of racial progress for African American churches and church leaders in the Southern Baptist Convention. Called "Ten Years of Racial Progress in the SBC, 1992–2002," a few of these findings noted such things as (a) progress in Baptist associations calling African Americans to serve as director of missions; (b) vice presidents elected to serve the International Mission Board and the North American Mission Board as well as one of the seminaries; and (c) Southern Baptist seminaries increasing the number of African American faculty and increasing their focus on African American church studies, "even to the point of a doctoral program in African American Church Leadership."[41]

Other findings noted (d) dramatic increases in attendance at Black Church Leadership Week at Ridgecrest and Glorieta; (e) SBC boards and committees included a "dramatic increase" in African Americans; (f) an African American delivered the annual sermon at the SBC; (g) two state conventions called "a man of color" to serve as executive director; and (h) SBC agencies opening mainstream management positions to African Americans.[42]

The final item on the list pointed to the "exponential proliferation of African American churches in the SBC" as "a contemporary phenomenon in church history," a fact attested to in the previous section of this report.[43]

Members of SBC Committees and Trustee Boards

It is widely perceived that the momentum Smith observed, that "SBC boards and committees included a 'dramatic increase' in African Americans," was not sustained into the twenty-first century. Statistical records of the racial or ethnic identity of individuals elected or appointed to serve on the boards and committees of the Southern Baptist Convention have not been solicited nor kept on a consistent basis, so there is no hard evidence to which one can point without doing an exhaustive review of thousands of individuals appointed to serve on SBC committees and elected to serve on SBC committees and boards.

Using the eighty-three-member Executive Committee as a representative body of the composition of the other board and committees of the Convention, the Executive Committee reviewed its own composition during the twenty years since the adoption of the Racial Reconciliation Resolution. If the membership of the Executive Committee serves as a microcosm of the other boards and committees, the presence of the intercultural make-up of the Convention was (and is) sorely lacking. Of the 249 individuals nominated and elected to serve on the Executive Committee since

1996, no more than eight were from non-Anglo racial or ethnic groups, representing only 3.2 percent of the members nominated and elected to this committee.[44]

The 2011 Report anticipated a formal, consistent mechanism would be set in place to encourage selection of a wider diversity of representation on the boards and committees of the Convention. In 2014, Executive Committee staff discovered that the nomination form used by the Committee on Committees had not been amended in 2011, a situation which has since been remedied (see below).

However, since the Ethnic Study Committee Report was adopted in 2011, as shown in the following section of the report, the three presidents who have been elected have taken the initiative to make appointments that reflect the intercultural diversity of the Convention. The fact that such a careful process on the part of the SBC presidents has yielded a more balanced intercultural mix of nominees points to the need for such a formal mechanism for *all* positions, whether appointed by the SBC President or nominated by the Committee on Committees and the Committee on Nominations.

AN UPDATE ON THE 2011 REPORT

In the four years since the adoption of the ten SBC-focused recommendations contained in the SBC-adopted "Directing the Executive Committee to Study Greater SBC Involvement for Ethnic Churches and Leaders," the following action steps have been taken by various SBC entities, committees, and leaders.

- In tandem with the adoption of the Ethnic Study Report in 2011, EC president and CEO Frank S. Page, during his inaugural Executive Committee report, invited leaders of each SBC entity, the cooperating state Baptist convention executive directors, and presidents of more than twenty ethnic fellowships that participate in Southern Baptist life and ministry to join him in signing an "Affirmation of Unity and Cooperation," pledging trust and cooperation between all ethnicities and races in order to "engage all people groups with the Gospel of Jesus Christ."[45]
- The Executive Committee, as part of its annual "data call" from the Southern Baptist Convention entities, has requested a descriptive report of participation of ethnic churches and church leaders in the life and ministry of the respective SBC entity for 2012, 2013, 2014, and 2015.[46]
- The Executive Committee amended the SBC President's Notebook given to each newly-elected president of the Southern Baptist Convention to include a section encouraging the president to give special attention to appointing individuals

who represent the diversity within the Convention, and particularly ethnic diversity, among his appointees to the various committees under his purview (Committee on Committees, Credentials Committee, Resolutions Committee, and Tellers) and encouraging the president to encourage the selection of annual meeting program personalities by the Committee on Order of Business that represent the ethnic diversity within the Southern Baptist Convention.[47]

- The SBC president reported the ethnic and racial diversity of appointees he selects for the committees under his purview in 2012, 2013, and 2015, with the descriptive information printed in the respective SBC *Daily Bulletins*, SBC *Annual*, or the SBC President's Page on SBC.net.[48]

- The Executive Committee has requested the seven-member SBC Committee on Order of Business (six elected members and the SBC President) to give due consideration to the ethnic identity of program personalities it enlists for each Southern Baptist Convention annual meeting, chronicling each year's program personalities.[49]

- In 2011, the Executive Committee amended the nomination form used by the Committee on Nominations to provide a place where a nominee may indicate his or her ethnic identity, should he or she so choose.[50] During the 2014 SBC annual meeting, the Executive Committee observed that the nomination form used by the Committee on Committees lacked a place where a nominee may indicate his or her ethnic identity. The Executive Committee has since amended the nomination form used by that committee.[51]

- The SBC entities continue to give due consideration to the recruitment of students, production of resources, offering of services, and employment of qualified individuals to serve in the various professional staff positions, on seminary faculty, and as appointed missionaries in order to reflect the intercultural diversity within Southern Baptist life as reported in the annual "data call" report contained in the Ministry Reports submitted to the Cooperative Program committee of the Executive Committee each winter and posted online at SBC.net/CP/Ministry Reports. The Executive Committee Communications Workgroup has reviewed the intercultural component of the Ministry Reports at its February meeting each year since 2011.[52]

- The Executive Committee, through its various publications and news outlets, continues to provide news coverage of interest to individuals of all ethnicities and to carry stories that demonstrate the wonderful works the Lord is accomplishing through the vital ministries of Baptists of "every tribe and tongue and people and nation." A search of *Baptist Press* and *SBC LIFE*, using search terms relative to specific ethnic and racial groups or fellowships such as, for example,

NAAF, Chinese churches, Korean churches, Native American, Deaf ministry, messianic, and a myriad of other terms, will yield scores of returns. Historical articles such as those written on the fiftieth anniversary in 2013 of the Birmingham church bombing[53] and an historical review of ethnic participation in the Convention at the time Fred Luter was elected SBC president in 2012[54] are also routinely sprinkled throughout these two news outlets for Southern Baptists.[55]

- Other Executive Committee-produced publications, such as the *Forged by Faith* film series, *Meet Southern Baptists*, and *The Southern Baptist Convention: A Closer Look*, include images that reflect the diversity of the Convention.[56]

- In concert with the North American Mission Board, the president of the Executive Committee has appointed four ethnic advisory councils (Hispanic, 2011; African American 2012; Asian American, 2013; and Multi-Ethnic, 2014), requesting reports from each advisory council designed to assist the EC, NAMB, and the other SBC entities in understanding and appreciating the perspectives the various racial and ethnic churches and church leaders bring to the common task of reaching the nation and the world with the Gospel, and to provide information, insight, and counsel to NAMB and EC staff relative to the special needs and concerns of the many ethnic churches and church leaders in the Southern Baptist network of churches.[57] The first two have completed their three-year assignments and have submitted their reports to Executive Committee President Frank S. Page. They are posted under the "Ethnic Participation" tab at www.sbc.net/cp/ministryreports/2014/sbcec.asp.

- In concert with the six seminaries and Union University, the Executive Committee hosted an Intercultural Educational Summit to further discussions with numerous racial and ethnic leaders about how best to deliver educational opportunities for God-called pastors from non-Anglo Southern Baptist churches.[58]

- Working in concert, the North American Mission Board and the Executive Committee have hosted the "Many Faces of the SBC" booth in the exhibit hall at the SBC annual meeting in 2012, 2013, 2014, and will again in 2015,[59] and has conducted numerous interviews with ethnic church leaders at the Cooperative Program booth in the exhibit area.[60] The high visibility of the many faces of the SBC in the exhibit hall and in the SBC annual meeting sessions of the SBC has raised the visibility of ethnic church leaders in Convention life and provided numerous opportunities for networking and ministry throughout the Convention.

- The SBC Executive Committee employed its first two non-Anglo professional employees, Diana Chandler, general feature writer/editor,[61] and Ken Weathersby, vice president for Convention advancement,[62] and has subsequently enlisted its first Hispanic and Asian ministry consultants.

- As noted above, the Southern Baptist Convention elected its first African American president in 2012, one of only five presidents over the past forty years who was elected by acclamation in two successive years,[63] and had a Korean presidential nominee in 2014 who received more than 40 percent of the vote.[64]
- In response to the killings of unarmed African Americans in 2014, ERLC hosted a Racial Reconciliation Summit in Nashville in late March 2015.[65]
- In light of the continuing "globalization" of the American population, NAMB hosted a two-day summit in April 2015 of more than twenty Southern Baptist leaders representing numerous ethnic and racial groups to discuss "current outreach efforts" and to "explore how NAMB can effectively help plant churches for diverse populations in cooperation with" the ethnic and racial fellowships that cooperate with the SBC.[66]

SUMMARY AND FINDINGS

The hundreds of pages of information referenced in this brief report demonstrate that much has been accomplished over the past twenty years in regard to increased racial and ethnic diversity in the life of the Convention, both in terms of awareness and participation. The data indicate that many potential barriers to participation have been identified and are being systematically addressed. There are also numerous sign-posts indicating a higher degree of inclusion of individuals of every race and tribe and tongue in the total fabric of Convention life. And, clearly the conversation has changed: increased participation of individuals of all ethnic and racial backgrounds is a topic of intense interest and frequent discussion at all levels of Southern Baptist life.

We rejoice that individuals of many races and ethnicities are routinely nominated and elected to key leadership roles in state Baptist convention and SBC life.

We celebrate the tremendous growth in the number of churches and church members from every kindred and tongue and tribe and nation that we have experienced since 1995.

We applaud the numerous proactive steps our SBC ministry entities have taken to enlist qualified individuals of all races and ethnicities for senior staff positions; to serve on faculty; to be appointed as missionaries and church planters; to write, edit, and produce Christian resources; to service the retirement needs of pastors and church staff; to raise awareness of the moral issues confronting our nation; to equip leaders; and to otherwise serve our churches in a variety of ways.

A Demographics Review

We affirm efforts taken by our ethnic fellowships and advisory councils to promote increased Cooperative Program support in their respective churches, encourage enrollment in all levels of Bible college and seminary training (including Ph.D. programs), challenge church members to respond to God's call for overseas and domestic missions and church planting, and serve as salt and light in their communities.

We humbly acknowledge the appropriateness of having repented of our Convention's past complicity with the systemic racism that marked our country, rather than having challenged our churches and our country to tear down entrenched social structures of inequality, hostility, and prejudice.

We further acknowledge the propriety of clearly stating in our confessional statement that racism is a sin against Almighty God and against our brothers and sisters in Christ.

Indeed, we give thanks that, as a network of autonomous churches, we seek to reflect the intercultural diversity that reflects what the gathered church *will* look like in heaven and *should* look like on earth as a display of God's glory.

However, the materials referenced in this report also reveal that more can and needs to be done. This is especially true in regard to proportional representation on SBC committees and boards.

To that end, the Executive Committee formally and humbly suggests the following action steps be undertaken for at least the next five years so that they become ingrained in our normal way of doing business.

1. That the president of the SBC report the racial and ethnic composition of the committees and group he appoints each year—the Committee on Committees, the Resolutions Committee, the Credentials Committee, and the Tellers—through *Baptist Press*; that the SBC Executive Committee include this report in the *Daily Bulletin*, Tuesday, Part 1; and that the SBC Recording Secretary include this report in the proceedings of the Convention when the president announces his appointments.

2. That each state/regional member of the Committee on Committees have a sufficient number of potential nominees to the Committee on Nominations to recommend to the full Committee on Committees so that the Committee on Committees will be able to propose a Committee on Nominations that reflects the racial and ethnic diversity of the Convention; and that the chairman of the Committee on Committees give special attention that, as much as possible, the final report reflects this intercultural diversity.

3. That each member of the Committee on Nominations solicit a sufficient number of potential nominees for the vacancies on the boards and committees of the Convention for which he or she is responsible so that the full Committee will be able to present to the Convention a list of nominees that builds or sustains equitable racial and ethnic diversity on each SBC board and committee; and that the chairman of the Committee on Nominations give special attention that, as much as possible, the final report reflects this intercultural diversity.

4. That the chairmen of the Committee on Committees and Committee on Nominations report the racial and ethnic composition of the committees and boards they nominate each year (along with other information such as representative church sizes, average CP giving of nominees' churches, baptism ratios, representative ages, and gender considerations) when their reports are released through Baptist Press; that the SBC Executive Committee include these reports in the Daily Bulletin, Tuesday, Part 2; and that the SBC Recording Secretary include these reports in the proceedings of the Convention when the chairmen move the adoption of their respective reports.

5. That the editors of *Baptist Press, SBC LIFE*, and the state Baptist publications make use of the information contained in the annual Ministry Reports submitted by the SBC entities to the SBC Executive Committee each February and the entity reports printed in the SBC Book of Reports each June to tell the good news of what God continues to do through the life and ministry of our SBC entities, giving particular attention to the participation of ethnic churches and church leaders in the ministries of the respective entities.

6. That our cooperating state Baptist conventions, local associations, and racial and ethnic fellowships encourage all cooperating Southern Baptist churches to submit an annual church profile for these prevailing reasons: (1) the information contained in the ACP routinely serves as the basis for determining whether a church, regardless of its racial or ethnic identity, fully cooperates with the Convention, and is used by the SBC President, Committee on Committees, and Committee on Nominations to determine if an appointee or a proposed nominee is "qualified" as representing a fully supportive, cooperating church; (2) it is unlikely that someone from churches that fail to submit an ACP will be selected to serve the Convention, with the result that the diversity their church brings to the Convention remains unknown, uncelebrated, and unrepresented; and (3) the information contained in the ACP becomes part of an aggregated total that serves as a report card to ourselves to inform us on how we are doing as a network of churches to impact the lostness across our nation through evangelism, discipleship, missions, church planting, attendance, and stewardship and to spur

us to address areas of apparent weakness in these key areas of Christian responsibility.

7. That the Executive Committee, each SBC entity, each cooperating state Baptist convention, and each racial and ethnic fellowship seek to educate all Southern Baptist churches, especially those that do not have a history with the SBC, that Cooperative Program giving serves as the primary means of measuring a church's support for its state Baptist convention and SBC missions and ministries. While the Convention celebrates the generous support of Southern Baptists as they channel giving to Great Commission causes through their churches, the Convention voted in 2010 to "continue to honor and affirm the Cooperative Program as the most effective means of mobilizing our churches and extending our outreach," affirming that "designated gifts to special causes are to be given as a supplement to the Cooperative Program and not as a substitute for Cooperative Program giving." (emphasis supplied)

The Executive Committee observes that none of these steps answers the fundamental question about whether reconciliation has occurred in individual Baptists' lives. Reconciliation is, at its core, a spiritual concept. True reconciliation is a condition of the heart. It is a restoring of right relationships between formerly estranged individuals or groups. It begins with fallen individuals being reconciled with God through Jesus Christ (2 Corinthians 5:18–21; Colossians 1:21–23). When separated from its redemptive roots, racial reconciliation, while laudable, is merely a humanistic achievement; but when grounded in the Gospel, it demonstrates the majesty and goodness of God's grace.

Once an individual has been reconciled with God through Jesus Christ, the indwelling Holy Spirit begins a sanctification process in his/her redeemed spirit, targeting such destructive emotions as prejudice, anger, malice, and bitterness (John 4:9–42; Ephesians 4:30–32), replacing them with divine qualities such as love, joy, longsuffering, gentleness, and self-control (Galatians 5:22–23).

Such a radical transformation provides the fertile soil for reconciliation between both individuals and groups. In Christ, the "dividing wall of hostility" between brothers and sisters is torn down (Ephesians 2:14). The Lord creates "in Himself one new man from the two" and reconciles "both to God in one body through the cross," putting the former "hostility to death" (Ephesians 2:15–16). The resultant peace cannot be given by the world (John 14:27). It is a transforming peace that "surpasses all understanding" (Philippians 4:7).

The referred motion raised the question about how Southern Baptists, facilitated by the Convention's entities and seminaries, can "better reach, make disciples, and raise up leadership from and among diverse racial and ethnic groups in North America."

Simply stated, the answer is to stay the course that is currently in place and intentionally implement the proactive steps enumerated above. Heightened awareness of the need to be more broadly inclusive leads to greater sensitivity to where we are and where we need to be. Greater sensitivity leads to intentional accountability, both in monitoring specific accomplishments and in celebrating continued progress through routine news reports and day-to-day conversations.

We pray God will use and bless this report for His Kingdom purposes.

Respectfully submitted,

The Executive Committee, June 15, 2015.

APPENDIX

Recommendations Related to the Executive Committee Report
A Review of Ethnic Church and Ethnic Church Leader Participation in SBC Life

Adopted by messengers to the 2011 Southern Baptist Convention Annual Meeting

Recommendation 5: SBC Referral: Directing the Executive Committee to Study Greater SBC Involvement for Ethnic Churches and Leaders

After extensive study of a 2009 motion, the Executive Committee of the Southern Baptist Convention makes the following recommendations designed to foster conscious awareness of the need to be proactive and intentional in the inclusion of individuals from all ethnic and racial identities within Southern Baptist life and recommends the Southern Baptist Convention request:

A. The Executive Committee to request from the Southern Baptist Convention entities to submit as part of its annual "data call" [as described in Bylaw 18E (12)], a descriptive report of participation of ethnic churches and church leaders in the life and ministry of the respective SBC entity; and

B. The Executive Committee to include a section in the SBC President's Notebook given to each newly-elected president of the Southern Baptist Convention encouraging the president to give special attention to appointing individuals who represent the diversity within the Convention, and particularly ethnic diversity, among his appointees to the various committees under his purview (Committee on Committees, Credentials Committee, Resolutions Committee, and Tellers Committee); and

C. The SBC president to report the total number of appointees he selects for the committees under his purview that represent the ethnic diversity within Southern Baptist life at the time the names of the committees are released to *Baptist Press*; and

D. The Executive Committee to include a section in the SBC President's Notebook encouraging the president to encourage the selection of annual meeting program personalities by the Committee on Order of Business that represent the ethnic diversity within the Southern Baptist Convention; and

E. The Committee on Order of Business to give due consideration to the ethnic identity of program personalities it enlists for each Southern Baptist Convention annual meeting; and

F. The Executive Committee to amend the nomination form for the Committee on Nominations to provide a place where a nominee may indicate his or her ethnic identity, should he or she so choose; and

G. The Committee on Nominations to include in its annual report the total number of new nominees and the total number of individuals among its nominees that represent the ethnic diversity within Southern Baptist life; and

H. The SBC entities to give due consideration to the recruitment and employment of qualified individuals to serve in the various professional staff positions, on seminary faculty, and as appointed missionaries in order to reflect well the ethnic diversity within Southern Baptist life; and

I. The Executive Committee, through its various publications and news outlets, to continue to provide news coverage of interest to individuals of all ethnic interests and to carry stories that demonstrate the wonderful works the Lord is accomplishing through the vital ministries of Baptists of "every tribe and tongue and people and nation"; and

J. The Executive Committee, through its Communications Workgroup, to receive a report from the Executive Committee staff in its February meeting each year concerning the participation of ethnic churches and church leaders in the life and ministry of the SBC entities as reported through the various means outlined in this recommendation (letters a. through i. above); and

The Executive Committee further recommends the Southern Baptist Convention respectfully request the Southern Baptist Pastor's Conference and other groups which meet as part of the larger event of the Southern Baptist Convention annual meeting be sensitive to the desire of our ethnic brothers and sisters in Christ to see and hear individuals from their respective cultural heritages address attendees of these related groups; and

The Executive Committee further recommends the Southern Baptist Convention strongly encourage church workers and leaders from all ethnic backgrounds within Southern Baptist life to involve themselves to the highest level possible in associational life and through state convention ministries so that their participation in broader denominational life becomes the platform from which their greater involvement in visible roles of leadership in the Convention will naturally follow.[68]

PART TWO
The Convention Mosaic

- African American — Robert Wilson
- Asian American — Peter Yanes, Paul Kim, Minh Ha Nguyen
- Hispanic — Daniel Sanchez and Bob Sena
- Native American — Gary Hawkins
- Multi-Ethnic — Lennox Zamore
- Anglo Church Planting and Ministry — Rodney Webb
- Bivocational and Smaller Church Ministry — Ray Gilder

African Americans in the SBC*

Robert E. Wilson, Sr.

"**Blest Be the Tie That Binds**" is not only the name of a popular hymn of benediction among Baptists, it is also a statement that points to the common ground of religious experience and insight shared by black and white Baptists. Without an understanding of their common heritage and history, it is difficult to understand and appreciate the involvements of African American Southern Baptist today.

"The history of both Black and White Baptists in America has been intertwined from the very beginning. In 1619, one year before the Mayflower landed the Pilgrims at Plymouth Rock, Massachusetts, the first shipload of African slaves landed at Jamestown, Virginia. The first record of a black Baptist dates to 1743 when the Newton, Rhode Island, Baptist church listed Quassey, a Black man, as one of fifty-one members."[1]

Blacks and whites in America have been intimately involved with one another for centuries, especially in the South. The dehumanizing institutions of slavery and segregation denied blacks the right to interact with whites as equals, but neither system could prevent the cross-cultural fertilization that occurred. Religion was no exception, for black and white Baptists have roots in the same soil, the revivalistic South.

For much of its history, the Southern Baptist Convention had no black members and, therefore, blacks were not directly involved with the life and work of the Convention. Despite this fact, it would be a mistake to conclude that blacks were not affected by or did not impact Southern Baptists.

Though there are differences in the way the majority of black and white Baptists express their religious convictions, the two are related whether they admit it or not.

Further, it is not too misleading to suggest that sociology, not theology, has kept them apart.

According to Rev. Chan Garrett, Blacks organized the first Black Baptist convention—known as the American Baptist Missionary Convention—in 1840 at the Abyssinian Baptist Church of New York.[2] It was in 1845 that northern and southern white Baptists split over the issue of slavery, specifically over whether slaveholders could be commissioned as foreign missionaries. From this chasm, the Southern Baptist Convention was formed with approximately 350,000 adherents, 100,000 of whom were Black.[3]

Some felt that Blacks were not relevant partners in the early days of the SBC and that the enslaved had no voice in the workings or formation of the Convention. I disagree with this line of thought because I believe that their mere presence had a major impact on the development of the Convention and its policies. It would have been practically impossible for their presence not to impact the thoughts and practices of the white Baptists who apparently were sincere in their desire to seek God's will. Their sincerity in seeking God's will is evidenced in the first charge given to the Domestic Mission Board (DMB) to: " ... take all prudent measures, for the religious instructions of our colored people."[4] This, in my opinion, offers proof that the concept of "theology of presence" matters. This phrase was popularized by Dr. Tom Kelly, who served for many years as director of African American ministries with the California Southern Baptist Convention.

The significant involvement of enslaved Blacks helped to both shape the SBC and propel it to the prominent place it holds today in the life of the 15.2 million Southern Baptists who comprise this multicultural body of believers. This Convention of believers has been shaped by both male and female heroes of nearly every race and color. Upon their shoulders we now stand; and hopefully they will continue to uphold us in the future.

Dr. Sid Smith, a champion for diversity within the SBC, reflected powerfully upon this odd history of Blacks in the Southern Baptist Convention: "The Black Southern Baptist experience may be likened to the sound of many [a] Black preacher's voice during the emotion of a sermon. It is bittersweet poetry in motion; it is pleasure in the midst of pain; it is progress despite resistance; it is struggle that yields movement; it is hope in the midst of uncertainty; it is a question mark with the potential of becoming an exclamation point!"[5]

Black and White Baptist Contacts Prior to 1845

Baptists began work in the South in the late seventeenth century, but it was not until the eighteenth century that their efforts were rewarded. Capitalizing on both the missionary spirit of northern Baptists, especially in Philadelphia, and the revivalist fervor of the First Great Awakening, the Baptist witness spread through Virginia, the Carolinas, and into Georgia. Blacks had limited exposure to Christianity,[6] but some slaves did respond to the Gospel, most often becoming members of predominantly white congregations. Yet, on the eve of the Revolutionary War, a black congregation developed at Silver Bluff, South Carolina. Often regarded as the first black Baptist church in America,[7] its history demonstrates the interdependence of black and white Baptists.

One of the men given credit for helping to found the Silver Bluff Church was George Liele (sometimes spelled Leile or Lisle). Liele was born a slave in Virginia around 1759. His master, Henry Sharpe, moved to Georgia, where Liele was converted and baptized some time prior to 1773. Sharpe, a deacon in his church, later gave Liele his freedom after Liele demonstrated satisfactory evidence of the genuineness of his call to preach. As an itinerant minister, Liele preached throughout the Savannah River region, which included the Silver Bluff plantation of George Galphin. Here Liele and a white minister, probably New Light Congregationalist Wait Palmer, organized the Silver Bluff Church between 1773 and 1775.

Following the Revolutionary War, Baptist strength increased. Baptist concepts of the church and religious liberty seemed to be in harmony with the ideals of the War of Independence, and most Baptists proved to be fiercely patriotic. At the end of the war, they reaped the benefits of that loyalty. The number of Black Baptists also grew as a result of the Second Great Awakening, which began around the turn of the century. Blacks were more directly involved in the protracted brush arbor meetings that characterized the second revival movement than they had been in the First Great Awakening. As a result, more blacks became Christian and many became Baptists. During the first decades of the 1800s, independent black Baptist congregations developed in the North, and several black churches developed in the South also. The southern black Baptist congregations most often operated under white observation, if not supervision, but the majority of black Baptists in the South became members of white churches. These blacks were allowed to worship with whites, sometimes in segregated sections of the church, but rarely were they allowed to be involved in the decision-making process of the body.

Despite the limits that were placed on the black Christian's freedom of religious expression, the possibility for black and white interaction and contact was evident in the development of the first organized mission efforts by black Baptists. A sound argument can be made for naming George Liele, who went to Jamaica in 1782 in order to keep his freedom, as the first black Baptist missionary. That motivation for going to the island does not detract from Liele's extraordinary mission work on the island; but it was Lott Cary who served as the first black Baptist missionary appointed to the foreign field. The formerly enslaved Cary purchased his freedom around 1813 and settled in Richmond, Virginia. Here he was converted and baptized into the First Baptist Church of the city. Soon afterward, he began preaching.

Cary was exposed to the rising concern for foreign missions that led to the creation of the Triennial Convention in 1814 and was so moved by the need for a Christian witness in West Africa that he was instrumental in the founding of the Richmond African Baptist Missionary Society in 1815. Luther Rice was one of the men who saw the society as a potentially powerful tool for Christianizing the continent. Six years after the society was founded, Cary sailed for West Africa with Collin Teague, a minister, and the constituent members of a mission church. They landed in Freetown, Sierra Leone, in 1821. Support for the endeavor came mainly from the Richmond African Baptist Missionary Society, but had additional support. The Triennial Convention made books available. Cary served in both Sierra Leone and Liberia until his accidental death in 1829.[8]

Despite the cooperation that took place among Baptists for much of the early nineteenth century, Baptist unity was extremely fragile, and in 1845 the bit of unity that existed was demolished. While other issues, such as disputes over the appointment of missionaries to the South and the Southwest and concern over whether the structure of the Triennial Convention was best for carrying out the mission task caused tensions within Baptist circles, the primary issue that led to the dissolution of the Triennial Convention was slavery.

Baptists such as John Leland in Virginia and David Barrow in Kentucky had argued against slavery in the closing years of the eighteenth and the opening years of the nineteenth centuries, but their voices were drowned out by an ever-increasing number of Baptists in the South who saw no contradiction between their Christian commitment and their support of slavery. South Carolina's Richard Furman, a leader in the Triennial Convention, was one of the leading defenders of slavery, arguing that the institution was sanctioned by the Bible.[9] In the 1830s, however, a more vocal abolitionist movement renewed its attack on slavery, and Baptists found themselves having to wrestle with where they would stand on the issue. The majority concluded that Baptist unity was to be preserved at all costs and managed to steer a dangerous middle course. Events soon made that option even more perilous.

In 1840, Elon Galusha, a vice-president of the Board of Foreign Missions, was elected president of the newly formed American Baptist Anti-Slavery Convention. His public denunciation of slavery in his inaugural address caused a stir in the South. Though the Triennial Convention avoided a major fight over slavery at the 1841 meeting, defections led to the formation of the American Free Mission Society in 1843. Abolitionist strength grew and was evident at the 1844 Triennial Convention, even though a resolution affirming the Convention's commitment to cooperate in the foreign mission enterprise and remain neutral on the matter of slavery was accepted. Later that year, however, the Home Mission Society refused to appoint a Georgia slaveholder as a missionary to Native Americans, indicating they would no longer appoint slaveholders as missionaries. A similar response from the board of managers of the Triennial Convention led the members of the Virginia Foreign Mission Society to call for a Convention of Baptists in the South. The result was that the Southern Baptist Convention was organized in May 1845 in Augusta, Georgia.[10] Blacks who were part of white churches that became members of the Convention formed a large percentage of the Southern Baptist membership for the next twenty years. Ironically, while Baptist fellowship was broken between the North and South, the interaction of black and white Baptists in the South continued.

The Southern Baptist Convention and Blacks, 1845–1900

The Southern Baptist Convention articulated its concern for Christianizing slaves from its inception and, through the Board of Domestic Missions, made efforts to carry out the Convention's directive. Laws against teaching slaves how to read and write, the general acceptance by Southern Baptists of black inferiority, as well as their acquiescence to the traditional views on race relations, however, combined effectively to limit the amount of work actually done among the slave population. Furthermore, the geographical vastness of the South, the number of whites who were not Christian, and limited financial resources also hindered formal evangelistic efforts by Southern Baptists among the slaves. For blacks who were converted and became Baptists, the church membership patterns established prior to the formation of the Southern Baptist Convention continued between 1845 and 1865. The majority of slaves became members of white churches, but others attended services for blacks that were conducted by white preachers or gathered together to hear approved black preachers.[11] As the Civil War began, black and white Baptists in the South were involved with one another, even if the involvement was based on a master-slave relationship.

The end of the Civil War did not end black-white involvement among Baptists, but it drastically altered the nature of the relationship. Almost immediately, black Baptists began to leave white churches. Although the evidence suggests that the parting was by mutual agreement, the split nevertheless reflected both black Baptist determination to be able to participate fully and freely in their own religious organizations and white Baptist inability to adjust to free blacks as equals in Christ.

After the Civil War and Reconstruction years, many of the Blacks who had been part of white churches left to form indigenous churches. Some remained, however, and worked alongside white missionaries to help disciple the masses.

Blacks formed their first state convention in North Carolina in 1866 and continued to develop other state conventions into the 1879s. The impetus for a national structure culminated in the formation of the Baptist Foreign Mission Convention in 1880, but even this momentous event once again reflected the ongoing involvement of black and white Baptists with one another.

The major person behind the formation of the Baptist Foreign Mission Convention was W. W. Colley, a Virginia native who had served as a missionary in Africa under appointment by the Foreign Mission Board of the Southern Baptist Convention. Upon his return to America in 1879, the black Baptists of Virginia commissioned him to determine whether there was enough support among blacks to establish a foreign mission agency under black control. Colley himself was convinced of the need for blacks to be more involved in the foreign mission enterprise and found enough support to hold a meeting in Montgomery, Alabama, on November 24, 1880, to establish a convention. Approximately 150 people, mainly ministers, attended the meeting, and the Baptist Foreign Mission Convention was born. William H. McAlpine, a leading Baptist minister in Alabama, was elected president, and Colley was elected corresponding secretary.[12]

Despite Colley's involvement with Southern Baptists and the positive results of that involvement, Southern Baptist involvements with blacks between 1865 and 1900 were hampered by financial problems and by Southern Baptists' inability to rise above the racial attitudes of the South.[13] The American Baptist Home Mission Society seized the initiative, especially in the establishment of school for the education of the freedmen, which eventually helped Southern Baptists engage more in educating blacks. Though some leading Southern Baptists had serious doubts about the educability of blacks,[14] there was support from the Home Mission Board for the education of ministers who would be responsible for leading the religious development of black people. In order to accomplish this, the board sponsored short-term institutes for black ministers, some in conjunction with Northern Baptists.

The board also helped sponsor some theology students at the Augusta Institute that had been established in 1867 in Augusta, Georgia, by the American Baptist

Home Mission Society.[15] Located in the basement of Springfield Baptist Church, the school's primary purpose was to prepare black men for ministry and teaching. In 1884 the board appointed Robert T. Pollard, a black Baptist minister in Alabama, to serve as a theological professor at Selma University in Alabama.[16] He later became president of that institution. The Home Mission Board also wanted Southern Baptists to begin a school for blacks, but that was not accomplished in the nineteenth century. Both Pollard and William H. McIntosh, who had served as both president and corresponding secretary of the Domestic Mission Board, continued to serve as theological instructors to black pastors in the various institutes supported by the Domestic Mission Board. Later, the Home Mission Board published a long article titled, "Our Honored Brother, Dr. McIntosh, Who Has Been Crowning a Long Life of Usefulness by Indefatigable Labors Among the Negroes of Georgia."[17]

Continued theological training of black pastors became a major emphasis for the Board, and as a new century was approaching, partnerships with Northern Baptists expanded. A plan had been put in place that allowed this partnership to develop leadership for preaching, providing aid to churches with vacant pulpits, to settle church disputes, to quell any strife that existed between churches and associations, and "to do all possible to promote the peace, purity, and efficiency of the Colored population."[18] This plan gave way to hiring several persons to give direct attention to the work of education among blacks. During the early part of the new century, joint work among black Baptist women and the National (black) Baptist Conventions elevated. By 1915, these SBC/NBC collaborative relationships had culminated in hiring nearly thirty missionaries. This joint committee brought on J. W. Bailey, the first evangelist hired by the department of evangelism.

While post-slavery black and white Baptists in the South continued their separate identities, their reaction to the American Baptist Publication Society's dominance in the field of religious literature also showed their kindred spirit, if not their actual involvement with one another. Following the Civil War, Southern Baptists began to feel the need to publish their own materials. Initial attempts to do this predated the Civil War, but became a casualty of the war. In 1863, the Convention established a Sunday school board to do the work of promotion and to develop materials for use in Southern Baptist Sunday schools. Because of periods of extreme financial difficulty, the board floundered and the Convention made it a part of the Board of Domestic and Indian Missions in 1873. Not until 1891 did the Sunday School Board emerge again as an independent entity. Black Baptists made extensive use of materials from the American Publication Society, and many black ministers worked as colporteurs. Increasing concern over the lack of materials designed to meet the needs of black Baptists, however, led many leaders to conclude that they needed their own publication facilities. The leadership was also concerned that the publication society did not use capable black writers. These concerns alone did not lead to the formation of the National Baptist Convention, USA, in 1895, but they were among the earliest concerns that the new convention tried to address. Both black and white Baptists in the South felt they needed to control the means of producing and distributing the materials used in their churches.[19]

From Midnight to the Dawn of a New Day, 1900–1950

The first half of the twentieth century witnessed radical changes in the health of the Southern Baptist Convention and corresponding alterations in its relationship with African Americans. The period was indeed so complex, including massive northern migrations by blacks, two world wars, near financial collapse for the nation, and financial and theological problems for Southern Baptists, that it is not possible to provide anything but the barest sketch of black and white Baptist involvements in a study of this nature. Yet, in this period seeds were planted that began to blossom as the era came to a close. Both the midnight and the dawn of new hope, therefore, merit some attention.

Few positive things can be said about the social, political, and economic condition of Baptists in the South as the new century began. Jim Crow laws, the systemic disenfranchisement of blacks, lynchings, the boll weevil, and low cotton prices all combined to make the plight of black people difficult. Little relief came from white Christians, many of whom were themselves victims of racist presuppositions and social traditions.[20] But even in the midst of an otherwise gloomy situation, there were continued positive contacts between black and white Baptists in the South, especially in the development of black Baptist denominational units and the education of black ministers. Given the fact that by 1900 there were well over 1.25 million black Baptists in America, the efforts were inadequate, but they were nonetheless welcomed signs of concern and continued the history of black and white involvement.

A plan had been devised as early as 1895 to help coordinate Northern, Southern, and black Baptist efforts to help black Baptists develop their churches and their denominational structures. The strategy, known as the New Era Plan, was modified in 1904 to include less northern Baptist participation. Under the modified plan missionaries were jointly appointed by the Southern Baptist Convention and the National Baptist Convention, USA.

By 1914, a total of forty-seven missionaries had been jointly appointed. This number was reduced by the split within the black convention in 1915 and by the beginnings of a severe economic crunch that confronted the Home Mission Board of the Southern Baptist Convention so that twenty fewer missionaries were jointly appointed in 1923. These missionaries worked with churches, black associations, and conventions in a variety of capacities. Some of them served as teachers in institutes or in other teaching positions. This continued the earlier concern for the education of black ministers. One of the most striking examples of this particular concern—which also demonstrates the continued involvements of black and white Baptists—was the ongoing discussion between National and Southern Baptists regarding the establishment of a seminary for black students. The discussions, which occurred over a period of twenty years, culminated in the founding of the American Baptist Theological Seminary in 1924, which was jointly support by the two conventions.

The financial problems of the Home Mission Board grew worse during the 1920s and necessitated further cuts in personnel. These cuts affected the number of missionaries that continued to serve under joint appointment. By 1932, only six missionaries remained in the program. Within five years, however, the future of black and white Baptist involvements improved. By 1937, Noble Y. Beall was appointed by Southern Baptists to direct the Home Mission Board's Department of Cooperative Work with Negroes. Under Beall, the position of teacher-missionary was begun.[21] Persons serving in this position were missionaries whose primary responsibilities were in the field of education as teachers in predominantly black schools. Beall was also successful in cultivating relationships with Northern Baptists, who provided support for him in return for his continued contact with Northern Baptist schools for blacks.

Other milestones in black-white Baptist involvement in the South were achieved in the 1940s. African Americans helped to establish many of the Baptist centers that were located across fourteen states. In 1953, a partnership between the HMB and the National Baptist Convention, USA, Incorporated, was established through the employment of Costello Trotter, a general evangelist. Another milestone was in Home Mission Board personnel and yet another was in the area of education. In 1942, during the time of Beall's leadership, the Home Mission Board employed its first black staff person, Roland Smith, who was an assistant secretary with responsibility to serve as a liaison between black and white Baptists. Although he did not have office space in the HMB building, his employment as a professional staffer was a major advance for the SBC. Smith served the board during the turbulent post-World War II years, resigning in 1949. The fruit of his work was the result of relationships that had been built by persons like A. E. L. Weeks, who in 1936 was appointed as a general missionary in cooperation with the Maryland State Mission Board. Even though African Americans could not share office space with their white counterparts or even sit and eat in the same facility, God had a much bigger plan. More than one hundred years after the formation of the SBC, a new day was dawning in the life of the SBC, according to Dr. Smith.[22]

The education milestone occurred in the same year, when Garland Offutt became the first black to receive a doctorate from a Southern Baptist school. Blacks had attended Golden Gate Baptist Theological Seminary, and Offutt had already received a ThM degree from The Southern Baptist Theological Seminary four years earlier. Because of segregation laws in Kentucky, however, Offutt was unable to attend regular day classes at the Louisville seminary. Rather, several teachers permitted him to do his work in their offices, which allowed him an opportunity to complete the ThD degree requirements.

The period after 1950 brought rays of hope that were much brighter in terms of black involvement within the SBC. The Mission Board continued to cross the barrier that race had established. The appointment of men to the Department of Cooperative Work with Negroes combined with the country's changing demographic, a shift took place in the strategy of the Home Mission efforts. Blacks, during this period, began to migrate from the states that had been part of the Confederacy. It is estimated that 1.5 million blacks had moved to the West, to the Northeast, and to the Great Lakes region. Since the work of the Mission Board related to developing continual relationships with blacks, the next logical step was to become more focused on how to enhance these relationships.

Early events indicated that at least two different approaches to black involvement with Southern Baptists might develop. On the one hand, the traditional ministries with and to blacks continued. Guy Bellamy was elected by the Home Mission Board in 1949 to continue the work of relating to blacks in National Baptist structures. Eight years later, the board employed S. E. Grinstead to develop Baptist Student Unions on predominantly black college campuses. Both the work of Bellamy and Grinstead, while somewhat different from previous work with blacks, had the same goals of providing a ministry to blacks. The work was paternalistic in the sense that Southern Baptists determined what was needed and moved to meet the perceived need, often without much black input and with little or no black oversight or control. The work was also geared to provide a ministry to blacks who were outside of the SBC.

On the other hand, a new thrust in the involvement of blacks within the SBC occurred in 1951, when the Community Baptist Church of Santa Rosa, California, and the Greater Friendship Baptist Church of Anchorage, Alaska, affiliated with Southern Baptist associations. These were the first black churches to become members of the

Convention since 1900. Although not made without a good deal of controversy, these advances meant that blacks were once again on the inside of Convention life and work.

Moving Beyond the 1950s

The 1960s were full of turmoil and uncertainty of change. The relationships and involvements of black and white Baptists did not escape the effects of that turmoil. The Civil Rights Movement shifted into high gear as the white church stood immobilized by fear of change and shackled by tradition. Yet even though the Southern Baptist response was inadequate in the eyes of many blacks, some meaningful changes were made. For example, more black preachers appeared before Southern Baptist audiences. Furthermore, a growing number of Southern Baptists began to see the need for a fully Christian response to the racism in America. Such men as Walker Knight, editor of *Home Missions*, Foy Valentine of the Christian Life Commission, Victor Glass of the Home Mission Board, T. B. Matson of Southwestern Baptist Theological Seminary, and the editors of some state papers began speaking and writing in ways that challenged long-held racial attitudes with biblical truths. The establishment of Race Relations Sunday on the Convention calendar in 1965 was also an important success. These occurrences indicated a changing mood among Southern Baptists that paved the way for closer relations with blacks within the Convention.

By 1968, the number of black Southern Baptist churches had risen to fifty-seven, and in that year the Home Mission Board elected Emmanuel McCall as an associate in the Department of Work with National Baptists, which was headed by Victor Glass. Earlier, Glass had hired Arvella Turnipseed as the first black secretary to work at the board's headquarters. Dr. McCall became the first black staff person to have an office in the HMB building. While questions remain unanswered about how much authority Roland Smith had to act during the time he was associated with the HMB, Dr. McCall had the same authority as any other staff associate. In this capacity, Dr. McCall was able to keep the respect he had among National Baptists while he cultivated the respect of Southern Baptists. His efforts did much to help Southern Baptists stretch in the area of racial reconciliation. He recruited other African Americans to work in his department and influenced the hiring of blacks in other SBC entities. It is very important to recognize that although Dr. McCall served as this change agent, many other blacks had preceded him in various areas. Nevertheless, his role there signaled a major shift in the movement of God in the life of the SBC. However, one hundred years of cooperative involvement had laid the foundation for this wind of change that had been inspired within the mindset of God's people.

Throughout the 1970s the HMB continued to work with National Baptists primarily through the Department of Cooperative Ministries with National Baptists. The preposition "with" was very important because it defined how the two entities would relate. The natural outgrowth of this name change was to hire a staff person who could facilitate the process of establishing ministry partnerships between Southern Baptists and National Baptists. The department's name reflected the new fraternal attitude of the department. Rather than setting the agenda unilaterally, Southern Baptists began the long and sometimes painful process of working cooperatively with National Baptists. Needs were assessed together, projects were planned jointly, and financing was agreed upon. This approach gave National Baptists joint ownership and responsibility for the success or failure of whatever was done. While not without its challenges and shortcomings, the new process helped create a more positive working relationship between black and white Baptists.

Dr. McCall (a mentor to me and countless other young African American Southern Baptists) best articulated this mentality:

> The history of the relationship of the Home Mission Board (HMB) of the Southern Baptist Convention to the black community has moved through three distinct phases. The movement has been from 'overtly paternal' to 'developing fraternal' to 'declared inclusivism.' The paternal period began with the Board's organization in 1845, and continued in strength until 1972. Some vestiges of the paternal spirit still remain, but are exceptions. While there were attempts at token fraternalism as early as 1904, the declared movement in that direction began as a result of a conference held April 24–27, 1972, at the Holiday Inn Central, Atlanta, Georgia. At that time, the HMB department staff, its 126 missionaries, and nine persons representing the three National Baptist Conventions, determined that a new direction would be forged that would reflect the highest ideals of Christian brotherhood. The 'declared inclusivism' phase began in 1975 as the board strategized for the development of black Southern Baptist churches.[23]

It would take more than another decade for equal access to find its place within the Southern Baptist Convention. The strategy of racial inclusion was focused on the development of black Southern Baptist churches. This process would require more than just gaining the allegiance of churches affiliated with one of the National Baptist churches or of those with no convention affiliation. The effort to develop black Southern Baptist churches would require church planters equipped with the tools to start from conception intentional black Southern Baptist churches. In 1989, the

Convention changed the name of the Department of Black Church Relations, then under the leadership of Dr. McCall, to the Black Church Extension Division.

During the closing two decades of the twentieth century, a new era in race relations was emerging for the Convention as cooperating churches, pastors, and members alike strove to repudiate the sordid conflict of human enslavement. Since its founding, black involvement within the Convention has grown in every area of denominational life—at the local church level, the associational level, the state convention level, and even at the national level. The following is an overview of black involvement in the life of Southern Baptists since the establishment of the first two African American churches affiliated in 1951:

1950–1960s

- Alvin Charles Daniels was appointed to serve as a teacher-missionary in Houma, Louisiana.
- The first black associational moderator was the Rev. William T. Vernon in Oakland County, Michigan.
- Dr. Samuel Simpson, fondly called the "Bishop of the Bronx," was appointed by the Home Mission Board as a pastor-director for the area.
- Race Relations Sunday was established in 1965.
- Dr. Emmanuel McCall began lecturing on church history at The Southern Baptist Theological Seminary in Louisville, Kentucky. In 1968, Dr. McCall became the first African American executive housed at the Home Mission Board's headquarters in Atlanta.
- Dr. Sid Smith, a home missionary in the Watts community of Los Angeles, graduated from Golden Gate Seminary in 1968.

1970–1980s

- Dr. Emmanuel McCall became the first African American department director at a denominational agency.
- Mrs. Margaret Perkins became the first African American hired as staff for the Woman's Missionary Union.
- Dr. Emmanuel McCall began teaching black church studies classes as an adjunct faculty member at The Southern Baptist Theological Seminary.

- Mrs. Verlene Farmer was commissioned as a teacher-missionary by the HMB to serve as director for the Baptist Student Union on the campus of Langston University in Oklahoma.
- Rev. James A. Wilborn, Jr. became the first African American chaplain (Air Force) endorsed by the Southern Baptist Convention.
- Rev. Austin Brown became the first African American male endorsed by the SBC Chaplains Commission to serve in the Florida state prison system.
- Chaplain Ivery De La Cruz was the first African American female endorsed by the SBC Chaplains Commission to serve in the US Army.
- Chaplain Kathryn Browder was the first African American female endorsed by the SBC Chaplains Commission to serve in the federal prison system.
- Rev. Jim Culp was appointed to head the Black Church Development Division for the Baptist General Convention of Texas.
- The descendants of the enslaved believers who formed Springfield Church (after breaking away from First Baptist Church of Greenville, South Carolina, a century prior) met with First Baptist descendants for the first time on Race Relations Sunday.
- Dr. Sid Smith was hired as Ethnic Liaison Consultant at the Baptist Sunday School Board (BSSB), thus becoming the first African American denominational executive at the agency. He became the first black denominational professional at BSSB. The Sunday School Board later expanded its focus on black church resources in 1987 and established the Black Church Development Section, over which Dr. Smith was appointed manager.
- Dr. Willie McPherson served Southern California's associations as a staff person for the California Southern Baptist Convention, and he later served as the California State Convention's director for African American ministries. He also served as a national associate in the HMB's Black Church Relations Department.
- Dr. Lincoln Bingham, pastor of St. Paul Missionary Baptist Church in Louisville, Kentucky, was the first African American employee for Baptist bookstores. He later became instrumental in Black Church Relations as a cooperative ministries consultant with the Kentucky Baptist Convention. After his retirement from KBC, Dr. Bingham continued his work in racial reconciliation. On August 23, 2009, St. Paul merged with the all-white Shively Heights Baptist Church congregation to form one body, known as St. Paul @ Shively Heights Baptist Church.
- Dr. Willie Simmons became the first African American staff person hired as an executive at the Foreign Mission Board.

- Rev. Tom Kelly served on the Long Beach Harbor Association staff in Long Beach, California, and later became director of African American Ministries for the California Southern Baptist Convention.
- Dr. Robert E. Wilson became one of two African American Church planter apprentices appointed by the Church Extension Division of HMB in 1984.
- Dr. Bill Perkins was elected as an associate in the Black Church Relations Department of the HMB.
- Dr. Victor Davis was appointed to a national leadership position at the Foreign Mission Board, succeeding Dr. Simmons in that capacity.
- Rev. Elgia (Jay) Wells began denominational work in Northern California on staff with Rev. Kelly in the California African American Ministries Division, as a church development associate.
- Dr. Sid Smith was appointed manager of the Black Church Development Section, an expansion of Black church work within the Baptist Sunday School Board.
- Over a two-year period, Reverends Samuel Beene, Olivia M. Cloud (the first African American female hired in a professional denominational position there), Elgia Wells, and Steven Warfield—all were hired as coordinators in Black Church Development. Upon the retirement of Dr. Sid Smith, Rev. Wells became the director of the department.
- Dr. Leroy Gainey became the first African American elected trustee-professor at a Southern Baptist institution, Golden Gate Baptist Theological Seminary, in 1987.

1990–2000s

- Dr. David Cornelius, who was commissioned by the Foreign Mission Board (now International Mission Board) as a missionary to Nigeria, was later appointed director of African American church relations, an IMB consultant for African American mobilization.
- Dr. Willie McPherson was one of the first African Americans to head a denominational division, upon his appointment as director of the newly named Black Church Extension Division.
- Rev. Michael Cox, hired as a Black Church Relations consultant at the HMB during the late 1980s, was elected assistant director of Mega Focus Cities.
- Dr. Lyman Alexander became associational missionary to two Southern California associations—Crescent Bay and Redwood Empire.

- Rev. Victor Ketchens was hired as African American church extension director for New York state.
- Dr. Robert E. Wilson was commissioned as a home missionary to South Central Los Angeles for the California Southern Baptist Convention in 1992. In 1994, he was elected associate director of the Black Church Extension Division of HMB. After the agency changed its name to the North American Mission Board in 1997, Dr. Wilson became manager of the African American Church Planting Unit.
- Rev. Michael Thurman was elected associate director in the HMB's Black Church Extension Division. Rev. Thurman was later called to pastor the historic Dexter Avenue King Memorial Baptist Church in Montgomery, Alabama.
- Rev. Herbert Brisbane was elected director of Black Church Evangelism, HMB.
- The African American Fellowship of the SBC held its first meeting during the Convention's 1984 annual meeting in Orlando, Florida.
- Rev. Roy Hopgood was named African American Ministry Consultant at Minnesota/Wisconsin Baptist Convention.
- Dr. Gary Frost, pastor of Rising Star Baptist Church in Youngstown, Ohio, became the first African American elected vice president of the Southern Baptist Convention. He was later elected to serve as Midwest vice president at the North American Mission Board (NAMB). He served for a time as executive director of missions for the Metropolitan New York Association.
- Dr. Sid Smith was the first African American to head a division in the Florida Baptist State Convention.
- Dr. Roy Cotton, who began African American denominational work in Virginia, was appointed director of African American work for the Baptist General Convention of Texas.
- Rev. Albert Holmes was elected the first African American associate to serve on the HMB chaplaincy staff in the area of Institutional and Business/Industrial Chaplaincy.
- Rev. Dennis Mitchell became associate director of the HMB's Black Church Extension Division in 1995, and later became director of NAMB's Multiplication Team. He now serves as executive director for the National African American Fellowship of the SBC.
- Dr. Phillip Davis was elected director of NAMB's Implementation Team, Church Planting Group.

- Rev. Hal Hopkins became the first African American elected to the State Convention of Pennsylvania/South Jersey staff as African American Director of Church Planting. He became the Team Leader for Greater Philadelphia Association.
- Rev. Leroy Fountain, who had served as an HMB church planter, became the first African American to serve at the SBC Annuity Board (now GuideStone Financial Services). He later returned under NAMB's Church Planting Group, and later engaged in work with the New Orleans Baptist Association.
- Army National Guard Chaplain Debra Berry was hired as a national consultant for the Woman's Missionary Union.
- Dr. Joshua Smith was commissioned as a national church-planting missionary to the US Virgin Islands.
- Dr. Jerome King, who had served on the Georgia Baptist Convention staff, was hired as an associate in NAMB's African American Church Planting Unit.
- Dr. Jeffrey Curtis, a former HMB missionary in California, was appointed as a national missionary under NAMB's Church Planting Group Mentoring Team, and later as a contextual leadership director at Golden Gate Seminary. He served for a time at LifeWay Christian Resources before becoming an adjunct faculty member at Golden Gate Seminary.
- Rev. Chris McNairy, at one time on the staff of the Tennessee and Michigan state conventions, was commissioned as a national missionary in Multi-Housing Church Planting, National Church Planting Missionary for African, African American, and Caribbean Church Planting. Eventually he was named NAMB Strategy Coordinator.
- Dr. Ken Weathersby, who served on state convention staff in Tennessee and Louisiana, became manager of NAMB's African American Church Planting Unit. He also served as Senior Strategist for Evangelism and Vice President for Church Planting at NAMB, and was an associate professor of Church Planting at New Orleans Baptist Theological Seminary. He was appointed to a joint position with the North American Mission Board and the SBC Executive Committee as presidential ambassador for ethnic church relations, and then became the first vice president to serve on the Executive Committee staff, where he currently serves as vice president for Convention advancement.
- Dr. Richard Lee was commissioned by NAMB as a national church planting missionary for African American church planting. He later became director of missions for the Philadelphia Baptist Association.
- Dr. E. W. McCall, a prominent pastor in Southern California and former president of the National African American Fellowship, was elected as SBC vice president.

After retiring as a pastor, he began serving the Texas convention as an African American consultant.

- Dr. Ken Ellis was named manager of NAMB's Multicultural Evangelism Unit, following his and his wife's service as SBC-endorsed prison chaplains in Florida. Dr. Ellis now serves as director of the Phillips Prison Seminary program under the auspices of New Orleans Baptist Theological Seminary.
- Rev Paul Brewer, who had served on the State Convention of Baptists in Ohio staff, was hired to serve in NAMB's Missionary Personnel Department.
- Dr. Robert Ndonga was appointed as an associate in NAMB's Apologetics and Evangelism Unit.
- Rev. Walter Mickels was appointed as a NAMB Strategy Coordinator.
- Rev. Keith Jefferson, who with his wife was commissioned as a missionary serving in Brazil, was appointed to serve the International Mission Board as African American mobilization manager.
- Dr. Fred Luter, pastor of Franklin Avenue Baptist Church in New Orleans, was the first African American president of the Southern Baptist Convention, serving two terms. He later was appointed NAMB Ambassador.
- Dr. Mark Croston, former pastor of East End Baptist Church in Suffolk, Virginia, and past association moderator and state convention president, was named national director of Black Church Partnerships at LifeWay.[24]

The work of the Master in the lives of African Americans in this Convention extends far beyond the pages of this chapter. Just as it would take all the books of the world to contain the works of the Lord Jesus and His Church, certainly many, many volumes would be needed to record the contributions of the many persons of African descent who have fought and paved the way for those who now stand upon their shoulders. But I close with this relevant quote from Dr. Emmanuel McCall, "Please permit a little 'boasting in the Lord.'"[25]

This chapter will never be complete until the Lord Jesus returns for His Church because red, brown, yellow, black, white, and every color in between is precious in His sight.

GOALS AND RECOMMENDATIONS[26]
Sharing Christ Among African Americans

Goal: Establish a national goal of baptizing 300,000+ African Americans by 2020, annually baptizing 50,000+ African Americans. This represents more than a 50 percent increase in annual reported baptisms.

● ● ● ● ● ●

RECOMMENDATION 1
Develop and implement effective urban evangelism strategies, as there are large concentrations of African Americans in major metropolitan areas.

Action Plans

1. Identify effective African American evangelism strategies among churches.
2. Convene leaders from effective churches to inform and index learnings.
3. Identify SBC staff with clear responsibility for urban evangelism strategies and implementation among African Americans.
4. Devise a major evangelism strategy for each Send City to reach African Americans.
5. Assist state conventions in developing and implementing evangelism strategies that impact lostness in metropolitan cities with significant African American populations.
6. Deploy sufficient missionary personnel and SBC staff to implement strategies that are developed.

RECOMMENDATION 2
Maintain support for national evangelism conferences that focus on reaching African Americans.

Action Plans

1. Continue support for the annual African American Men's Conference (Be the Man).
2. Implement a national African American youth evangelism conference with a focus on Saving the Seed (African American males are being lost at an alarming rate to death, prison, and general environmental dysfunction).

3. Conduct national youth evangelism trainings to enlist, equip, and engage five hundred youth at various venues, such as Black Church Leadership Week, Collegiate Week, etc.

RECOMMENDATION 3
Develop major communications plans for reaching African Americans.

Action Plans

1. Create a communication resource (marketing) on evangelism targeted to reach African Americans.
2. Develop culturally relevant evangelism resources. African American churches are highly relational, and typical SBC contact or promotional tools are largely ineffective as they are culturally insensitive.
3. Educate and equip African American leaders regarding the purpose and use of the Evangelism Response Center.
4. Assist churches in airing radio, television, and Internet promotional campaigns in urban areas where 100,000+ African Americans reside.

RECOMMENDATION 4
Assist African American churches in becoming aware of SBC evangelism resources that can help them impact lostness in indigenous communities.

Action Plans

1. Assist state conventions and associations in hosting orientation sessions for African American pastors.
2. Engage and/or train majority culture SBC staff in resourcing the African American community.
3. Identify strategic churches and church leaders that already may be aware of SBC evangelism resources.
4. Establish a national evangelism awareness training process targeted to the needs of African American churches.
5. Identify internal SBC personnel and processes that will provide oversight and implementation of African American focused evangelistic initiatives.

RECOMMENDATION 5

Develop strategies to equip African American churches to present the Gospel to unreached persons of African American subcultures, such as prisoners and their families.

Action Plans

1. Study best practices among African American churches effectively addressing fatherlessness, and develop an effective training module.
2. Study how African American churches are ministering to current and former prison inmates and their families, and provide effective training for churches to minister to these groups.
3. Develop relevant ministry models to assist African American churches to effectively minister to pressing needs of African Americans (e.g., parenting, prisons, finances, abstinence).
4. Focus on prison ministry to reduce the high concentration of incarcerated African Americans.
5. Adopt-a-Prison: each church reach one correctional facility, with a national goal to adopt fifty prisons by 2020.
6. Hire a national strategist to equip and enable African American churches to strengthen their SBC connections locally and nationally. A national leader is essential to accomplish this strategy.

STARTING CHURCHES AMONG AFRICAN AMERICANS

Goal: Establish New Testament congregations to fulfill the biblical mandate to make disciples. In 2011, there were 3,484 African American SBC congregations. Our vision is to increase to a total of six thousand African American Southern Baptist churches by 2020. This can be accomplished by planting four hundred African American churches annually. We also hope to enlist, equip, and engage one thousand African American churches to sponsor healthy church plants within five years.

RECOMMENDATION 1

Increase the number of church plants and sponsoring churches, while impacting lostness in the African American community.

Action Plans

1. Assist church planters in securing church sponsors and then identifying creative methods for funding the church plant.
2. Provide contextual training and resources for planters and sponsoring churches in urban areas.
3. Enlist, engage, and equip strong urban churches in the African American community to be urban church planting training centers. Identify one church in every urban area to become an Urban Church Planting center.
4. Develop a pool of qualified coaches /mentors for church planters.
5. Identify cooperatively committed churches that have never sponsored a church and provide training, support, and coaching for both the planter and sponsoring church.
6. Develop transitional church planting strategies, teams, and networks that focus on churches in transition (or decline) who are partnered to plant African American churches in transitional communities to keep continual SBC presence and provide a jump start for new church plants.
7. Establish at least one African American church planting center in every Send City.

RECOMMENDATION 2
Develop leaders in local African American churches to plant new churches.

Action Plans

1. Develop a church planting school for Black Church Leadership Week that provides a course of study for equipping and training both sponsor church leaders and potential church planters. These courses will lead to certification in church leadership.
2. Develop and implement a strategy to utilize associate ministers in African American churches in church planting.
3. Permit the SBC African American Fellowship to assist by giving input in planting additional African American works in strategic cities.
4. Assist and encourage state partners in hiring African American church planting leadership at the state convention level in areas where the African American population exceeds 500,000, and part-time African American consultants at the state level for populations between 100,000 and 500,000.

5. Create a national African American church planting office with sufficient staff to impact lostness among African Americans through church planting.

STRENGTHENING AFRICAN AMERICAN LEADERS

Goal: Lostness among black people in America is rising faster than that lostness is being addressed. The African American Council believes new strategies should be implemented in order to win more souls for the kingdom of God. Some of these new strategies should be focused on equipping African American leaders, enlisting African American churches within the Southern Baptist Convention, and engaging African American culture through the power of the Holy Spirit.

RECOMMENDATION 1
Implement a strategy to equip African American leaders in the SBC.

Action Plans

1. Train more African American pastors to be facilitators at training conferences.
2. Train more African American pastors and church leaders to improve their knowledge base regarding all SBC ministries.
3. Equip more African American pastors to become more deeply engaged in denominational work.
4. Create a database of African Americans and their skill set to fill denominational and church positions as they become available.
5. Engage younger leaders in African American churches by identifying internships and mentorship opportunities for young African American leaders.
6. Increase gifts to the Cooperative Program, Annie Armstrong, and Lottie Moon offerings through promotional CDs and DVDs by highlighting direct African American involvement and African Americans telling mission stories.
7. Encourage alignment with the biblical requirements for leadership in 1 Timothy 3.

RECOMMENDATION 2
The African American Council believes the connection between the people and leaders of the Convention can be stronger if a mechanism, which includes African American engagement, is created to oversee the implementation of the African American Council strategies. The culture can be impacted with the power of Christ. Churches will

be reenergized to become more actively involved with people and resources if they see persons that they are able to identify with in leadership.

Action Plan

1. Appoint personnel to oversee the implementation of the Council's strategies.

AFRICAN AMERICANS STRATEGICALLY IMPACTING THE CONVENTION AND CULTURE

Goal: If change and winning lost souls are the key outcomes, impacting African American culture is most effectively done by African Americans. There are over 46 million African Americans in the United States. The great majority dwell in large urban centers, as already recognized by the SBC. Research and reality must make a connection somewhere.

RECOMMENDATION 1

Implement a strategy to impact the African American culture.

Action Plans

1. Start high-impact churches in strategic urban centers.
2. Study the methods and philosophies of successful African American churches in urban cities and develop an equipping module.
3. Assist churches in developing and identifying ministries to impact a growing youth culture in the following areas: music, abortions, abstinence, gangs, and lifestyle witnessing.
4. African Americans are the largest audience in the major cities of the South; therefore, African Americans should be used in direct advertisement when developing marketing strategies for evangelism and appeals to churches.
5. Develop a discipleship process that impacts the church and culture.

RECOMMENDATION 2

Implement a strategy to impact the Southern Baptist Convention culture.

Action Plans

1. Continue ongoing dialogue to help sensitize SBC constituents and entities.
2. Encourage the SBC Executive Committee and SBC entities to seek continuing input from the NAAF.
3. Develop a database of African Americans for recommendation to strategic SBC entity positions.

AFRICAN AMERICANS SENDING VOLUNTEER MISSION TEAMS

Goal: Increase annual Mission Project involvement among African Americans by 100 percent to over 50,000 by the year 2020. We also aim for the SBC to lead in communicating North American and International Mission opportunities to African American churches.

RECOMMENDATION 1

Assist state conventions, associations, and African American churches in identifying, tracking, and reporting mission activity.

Action Plans

1. Assist local churches in tracking and reporting volunteer mission activities already being done such as summer camps, food pantries, clothing closets, hot meals for the homeless, etc.
2. Make ACP completion a Convention-wide promotion during the month of September each year.
3. Assist in development of an ACP Short Form highlighting the most crucial data for churches, including African American churches that have not returned the ACP form in prior years, the purpose being to capture critical data.

RECOMMENDATION 2

Increase African American awareness of opportunities for missions.

Action Plans

1. Enlist key leaders in local African American churches to participate on short-term mission trips with existing mission-minded churches and/or other SBC personnel.

a. Focus on high density African American population areas.
b. Share past experiences of successful National African American Fellowship /NAMB/IMB projects, such as Paint the Town project.
c. NAMB and IMB can help create opportunities (awareness of need).
2. Create more projects that are easy to buy into in strategic urban areas and around the world. Example: Bronx Middle School Paint Projects.
3. NAMB and IMB can provide undated African American sensitive mission media to promote Annie Armstrong and Lottie Moon missions giving within the African American Church. (Provides a more relevant delivery system to African American church). Examples range from DVD, to print, to web casting, etc.
4. Communicate activity in Disaster Relief ministries and other mission projects by African American churches.

RECOMMENDATION 3
Highlight models within the African American church community who are volunteering in missions.

Action Plans
1. Identify local churches that exemplify the use of volunteers in missions.
2. Team up African Americans churches that are not volunteering in missions with others who are, for exposure.
3. Tell the stories of missions from the African American experience.
4. Teach mission action from an African American perspective.
5. Include African American testimony of life changes that have taken place as the result of mission involvement.
6. Assist African American churches in clearly defining objectives and mission purposes.
7. Document and share feedback from mission projects.

RECOMMENDATION 4
Engage African American churches in understanding and participating in the Annie Armstrong and Lottie Moon missions offerings.

Action Plans

1. Engage African American churches to invest in the church in Baltimore in which Annie Armstrong was baptized and a member. The church building is in dire need of refurbishing at the physical plant located in Baltimore, Maryland. It is a critical church in an urban setting and is currently pastored by an African American.
2. Make Annie Armstrong's former church a mission laboratory to help tell the story of missions to increase African American giving and volunteer missions project involvement.
3. Plan mission trips to China to explore the path blazed by Lottie Moon.
4. Enlist and engage African American pastors to pray for volunteers in missions in key population areas.
5. NAMB and IMB can assist African American churches in missions promotion and prayer by telling our story in print media or in audio (CDs, DVDs, web casting, etc.).

AFRICAN AMERICAN VOCATIONAL MISSIONARIES

Goal: To enlist, equip, engage and challenge African Americans to fill at least 10 percent of the North American Mission Board's and International Mission Board's goals for sending missionaries. This will result in over 1,500 African American missionaries and chaplains and over 200 student missionaries.

RECOMMENDATION

The North American Mission Board and International Mission Board should lead in assisting African American churches in calling out the called through specific enlistment efforts focused on African Americans.

Action Plans

1. Provide regional and national conferences informing pastors and key leaders about funded and jointly funded mission service opportunities.
2. Over the next six years, focus on key pastors in twelve regions with high African American populations to host strategic mission conferences to raise mission awareness, spiritual growth, and mission participation.

3. Provide culturally sensitive DVDs and other electronic media that will challenge young African American believers about God's purpose and the mission challenge, the careers available, and the process to become an appointed missionary.

4. Develop culturally sensitive Week of Prayer materials including prayer for current missionaries, prayer for those God is calling to missions, and greater missions giving through the Christmas and Easter offerings.

4. Find more ways to encourage African Americans to participate in the Mission Pathways options.

---

*Portions of this chapter were extracted from "An Overview of Black Southern Baptist Involvements," by Dr. Edward L. Wheeler, *Baptist History and Heritage* (July 1981, Vol. 16, No. 3), published by the Historical Commission of the SBC and the Southern Baptist Historical Society. Dr. Wheeler served as a consultant in the Black Church Relations Department of the Home Mission Board under Dr. Emmanuel McCall and is currently president of the Morehouse School of Religion in Atlanta, Georgia.

BIBLIOGRAPHY

Black Churches Developing Strategies for the 1980's. Atlanta: The Home Mission Board, 1981.

Branch, Taylor. *Parting the Waters: America in the King Years 1954–63*. New York: Simon and Schuster, 1998.

Ellis, Ken. "Developing a Ministry Team to Disciple Young African Men in Prison." DMin Project, Southern Baptist Theological Seminary, 2006.

Fitts, Leroy. *A History of Black Baptists*. Nashville: Broadman Press, 1985.

Frazier, E. Franklin, and C. Eric Lincoln. *The Negro Church in America/The Black Church Since Frazier*. New York: Schocken Books, 1974.

Lincoln, C. Eric, and Lawrence H. Mamiya. *The Black Church in the African American Experience*. Durham and London: Duke University Press, 1990.

McNairy, Chris, Compiler. *A Southern Baptist Convention Orientation for the African American Ministry Context*. Atlanta: A CMC Production, 2006.

Paris, Peter. J. *Black Religious Leaders: Conflict in Unity*. Louisville: Westminster/John Knox Press, 1991.

Robinson, Paulette J., and B. J. Tidwell, eds. *The State of Black America 1995*. New York: National Urban League, Inc., 1995.

Rutledge, Arthur. B., and William. G. Tanner. *Mission to America: A History of Southern Baptist Home Missions*. Nashville: Broadman Press, 1969.

Sernett, Milton C., ed. *Afro-American Religious History: A Documentary Witness*. Durham: Duke University Press, 1985.

Sertima, Ivan Van. *They Came Before Columbus: The African Presence in Ancient America*. New York: Random House, 1976.

Smith, J. Alfred, ed. *The Church in Bold Mission: A Guidebook on Black Church Development*. Atlanta: Home Mission Board, 1977.

Smith, Sidney, ed. *An Orientation to the Southern Baptist Convention for Southern Baptists*. Nashville: Sunday School Board, 1984.

Wilson, Robert. E. "Establishing a Process at Sandtown Baptist Church, Atlanta, Georgia, to Mobilize Volunteers to Plant an African American Church in the Greater Atlanta Area," DMin Project, Southern Baptist Theological Seminary, 2003.

Asian Americans in the SBC

Peter Yanes, Paul Kim, Minh Ha Nguyen

In 1620, a small group of faithful **pilgrims** sailed on the Mayflower from England and landed on the shores of Massachusetts. They dreamed of religious freedom in the New World as they fled persecution in their homeland. They settled in the New World and built a new nation—America. About three centuries later, another group of immigrants and refugees came to America's shores from Asia. They came from Cambodia, China, Hmong, Japan, Korea, Laos, the Philippines, and Vietnam. Their dreams were similar to those of the Pilgrims—to raise their children in a land where they could obtain better education and better living, and be free from political persecution. These migrants are identified in this chapter as "Asian Americans."

Asian immigration dates back to the nineteenth century, when the first groups of Chinese citizens migrated to America to work in the nation's railroad

Asian Americans

Congregations	1,936
Members	155,087
Population	16,235,305
Foreign Born	67%
2nd and 3rd Generation	33%

Number of Asian Americans without a personal relationship with Christ

15,497,386

This represents
95%
of the total Asian American population

1 to 8,133

is the ratio of Southern Baptist congregations to population of Asian Americans[1] and gold-mining industries. They banded together and built their own communities that became known as "Chinatown." Other Asian immigrants journeyed to the islands of Hawaii to work on sugarcane plantations. Still other Asians came to study as international students. Vietnamese migration to the United States began mainly as a humanitarian response after the end of the Vietnam War in 1975, and over time transformed into migration for family reunification.[1]

These first-generation Asian Americans are rooted in a unique culture, language, and set of religious beliefs. They worship in their native language. Their children born in this country are known as second-generation Asian Americans. This next generation differs from their parents and grandparents. For them, America is their homeland and English is their first language.

Currently, there are 1,936 Asian Southern Baptist churches.[2] Some are strong and healthy churches, but the majority are too small to survive in their communities. Some Asian pastors need more theological education and training to minister more effectively to their people groups. In addition, many US-born second and third generations need to hear the Gospel of Jesus Christ within the context of their respective Asian cultural affinities in English-speaking churches, independently of first-generation churches.

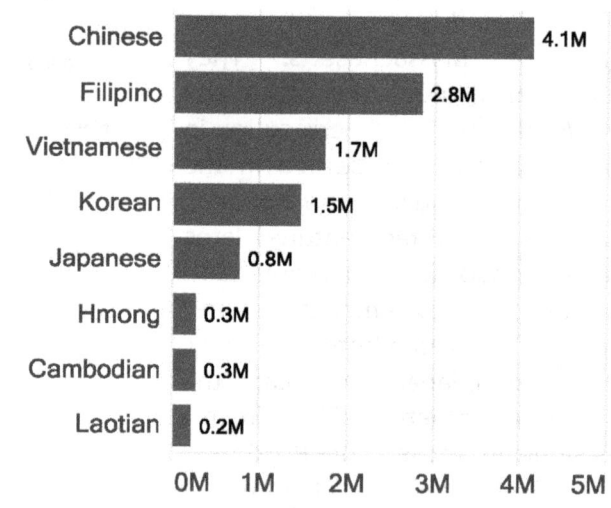

Population by Ethnic Groups

Chinese	4.1M
Filipino	2.8M
Vietnamese	1.7M
Korean	1.5M
Japanese	0.8M
Hmong	0.3M
Cambodian	0.3M
Laotian	0.2M

I thank Peter Yanes and Minh Ha Nguyen, members of the SBC Executive Committee's Convention Advancement Advisory Council, who spent many hours compiling this valuable chapter. Others have contributed in their Asian Advisory Council Report in 2014. As the first-ever Asian American Relations Consultant of the SBC Executive Committee, I thank them all as partners in spreading the Gospel.

SBC Asian American Churches by Ethnic Groups

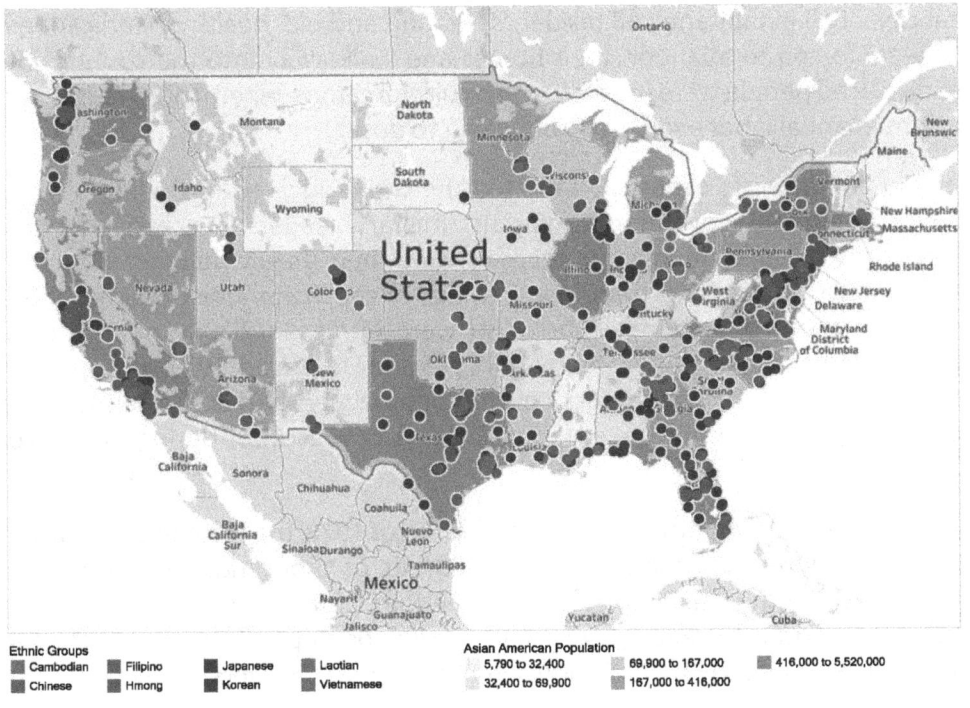

Ethnic Groups: Cambodian, Chinese, Filipino, Hmong, Japanese, Korean, Laotian, Vietnamese

Asian American Population: 5,790 to 32,400; 32,400 to 69,900; 69,900 to 167,000; 167,000 to 416,000; 416,000 to 5,520,000

CAMBODIAN SOUTHERN BAPTIST FELLOWSHIP

Brief History of Cambodia

The Khmer (Cambodian) people are immigrants who came en masse to the United States during the 1980s and 1990s, after dictator Pol Pot's Khmer Rouge movement. He annihilated more than one million Cambodians at several interment camps that became known as the Killing Fields of Pol Pot.

Within days of coming to power, and applying a radical communist ideology, Pol Pot, the top ruler of the Cambodian

Cambodian

Congregations	39
Members	2,157
Population	275,738
Foreign Born	56%
2nd and 3rd Generation	44%

Communist Party, began emptying all large cities, including Phnom Penh, the capital city, of all inhabitants. All residents—young and old, healthy, handicapped, or ill—were forced to abandon their homes and walk away into the countryside. These displaced people were ushered to agricultural camps, where they were forced to perform manual labor every day from dawn to dusk.

The ruling communists especially targeted the well educated (including anyone who wore glasses)—government officials, military leaders, teachers, doctors, engineers, city dwellers, merchants, etc.—viewing them as having been corrupted by the Western culture, and therefore enemies of the Communist regime. These groups were the first to be executed, and were buried in 20,000 mass graves[2] scattered across the country. Between April 1975 and December 1978, an estimated one-third of the population (around 2 million people) perished at the hands of the communists from starvation, forced labor, illnesses, or execution, during a period of just under four years.[3]

When the Pol Pot Communist regime fell at the end of 1978, the Vietnamese invasion of Cambodia triggered a mass exodus. Hundreds of thousands of Cambodians flocked to neighboring Thailand in search of freedom. Unfortunately, as they crossed the borders, thousands more fell victim to bandits or stepped on minefields that had been planted by the Khmer Rouge along the nation's borders.

Furthermore, the Thai people refused to accept Cambodians into their country and pushed them back into their own land. A humanitarian relief operation came in response to an international outcry, leading to the establishment of refugee camps at the borders.

The Beginning of Cambodian Churches

Numerous relief agencies came to the Cambodians' rescue, and among them were many Christian teams. They came not just with humanitarian aid, but also with the message of hope in the Lord Jesus Christ. Thousands gave their lives to the Lord, and churches began to spring up in the camps. Key to this rapid church development was a few hundred believers who had survived the Killing Fields and became crucial players in early Christian work within these camps.

Within months of the US government-sponsored resettlement process, several thousand Cambodian refugees were transported to the United States. Many of them settled in California, especially in the greater Long Beach area, after a short stay in Camp Pendleton. Several thousand more were scattered in large cities across the country, including: Philadelphia, Atlanta, Houston, Dallas, Jose, Seattle,

St. Paul, Chicago, Boston, Lowell (Massachusetts), Columbus (Ohio), and Richmond (Virginia). Many sponsoring churches took up the crucial task of helping refugees start a new life by assisting them in finding employment, registering their children in school, or integrating them into the larger society. Many believers kept their faith after resettlement, and new believers were added. As a result, a number of churches were planted in these cities. Most of them still worship the Lord today.

Cambodian Southern Baptist Fellowship

The Cambodian Southern Baptist Fellowship is one of the largest association of Cambodian Christian churches in the United States. The Fellowship was formed in the mid-1980s, after a historic gathering of the newly arrived Cambodians at the SBC Annual Meeting. Since that time, Cambodian Baptists have come together for annual conferences. Typically, between 150 to 250 people attend the three-day conference, held during the Fourth of July weekend.

At the conference, first-generation Cambodians worship in their native language, whereas the second generation speaks English. Out of the thirty or so churches in the Fellowship, a few have acquired their own church buildings. Some Cambodian pastors are Christian converts from the refugee camps who had a chance to obtain a theological education.

At the same time, the church of Cambodia has grown at a very good pace, thanks to the relative openness of the government.

The Status of Cambodian Churches Today

Ministry among Cambodians in the United States, which was quite fruitful when refugees first arrived in the 1980s and 1990s, has leveled. Today, only a few churches experience baptism and growth. Although the Cambodian Baptist Fellowship annual conference attracts a respectable number of participants, the church planting movement has flagged due to a lack of leadership. We do need an awakening!

Nevertheless, the Baptist movement in Cambodia, led by Fellowship members who travel there regularly, seems to have produced a significant number of new churches, especially in the poorest and remote rural areas. Our Fellowship is in contact with nearly 400 churches in at least twelve (out of twenty-five) provinces. The Lord adds more believers every time a leader from our Fellowship travels to the provinces to conduct teaching and training classes for the villagers.

Unlike its neighboring countries, today's Cambodia is receptive to the Gospel and the current government under Hun Sen seems to be lenient in allowing the Gospel to be preached freely. A few thousand churches already have been planted throughout the land, including the countryside. Currently, there are approximately 20,000 believers and about 1,200 churches and home-based churches throughout Cambodia.

The pioneer work of Southern Baptist missionaries there was started in the early 1990s by Rev. Bruce Carlton and his team. Their early efforts are part of the foundation of the Cambodian Baptist Union (CBU).

Challenges for Partnership

Theological Education—Cambodians need a significantly greater number of seminary-trained teachers and preachers. This deficiency has translated into a shortage of capable teachers of the Word among first-generation Cambodians. An obvious remedy should be for our Baptist seminaries to offer scholarships, making theological education affordable to prospective students.

Church Planting—It is difficult to find leaders who are interested in church planting and who are willing to relocate to where a plant is needed.

Literature—The Cambodian Baptist churches generally use Bibles, hymnbooks, and other church resources printed in the Cambodian language, but these materials are produced by other denominations. This lack of Southern Baptist literature in Khmer (which would help describe our Southern Baptist identity) often puts our Baptist members in a difficult position to explain our heritage and distinctiveness. A short booklet, which would briefly summarize basic Southern Baptist beliefs, practices, and history, and include the work among the ethnic groups, would help us explain Baptist tenets with proper perspectives.

Church Revitalization—The Cambodian Baptist Fellowship plays a vital role in encouraging its members and in keeping the connection and communication among churches alive. Another critical task is to draw more of the younger generations into the Fellowship. Each year, attendants receive discipleship training and return home energized for service.

"From the Killing Fields to the Blessing Field" was the theme from which the name Blessing Field was inspired. The Blessing Field is located in Macon, Georgia, where the camp and conference have been held every year since 2007. It is a strategic gathering point for churches in the eastern United States, where most Cambodian

Southern Baptist churches are located. The Fellowship is contemplating a more frequent use of the camp for training, retreats, and discipleship, which would further benefit churches in the area. The Blessing Field is now recognized as a 501(c)(3) organization by the IRS and opens its doors to non-Cambodian Baptist church groups for use.

CHINESE BAPTIST FELLOWSHIP

Chinese Population in North America

Chinese people have an extensive history in North America. Many from southern China came to North America in the early nineteenth century to escape famine in their homeland. After World War II, the Chinese population in America began to grow significantly as laws that limited Chinese immigration were amended or abolished. After the Communist Party took over China in 1949, many Chinese living in the United States could no longer return to their home country. As a result, many highly educated Chinese immigrants were granted refugee status in the US. During this same time, students from Taiwan, Hong Kong, and Southeast Asia came to North America to pursue higher education and professional careers.[4]

Since the People's Republic of China adopted an Open-Door emigration policy in the early 1980s, large numbers of people from Mainland China migrated to North America to reunite with their families and seek a better life. As the economy in Mainland China improved, more people came to North America to study, and then made this land their home. As the Chinese economy has

Chinese

Congregations	245
Members	28,510
Population	4,133,674
Foreign Born	70%
2nd and 3rd Generation	30%

Number of persons of this ethnic group without a personal relationship with Christ

3,978,849

This represents

96%

of the ethnic group total population

1 to 15,526

Is the ratio of Southern Baptist congregations to population of this ethnic group

continued to expand in recent years, many of its citizens have come to conduct business and invest in North America.

Among the Chinese population in the US are immigrants from Southeast Asia who hail from countries such as Indonesia, Malaysia, the Philippines, Singapore, Thailand, and Vietnam.

From these immigrants, four types of Chinese cultures developed in North America:
1. Cantonese-speaking Chinese from Hong Kong
2. Mandarin-speaking Chinese from Taiwan
3. Chinese from Mainland China
4. American- or Canadian-born Chinese (ABC and CBC, respectively)

There are vast differences in their habits, values, political views, and their adaptation to North American culture. Chinese churches in this melting pot have faced the challenges of having two cultures and three languages among one people, which makes pastoring more complicated than among some other ethnic groups.[5]

Language Variations

In the early days, most Chinese were from counties in the western Guangdong province and spoke the dialects of their home villages. After WWII, the Chinese migrants from Hong Kong spoke Cantonese, while those from Taiwan spoke Mandarin. Since the large number of immigrants came to the US from Mainland China after the 1980s, the common language among Chinese immigrants is Mandarin, though many also speak their own dialects, such as Fujianese.

The second generation of Chinese, those born in North America or who came as children, speak English, with many of them speaking English only.[6]

Chinese Population Growth

According to American census records from 2000, the Chinese population in the United States was 2,432,585, or 0.9 percent of the total population. According to the latest census data, the Chinese population has grown close to over four million, a 40 percent increase in a single decade. The four states with the highest Chinese populations are California (1,253,100), New York (577,000), Texas (157,000), and New Jersey (134,500).

Send Cities

The major cities that NAMB's Send North America strategy (locations where NAMB has prioritized its work in the cities with the greatest spiritual need and potential influence throughout North America) has targeted are some of the same cities with large Chinese populations. For example, San Francisco, Los Angeles, and New York all have Chinese populations of over half a million each, while Chicago has close to 100,000 residents of Chinese ancestry.

Chinese Southern Baptist Work

Chinese Southern Baptist work can be dated back to 1854, with the Chinese Baptist Chapel of the Baptist Church in Sacramento, California. By 1987, there were 156 Chinese Southern Baptist ministries (including ministry locations in western Canada). Per the 2015 Annual Church Profile, there are 245 Chinese congregations that cooperate with the Southern Baptist Convention. Their Cooperative Program giving per resident member is higher than the national average of all churches.

The Chinese Baptist Fellowship

The Chinese Baptist Fellowship of the United States and Canada was organized in 1980, when Chinese Baptists worldwide attended the Baptist World Alliance in Toronto to connect with Chinese Baptists in North America. As of February 2015, there are 194 Chinese Baptist churches that cooperate with the SBC in the United States and 82 Chinese Baptist churches affiliated with the CNBC (Canadian National Baptist Convention; formerly the CCSB, Canadian Convention of Southern Baptists) and CBOQ (Chinese Baptists of Ontario and Quebec).

Since 2010, the Chinese Baptist Fellowship and NAMB have shared and promoted the singular vision of planting Chinese Baptist churches. As of February 2015, there have been 65 Chinese church plants, with the majority being in the United States. This church planting movement has a dual focus:

1. Many Chinese from Mainland China are concentrated in the newly developed areas, and there is great need for the Gospel. We call and send church planters to go there to establish Bible study and home groups. We also rent churches or schools to start worship services. English-speaking churches often adopt these church plants and make them their Chinese ministries. This model stabilizes and grows the Chinese work.

2. Strong churches, after research and analysis of the population in the new cities, can send pastors or equipped Christians to Chinese population centers to start new work. With the support and supervision of the mother church, the success rate of developing a healthy and growing Chinese church plant is phenomenally greater.

If Southern Baptist churches open their facilities to a church plant, and even serve as its mother church, this will reduce the failure rate of these church plants.

English-Speaking Chinese Ministry

The challenge for an English ministry in Chinese Baptist churches in the United States involves balancing the outreach needs of new immigrant Chinese with the needs of second or third generation Chinese born in the US. The growth of Chinese-only worship services is projected to continue with the ongoing influx of immigrants, many of whom have children. As these Chinese children grow up in America and assimilate (this is the 1.5 generation), they become proficient in English, expanding the need for an English ministry.

There is also a growing number of children of Chinese ancestry who are born in the US. Ministry to the 1.5 generation born overseas is similar to that of their parents, yet much different from the ministry to the American-born Chinese. There are over a half million second-, third-, and fourth-generation Chinese in the US.

Some Chinese churches address this need by providing interpretations of the services in English. But hearing the Word preached second-hand becomes a burden for the next generation. The problems of limited resources and few English workers can be overcome, however, as the church grows larger. Notice the column with separate Chinese and English services in the western parts of the US. However, many Chinese Baptist churches do not get to this stage, as succeeding generations often leave the church. Some join non-Chinese, multi-ethnic churches, but many drop out and do not attend any church. Some churches may encourage this group to form English-only church plants, as has been done in Southern California. This can also motivate those from smaller Chinese-speaking churches to gather in significant numbers in this mission church. NAMB can assist in starting such English-speaking next-generation mission churches.

Larger churches in heavily Chinese-populated areas can minister by developing separate Cantonese (or Mandarin) and English services. Some can provide all three languages. Most Chinese Baptist churches are small, however, and cannot offer English on their own, as indicated by the large number of Chinese-only services and

Chinese-to-English translated services. NAMB can assist in recruiting non-Chinese English-speaking ministers to begin a separate English service.

One of the needs of the next generation is to be included in the church's decision-making process, and Baptist polity in Chinese Baptist churches may take longer than this generation can tolerate. They desire more technology and social-media solutions, which they already use at work, in helping the church. NAMB can train church members to share effective congregational/committee/small-group decision making to promote church unity. NAMB also can create dialogue between pastors born overseas and English workers to foster acceptance and team ministry.

The next generation may also feel discouraged that the biblical mandate to move beyond an exclusively Chinese church environment is not being implemented. They desire community involvement, especially multi-ethnic cooperation. They want hands-on, practical ministry in the community. They also want to follow the first generation's model to obey the Great Commission and to work with them to do missions beyond the Chinese culture and reach other ethnic groups. (NAMB can assist in community efforts to reach other ethnic groups to model Christ-like outreach.)

Resources from Baptist associations, state conventions, and the Southern Baptist Convention can be used to encourage monetary contributions and personnel for calling out and training English workers. Perhaps both Chinese and non-Chinese workers from one part of the United States can be sent to those churches with limited resources to do English ministry.

Challenges for Partnership

Funding: The Cooperative Baptist Fellowship has put together a $50,000 budget to cover church planting tasks in two years. This effort is commendable, but such limited funding can only provide for the promotion, training and planter retreat, as well as some startup funding for equipment and materials. The budget is not sufficient to supplement a church planter's monthly salary. We are 100 percent dependent on the support from partnership churches, local associations, state conventions and NAMB to fund church planter's monthly supplements.

Training: There are two types of new pastors: recent seminary graduates and pastors with a wealth of experience from other denominations, but with no background in the Baptist faith. Orientation is a definite help to them. Some Baptist churches will require these pastors to attend a Baptist seminary to learn Baptist faith and polity. Some of these pastors refuse to attend. Due to the shortage of pastors, however, this requirement is often overlooked. Even deacons may not have Baptist backgrounds. As a result, the congregation's demand for their leaders to embrace Baptist faith and polity is lessened. This is a serious situation among the churches.

The growth of the Chinese population presents both opportunities and challenges. The big opportunity is that the harvest field is ripe here in North America. Chinese Southern Baptist churches are a growing force for the Great Commission. Many new churches have to be planted among the new immigrants and the next generations. The SBC has to develop resources to disciple believers from different backgrounds and cultures, as well as mobilize and develop workers for the harvest.

FILIPINO SOUTHERN BAPTIST FELLOWSHIP OF NORTH AMERICA

The Philippines started as a colony of Spain in the early 1500s, and remained under Spanish rule for over three hundred years.[7] Spanish colonization introduced a political and religious system according to their model, thus making the Philippines the only "Christian country" in Asia (surrounded by Hindu, Muslim, and Buddhist neighbors). Overall, the Philippine population is 85 percent Roman Catholic, 10 percent Protestant, and 5 percent Muslim and other religions.[8] American missionaries introduced Protestantism to the islands in the early 1900s.[9] Thus, most Filipinos migrating to North America are members of Roman Catholic churches, while a small number belong to Protestant and evangelical denominations.

Filipino

Congregations	192
Members	12,881
Population	2,848,148
Foreign Born	66%
2nd and 3rd Generation	34%

Number of persons of this ethnic group without a personal relationship with Christ

2,566,918

This represents
90%
of the ethnic group total population

1 to 14,155

is the ratio of Southern Baptist congregations to population of this ethnic group

Filipino Americans

Filipino Americans in the United States America are a diverse group with a population of about four million, according to the US State

Department, with the largest numbers residing in the California and tri-state areas (Connecticut, New Jersey, and New York).[10] Filipino Americans rank as the second most populous Asian American subgroup in the United States. With strong historical ties to the US, Filipinos are proficient in English.

Attracted by economic and educational opportunities, Filipino Americans tend to live in and around metropolitan areas or in other urban areas. A high proportion of Filipinos immigrate to the US as professionals, many of them having acquired college or graduate degrees from the Philippines. Significant proportions are nurses, students, and from families of immigrants. Filipino females represent the largest number of Asian nurses in the US. With household incomes in the middle and upper-middle income brackets, many Filipino Americans enjoy a higher standard of living, as compared to other Asian American subgroups.[11]

Knowing the differences in Filipino generations in the United States can be helpful in witnessing to them. Three cultural influences affect Filipino thoughts and decisions: (1) Malayan timid passivity; (2) superficially absorbed Spanish pride; and (3) Americanized democratic ideals. Furthermore, Filipinos in the US may be classified according to their place of origin, dialect, religion, education, profession, economic standing, and length of residency. First-generation Filipinos bring to the United States their cultural and linguistic lives and values. Second-generation Filipinos (Filipino Americans) endeavor to assimilate into American society. Third-generation Filipinos (American Filipinos) easily assimilate into American society. Fourth-generation Filipinos are Americans by language and by culture. Each of these generations demands an indigenous approach for evangelism and church-planting strategies. It is important to have compatible leadership and ministries targeted to each generation of Filipinos in North America, as significant positive behavioral differences can be observed after Filipinos experience conversion to Jesus Christ.

Filipino Canadians

Filipino immigration to Canada began in 1930. These first immigrants were mainly women who worked as nurses, teachers, or other healthcare workers. During the 1990s, more Filipinos came as families and independents instead of being sponsored by family or recruited as contract workers. Since the 1990s, there has been a steady increase in the flow of Filipinos entering Canada. As of 2006, Filipinos comprise the largest group of new immigrants to Canada, surpassing groups from both China and India.[12]

According to the 2011 Canadian census, there are around 660,000 Filipinos living in Canada,[13] most of them living in urbanized areas, especially Greater Toronto and Winnipeg. This number is growing yearly due to Canada's more liberal immigration laws to compensate for their low population growth. Filipino Canadians are the third-largest Asian-Canadian group in the nation after the Indian and Chinese communities. On average, Canada received about 20,500 Filipino immigrants every year from 2001 to 2006.[14]

Overwhelming Challenges

The population growth of immigrant Filipinos over the last decade is overwhelming and presses an urgent need for Gospel partnerships among churches and mission organizations. Currently, only about 200 Filipino Baptist churches in the US and Canada work with Southern Baptists. Indeed, the harvest is great (Luke 10:2)! In response to the challenging need, the Filipino Church Planting Network of North America was formed in 2010 through a partnership of passionate Filipino pastors from various state conventions and the North American Mission Board.

The creation of the network gave birth to 20/20 Vision, a national shared-strategy of starting 100 Filipino churches by the year 2020. The national fellowship adopted its process as part of the campaign across North America. The church-planting strategy covers three important key processes to realize the vision: (1) Discover (Identify Places, Partners, and Planters); (2) Develop (Planter, Sponsoring Church, Church Planting team); and (3) Deploy (Church Planter, Sending Church, Partner Agencies). This process is in line with our partnership with NAMB and several state conventions.

Opportunities for Partnership

- Intentionally promote our two viable options to reach the four million with the Gospel in partnership with our 200 churches to develop homegrown church planters and the legally sponsored importation of church planters from the Philippines.
- Proactively promote and partner in Filipino American Church Planting in North America for funding and resourcing.
- Allow Filipino Americans the opportunity to reach their own people with the Gospel as IMB missionaries to the Philippines.

HMONG BAPTIST ASSOCIATION

The Hmong people are a Southeast Asian highland people who are predominantly hill farmers, raising livestock, and cultivating rice and other grain for their needs. The Hmong trace their ancestry back to China and claim China as their native homeland. They are relatively new arrivals on the Southeast Asian peninsula, many moving south in order to avoid harassment by Chinese emperors.

Today, there are more than nine million Hmong people living in China (Guizhou, Yunnan, Hunan). There are also significant numbers living in Laos, Thailand, Vietnam, and Burma. Animism is the basis of faith for most Hmong people, including the practice of ancestral worship and shamanism.[15]

Hmong

Congregations	48
Members	4,308
Population	285,064
Foreign Born	37%
2nd and 3rd Generation	63%

Number of persons of this ethnic group without a personal relationship with Christ

280,756

This represents

98%

of the ethnic group total population

1 to **5,806**

is the ratio of Southern Baptist congregations to population of this ethnic group

Hmong Believers in the Southern Baptist Convention

An amendment passed by the American government in 1976 made it possible for many Hmong refugees to migrate to the United States. There are more than 300,000 Hmong people living in the US today. The three states that have the highest number of Hmong people are (in descending order): California, Wisconsin, and Minnesota.[16]

At the start of 1975, Southern Baptists and other Christian denominations began to sponsor Hmong refugees to the United States. This eventually led to the conversion of many Hmong people and the start of Hmong churches. Today, five percent of the Hmong population have been reached with the Gospel of Jesus Christ in the United States.

The influence and leadership of Southern Baptists has been the reason for the many Hmong people who have given their lives to Jesus Christ and for the start of Hmong-speaking churches across the United States. Among those leaders, Rev. Joshua Vang was the first Hmong leader appointed by the Home Mission Board as ethnic missionary for Indochinese refugees in the USA. He coordinated Lao and Hmong refugees joining Southern Baptists in 1976.

Hmong Baptist National Association

While many Hmong churches were planted and established through the help of Southern Baptist leaders, these churches were facing difficulties such as language barriers, lack of printed material, and no worship facilities. In 1991, leaders from Hmong Baptist churches came together in Kansas City, Kansas, to discuss and establish a coordinating office for all Hmong churches. The Hmong Baptist Fellowship came into existence through their recognition of the need for guidance and leadership. Pastor Tong Zong Vang was elected as the first executive director of Hmong Baptist National Association (HBNA), headquartered in St. Paul, Minnesota.

The association adopted as its mission: "To equip and empower churches and Christian leaders to effectively serve and to make a difference in the growing Body of Christ around the world until we all reach unity in the faith and in the knowledge of the Son of God and become mature, attaining to the whole measure of the fullness of Christ (Ephesians 4:12–14)." Further, the association has a vision: "To see effective Christian leaders and churches fulfill the Great Commission (Matthew 29:18–21) and the mobilization of all Hmong Baptist Churches to fulfill the Great Commission. Matthew 28:18–20."

The Work of the Hmong Baptist National Association

Currently there are 56 Hmong Baptist congregations across the United States: Georgia (5); North Carolina (6); Tennessee (1); Arkansas (4); Oklahoma (2); Texas (2); Michigan (4); Minneapolis (10); Wisconsin (8); Kansas (1); Ohio (1); Missouri (1); California (9); and Colorado (2).

The Hmong Baptist National Association has the following ministries: men's, women's, youth, love and care, education, Sunday school and small group, and collegiates. On leadership and church strengthening, the association has offices for pastoral leadership, church administration, church finance, evangelism, discipleship, and stewardship.[17]

HBNA also has home missions components that include WMU and Brotherhood organizations, and global missions focusing on Hmong works in Vietnam and

Thailand. HBNA also has a church planting team with leaders that are responsible for the western, northern, and southern regions.

CHALLENGES FOR PARTNERSHIP

How the SBC can help HBNA

1. Develop resources for discipleship materials.
2. Learn and grow into a better way of structuring Hmong Fellowship churches.
3. Arrange for SBC seminaries and their colleges to meet with high school students and share information during summer camps and annual meetings about their programs and education possibilities.
4. Develop a pastoral study program for Hmong pastors who have been unable to attend seminary or engage in other higher education opportunities.

How HBNA Can Help the SBC

1. Promote and challenge local Hmong churches to be more involved with their local associations and state conventions.
2. Partner with LifeWay to translate discipleship materials into Hmong language.
3. Develop more leaders who will have a sense of passion for joining SBC leadership and the mission field.

JAPANESE CHURCH PLANTING NETWORK

Background

The SBC's Japanese Church Planting Network (JCPN) was organized in March 2003 by seven Japanese churches. Since 2000, the network has planted eleven Japanese churches, and fifteen additional churches are working with the cooperation of JCPN, the local association, state conventions, and the SBC.[18]

JCPN churches are located in Lynnwood and Tacoma (Washington); Portland and Eugene (Oregon); Pasadena, Paloma, and San Diego (California); Phoenix (Arizona); Denver (Colorado); St. Louis (Missouri); San Antonio (Texas); Pittsburgh (Pennsylvania); Washington, D.C; Orlando (Florida); and Pearl City (Hawaii).

Demographics

Total population of Japanese in USA and Canada

- USA: 841,825 (US Census Bureau, 2010)
- Canada: 73,315 (The visible minority population by ethnic origin for CMAs: 2001)

Currently there are about thirty Japanese churches and thirty Japanese mission churches in the SBC. The Network plans to plant an additional thirty churches.

Japanese

Congregations	46
Members	4,461
Population	757,468
Foreign Born	41%
2nd and 3rd Generation	59%

Number of persons of this ethnic group without a personal relationship with Christ

745,438

This represents

98%

of the ethnic group total population

Opportunities for Partnership

1. We continue to work with SBC entities to plant new Japanese churches and will expand our work to Asian American church planting for the second generation. We will also plant new churches in Japan and support church planters in 10/40 Window nations.

1 to **17,144**

is the ratio of Southern Baptist congregations to population of this ethnic group

2. The Network appreciates the SBC's cooperation in supporting church planters, but greater cooperation is needed. The following are the basic steps to effectively start a church working with state conventions, association, and local churches:

    - JCPN identifies a city that has no Japanese Southern Baptist church, putting a priority on the size of the Japanese population and the number of existing Japanese churches.
    - JCPN finds core families willing to start a Bible study. The Network waits until we identify someone to start a Bible study in Japanese.
    - The Network connects partners with the help of the North American Mission Board. We continue to want NAMB to serve as the connection between JCPN and state conventions and local associations to start Japanese church planting in any city, just as Brother Jeremy Sin has done until now.
    - The Network recruits Japanese church planters in the USA and Japan.

- The Network starts a Japanese Bible study before the church planter comes in because it takes time to get a visa, and even more preparation to deploy the church planter.
- The Network decides on sponsoring churches.
- The Network organizes the church-planting team with the state convention, association, and local sponsoring church and designs a financial plan to support the church planter.

3. The Network needs SBC assistance or sponsorship for immigration visas for Japanese church planters to come to the US.
4. The Network needs Southern Baptist churches for partnerships. All JCPN staff are local pastors, working as volunteers for the Network. The work of the board of directors is limited because of their pastoral care for their own congregations.

KOREAN BAPTIST FELLOWSHIP

Korean Americans, or Americans of Korean descent, are mostly from South Korea, with a small percentage from North Korea. There are more than 1.4 million Korean Americans in the United States, according to the latest US census, up by 41 percent since 2000. In 2011, they made up 9.5 percent of the total Asian American population in the United States. Nearly 62 percent are foreign born. Koreans are the fifth largest Asian American community, after Chinese, Indians, Filipinos, and Vietnamese.

Many Korean immigrants attain US citizenship, ranking them twelfth among all US naturalizations in 2012, and fifth among Asians. The US is home to the second largest Korean diaspora community in the world, after the People's Republic of China.[19]

Here are the ten states, based on 2010 US Census Bureau statistics, with the largest Korean American populations: California

Korean

Congregations	872
Members	72,584
Population	1,460,483
Foreign Born	72%
2nd and 3rd Generation	28%

Number of persons of this ethnic group without a personal relationship with Christ

1,270,483

This represents

87%

of the ethnic group total population

1 to **1,655**

is the ratio of Southern Baptist congregations to population of this ethnic group

(505,225), New York (153,609), New Jersey (100,334), Virginia (82,006), Texas (85,332), Washington (80,049), Illinois (70,263), Georgia (60,836), Maryland (55,051), and Pennsylvania (47,429). Hawaii was the state with the highest concentration of Korean Americans, compared to its total state population, with 48,699 residents of Korean descent.

History and Current Status

The Korean Baptist Fellowship, which was established with the support of the Southern Baptist Convention in the 1960s, rapidly developed during the late 1970s after revision of the Immigration Act under President John F. Kennedy. The Korean Fellowship Group has now reached more than 850 churches that are widely spread throughout America, with the foundational support of the Language Missions Division of the Home Mission Board.

However, due to a severe language barrier and cultural differences, Korean immigrants could not fully participate within the full range of Southern Baptist life. This prevented most Korean pastors and leaders from participating in association and state convention activities, which were conducting businesses in English. Most were unable to take advantage of English resources provided by the associations and state conventions.

With help from the Language Mission Division of the Home Mission Board, Korean churches met in 1981 for the purpose of fellowship and encouragement, as well as to share ministry information. The following year, they were able to establish the Council of Korean Southern Baptist Churches in America. With this new entity, Korean churches were able to engage its ministries at the association and state convention levels.

The Korean Fellowship has officers (president, first vice president, second vice president, executive director, secretary, and treasurer) and eight agencies (Korean Baptist Overseas Mission Board, Home Mission Board, Education Department, Pastoral Department, English Ministry Department, WMU, Brotherhood, and the Seminary Department) to meet and support the needs of the Korean Baptist churches in America.[20]

The Korean Baptist Overseas Mission Board, in close cooperation with IMB, has sent approximately 320 missionaries worldwide through IMB, and currently has 188 in mission fields. It has also sent out over 45 missionaries on its own.[21]

The Korean Home Mission Board, in cooperation with NAMB, has initiated three mission conferences to mobilize church planters for the Koreans and for other ethnic groups. They have worked diligently to plant a new Korean church and raised a special mission fund to sponsor thirty-seven Korean church plants.

The Education Department and the Pastoral Department each held annual conferences to meet various pastoral needs and to provide resources on evangelism, discipleship, preaching, and spiritual renewal. The English Ministry Department has supported the English-speaking Korean churches in planting new churches and providing pastoral fellowship and mentorship.

The WMU has conducted its own annual seminar to promote missions, to cultivate future WMU leaders, and to promote annual missions offerings.

The Brotherhood, in cooperation with the Annuity Board, has promoted the annuity program for Korean pastors. The Seminary Department has compiled information about Korean or Korean American students enrolled at the six SBC seminaries and given it to Korean churches. This program also helps the students find ministry fields upon graduation.

The Council of Korean Southern Baptist Churches has organized thirty associations in all fifty states. The council has two major committees: the operating committee, which is composed of six elected officers and eight department leaders; and the executive committee, which is composed of twenty delegates from the thirty Korean associations. The Council holds its annual convention in June, where it elects new officers and committee members and adopts a new operating budget and various resolutions. The Council executive director is a full-time position that directs all business while working closely with other offices and department leaders.

Challenges for Partnership

Korean Southern Baptist churches in America have operated within their own council since 1981 in order to accomplish greater mission work. To fulfill this purpose, the Korean churches have pledged to give double or triple their Cooperative Program mission offerings.

With the help of the Home Mission Board, Korean churches started the Korean Fellowship, which was truly to foster fellowship among Korean pastors. Over the years it has expanded to the Council of Korean Southern Baptist Churches in America, mirroring the Convention's structure. The Council, with limited resources, has been serving Korean churches and their various ministry needs, just as associations, state conventions, NAMB, and IMB do for all Southern Baptist churches.

Historically, Koreans have found it difficult to assimilate to Western culture due to unique language and cultural barriers. Therefore, the Fellowship seeks guidance from the SBC Executive Committee for better solutions. Since the beginning, the leadership of the Council has been working hard to find better solutions for its fellowshipping churches.

LAOTIAN BAPTIST FELLOWSHIP

Laotian History/Heritage

Lao or Laotian people arrived onto the shores of the United States because of the Indo-China War. They came from Laos, a small landlocked country in Southeast Asia situated between Thailand to the west, Vietnam to the east, Cambodia to the south, Myanmar to the northwest, and China to the north.

Laos became a French protectorate in 1893 and gained its independence from France in 1954 as a constitutional monarchical state. From French colony to a self-governed country with Western influence, the country was under a kingship and a democratically elected government. As soon as the country became an independent state, it was unable to meet its own needs politically, economically, and militarily. The people were dependent upon financial, economic, and military aid from Western countries such as the United States, England, France, and others for basic needs. Because of that, the Communist political segment of Lao society fought against a democratically elected government. That faction received its political influence and support from

Laotian

Congregations	43
Members	2,392
Population	213,954
Foreign Born	58%
2nd and 3rd Generation	42%

Number of persons of this ethnic group without a personal relationship with Christ

205,903

This represents
96%
of the ethnic group total population

1 to **5,023**

is the ratio of Southern Baptist congregations to population of this ethnic group

countries like the Soviet Union, China, and communist or socialist countries, but most importantly, North Vietnam.

The country received its independence, but it involved itself in a civil war. Three factions, the neutralist, the communist, and the conservative, fought over the ideology of the West versus the East. War ensued for over thirty years. After US armed forces withdrew from Vietnam in July 1975, the Pathet Lao or Lao Hak Xat, the communist faction, took control of the country.

Laotian Refugees

When communists took control of the country politically, there was much chaos and uncertainty. Laotian citizens, especially those who formerly worked for the government and those who aided the United States in the war effort, were afraid of retaliation. They fled from their families and their homes by thousands. They crossed the Mekong River under the cover of night into Thailand. From 1975 to the mid-1980s, more than 300,000 crowded the few refugee camps available in Thailand. Unsanitary living conditions and harsh treatment by camp officials made life extremely hard and horrible for the Lao refugees.[22]

After 1980, the government of Thailand tried to stop or slow the flow of Laotian refugees pouring into the country by turning them back or not admitting them into already crowded refugee camps. The purpose of doing so was to close these refugee camps as soon as it was feasible. The policy created an enormous international outcry and controversy among countries that supported humanitarian aid to homeless people. Out of this chaos, the suggestions were to screen economic refugees. Only political refugees would be admitted into refugee camps. After these people were admitted into the camps, they could be given opportunities for resettlement in countries such as the United States, Canada, France, Argentina, China, and others. Once they were found qualified, they could be processed speedily for resettlement in order to close those camps by certain target dates.[23]

Resettlement Programs

For the sake of humanitarianism, the United States government established a resettlement program for Laotian refugees who had worked closely with the American aid agencies, armed forces, and those who were ex-government employees, including those who were part of armed forces, Lao royal army, policemen, and other civilian state servants.

According to information published by the UCLA Asian American Studies Center, citing the 2000 Census, 198,203 Laotians lived throughout the United States. It explained further that from 1979 to 1981, an estimated 105,477 "first wave" Laotian refugees were admitted into the United States under the Indochina Migration and Refugee Assistance Act. From 1986 to 1989, a total of 52,864 "second wave" Laotian refugees arrived in the US and settled in communities across the country, and were sponsored by resettlement agencies, religious organizations, churches, and American families. Laotian people often settled in medium-sized cities such as Fresno, San Diego, Stockton, and Sacramento in California.[24]

According to the 2001 Canadian census, there were 16,950 living in Canada. The largest Laotian concentrations in Canada were in Toronto, Montreal, Quebec, Vancouver, Calgary, and Winnipeg.[25]

The Growth of Laotian Communities

Though the numbers from these sources are slightly different, according to the US census of 2000, the Laotian population grew to 168,707.[26] Ten years later, the US census indicated that the Laotian population in the United States further grew to 191,200.[27] This figure of Laotian people is included in total Asian population growth according to the 2010 US census.

States with fewer than 937 Laotians were not listed. These numbers could shift due to secondary migration to different states where their employment took them. Normally, the people also liked to congregate near relatives and friends to benefit from mutual support and to encourage one another in coping with difficulties and barriers to full resettlement.

According to the 2010 US census, Laotian population distribution was only slightly different from the 2000 census. Some of the Laotian population numbers in certain localities were collected through Buddhist temples, Laotian associations, and Lao American Societies, which would have the most accurate numbers since they worked with Laotian residents on a regular basis.

Challenges for Partnership

Change in Church Planting Strategy

Some Baptist associations have more than one people group; however, church-planting efforts should not be limited to only one church plant for a particular group. Instead, more churches should be planted to encourage churches to reach more.

The effort for church planting should not be limited only to the state Baptist convention and/or NAMB levels. Strategies should include the local church level and should work hand-in-hand with local ethnic minority leaders. Current strategies frequently posture NAMB and state conventions as experts without taking into consideration input from local Baptists who know the people and the culture.

NAMB and the local Southern Baptists should partner with local Lao leaders to recruit, invest in, and train future local leaders. Currently, fewer and fewer Laotians are qualified for church planter positions due to their lack of seminary experience.

Global Need

Laotian people are scattered around the world. In fact, there are more Laotians outside of Laos than are within the borders of Laos. Cambodia is home to approximately 1.5 million Lao, known as Cambodian-Lao. Thai-Lao, Laotians living in Thailand, number more than 40 million. Millions of people living in southern China speak Lao, as do millions more in northern Vietnam. In addition, a large number of Laotians live in various countries in Europe, as well as Argentina.

VIETNAMESE BAPTIST FELLOWSHIP

The history of Vietnamese Americans begins with the end of the Vietnam War in April 1975. After an almost twenty-year involvement in Vietnam, the United States government unenthusiastically agreed to withdraw its financial and military support for South Vietnam by signing the Paris Agreement. The US government changed its direction toward the Vietnam War. There were many reasons leading to this troop withdrawal policy—increased anti-war protest, the overwhelming loss of pride regarding the war, the depressed economy, the decreased global credibility, and a loss of faith in the government.

After twenty years at war, Vietnamese people longed for peace. They expected all sides to honor the promises of the Paris Peace Agreement. However, soon after the withdrawal of the United States' military and economic support, the Communist regime from the North invaded South Vietnam. The North Vietnamese army attacked Phuoc-Long Province, located about fifty-eight miles from Saigon, to test the US government's policy. President Gerald Ford responded to the Communist invasion by holding a press conference stating that the US government was unwilling to re-enter the war in Vietnam.

Knowing the US government's unwillingness to fight, in mid-March and early April 1975 the North Vietnamese army attacked the South highland and took control of areas such as Pleiku, Kontum, and Ban-me-thuot. As a result of this military offensive, about one million refugees poured out of these areas and headed for Saigon and the coast. Saigon, the former capital of South Vietnam, fell to the North Vietnamese regime and Viet Cong on April 30, 1975. The first wave of Vietnamese refugees to the United States took place at that time.

Vietnamese

Congregations	151
Members	11,809
Population	1,738,848
Foreign Born	68%
2nd and 3rd Generation	32%

Number of persons of this ethnic group without a personal relationship with Christ

1,705,148

This represents
98%
of the ethnic group total population

1 to 11,469
is the ratio of Southern Baptist congregations to population of this ethnic group

Pre-1975

In over a thousand years of history, Vietnamese have rarely escaped their homeland. During nearly one hundred years under French rule (1858–1945), some Vietnamese were forced to leave their country to labor in French colonies.

Before the 1950s, there was a small number of Vietnamese Americans. During the 1950s and 1960s, a few hundred Vietnamese arrived in the United States for academic and military training purposes. According to the US Immigration and Naturalization Services, only 650 Vietnamese arrived in the United States from 1950 to 1974.

Post-1975

Most Vietnamese Americans arrived in the United States after the end of the Vietnam War. According to the US Census Bureau, in 2015 there were more than 1.7 million Vietnamese living in the United States, including 1.2 million refugees and immigrants, and about 550,000 US-born citizens of Vietnamese heritage. They became the fourth largest group of Asian Americans, after Chinese Americans, Filipino Americans, and Asian Indian Americans. Between 2000 and 2015, the US Vietnamese population gained approximately 600,000 residents.

Vietnamese Americans mainly live in metropolitan areas, including Orange County, San Jose, and San Diego, California; Houston, Texas; Fairfax County, Virginia; King County, Washington; and Chicago, Illinois.

VIETNAM REFUGEES AND IMMIGRANTS

The First Wave 1975–1977

The Vietnamese Communists took over Vietnam on April 30, 1975. In an attempt to pursue the gift of God that is called liberty, Vietnamese people decided to escape their homeland. Within the first week after the end of the Vietnam War, about 130,000 Vietnamese fled Vietnam (US Immigration, 2000). They were airlifted and sealifted out of Vietnam by US military forces. This created the first massive wave of Vietnamese from Vietnam to the US. Many of these Vietnamese served with the South Vietnamese government and fought alongside the American forces. Religious leaders also escaped Vietnam. Vietnamese people left Vietnam during this first wave for political and religious purposes. Most of them had political connections with the US government, high levels of English proficiency, education, and wealth.

These early Vietnamese refugees faced many difficulties when they first came to the New World. They were moved to a military camp and had to live there until an American citizen sponsored them. Many churches and non-profit organizations were their main sponsors.

The Second Wave 1978–1986

Shortly after the end of the Vietnam War, the Vietnamese Communist government sent leaders of the former South Vietnamese government, leaders of political parties, and religious leaders to prisons called "re-education camps" and their families to "new economic zones." These sites had been undeveloped or abandoned during the turbulence of war. Most of the leaders had a close relationship with the first wave of Vietnamese refugees and were associated with the South Vietnamese government. Their connection to both the former South Vietnam government and the United States government made them targets of persecution for the Vietnamese Communist government.

Scholars A. Do, T. Phan, and E. Garcia (2009) believe that about one million people were imprisoned without formal charges or trials, and approximately 165,000 people died in the Socialist Republic of Vietnam's re-education camps. These horrible situations caused hundreds of thousands of Vietnamese to flee the country.

They left Vietnam's shores by sea on makeshift boats and rafts. Additionally, in 1979, Vietnam was at war with the People's Republic of China (PRC). Many Chinese Vietnamese living in North Vietnam were the targets of that government's policies and made their escapes by boat.[28]

The second wave of Vietnamese refugees seemed to be poorer, less educated, and subject to greater trauma than the first wave (Chung & Bemak, 1998; Matsuoka, 1993). According to stories of the boat people, they often feared Vietnamese policemen, suffered from dehydration, and lost family members and friends during their escape. They were victims of hunger, malnutrition, assault, rape, and robbery by Thai pirates. Many children witnessed these violent behaviors.[29]

Some boat people escaped from Vietnam on large vessels. However, many boat people left their homeland on little wooden boats with old rebuilt engines. Dozens and sometimes hundreds of refugees crowded into small boats. They sat next to each other like fish tightly packed in a can of sardines. Days and nights went by, and sometimes the engine would suddenly stop. They would float with the wind without food and water. They dealt with fear from the crashing waves every minute. They suffered storms, robbery, and rape repeatedly. Many lost husbands, wives, children, parents, and relatives in their desperate search for relief. Some of them were kidnapped and others were killed and buried at sea.

After traveling on the ocean, many boat people came to refugee camps in Malaysia, Thailand, the Philippines, Hong Kong, and Indonesia. The conditions at these camps were very poor. The Vietnamese boat people in the camps were treated horribly, with frequent camp inspections and constant police oppression. An entire generation of children born in the camps had never known life outside the hurtful wire that surrounded them.

Without boat people's strength in seeking liberty and freedom, escape would have been impossible. No words can describe how terribly boat people suffered on these unforgettable escapes. The number of Vietnamese boat people was estimated at 600,000. They confronted death and risked their lives on the high seas to escape the unimaginably terrible reign of the Vietnamese Communist government. According to the report of the Office of the United Nations High Commissioner for Refugees, one-third of the boat people died at sea by murder, storms, illness, and food shortages. Many women were captured, molested, and raped by pirates.

In addition to the boat people of the second wave, another group of Vietnamese refugees escaped by land across the Cambodian border. They came to Thailand and ended up at the same camps, just like those who escaped by sea.

The Third Wave 1987–2000

Under Communist leadership, Vietnam became one of the poorest, most isolated countries of the world. This caused many Vietnamese people to leave the country in search of a better life. Alongside the second wave of Vietnamese refugees, the third wave began to rise up. These refugees came to the US by airplane directly from Vietnam. The third wave of Vietnamese immigrants to the US included the combination of Vietnamese refugees and immigrants in the Orderly Departure Program (ODP).

In 1987, the United States Congress passed the Amerasian Homecoming Act to welcome the US Amerasian children and their families to America. Many of these children were the progeny of US soldiers and Vietnamese women. Under this act, about 75,000 Amerasians and their family members arrived in the US. Phan (2003) cites a study from Ohio State University that found that 76 percent of Amerasians wanted to meet their fathers when they came to the United States, but 70 percent did not know their father's name. About 22 percent of them had tried to make contact, and only 3 percent had actually succeeded in meeting their biological fathers. In reality, many American fathers did not want to meet their left-behind children, because of fear, embarrassment, or lack of desire to take responsibility.[30]

In 1989, the US government signed an agreement with the Vietnamese government about releasing the political prisoners. This agreement requested the Vietnamese government to free all former South Vietnamese soldiers, officials, and religious leaders who were held in re-education camps and to allow them to come to the United States. According to the Encyclopedia of the New American Nation, the Vietnamese government released more than six thousand military and political prisoners in September 1987. In 1990, the first group of former Vietnamese political and re-education camp prisoners arrived in the United States under the Humanitarian Operation or "HO" Program.[31]

The Fourth Wave 2001–Present

The Vietnam Communist Party implemented a free-market economic reform program, known as Doi Moi (reform or renovation), which carefully managed the transition from a centrally-planned economy to a Socialist-oriented market economy. With the authority of the government remaining unchallenged, private ownership of farms languished and large companies engaged in commodity production and deregulation. Foreign investment was encouraged, while the government maintained control over strategic industry. The economy of Vietnam achieved rapid growth in agricultural and industrial production, construction and housing, exports and foreign investment.

During the Clinton administration, the US government established full diplomatic and economic relations with Vietnam in 1995. A new chapter in Vietnam was opened. Vietnamese exports to the United States increased near the $800 million mark in 2001; $3 billion in 2005; and $12.9 billion in 2008. The increase in business, trade, and educational relations between the US and Vietnam continued the flow of Vietnamese immigrants and Vietnamese international students to the US in the twenty-first century. Many of these people chose to live in the United States permanently. In addition, Vietnamese Americans usually seek to bring relatives to the US. Some Vietnamese Americans and US citizens of other ethnicities travel to Vietnam to marry Vietnamese citizens and start a new round of immigration for their spouses.

Resettlement Process

At the end of the Vietnam War, the majority of US citizens did not support a large-scale program to bring refugees to the United States. The majority was unfriendly toward Vietnamese refugees. The oppositional concerns of Americans were based on political conservatism, refugee crisis, and economic self-interest, such as job losses and increased public welfare expenditures.

The United States government used the Dispersal Policy on Refugees to reduce the social and economic impact of this large arrival of Vietnamese refugees. Do Hien Duc states that the main purposes of this policy were to: (1) relocate the Vietnamese refugees as quickly as possible so that they could achieve financial independence; (2) ease the impact of a large group of refugees on a given community which might otherwise increase the competition for jobs; (3) make it easier logistically to find sponsors; and (4) prevent the development of an ethnic ghetto.[32] A ghetto is defined as a "portion of a city in which members of a minority group live, especially because of social, legal, or economic pressure" (*Merriam-Webster Online Dictionary*, www.merriam-webster.com). Vietnamese refugees and immigrants were spread across the country by this policy.

The government's Interagency Task Force contracted with nine voluntary agencies to oversee the refugee resettlement process: Church World Service, the Lutheran Immigration and Refugee Service, the United Hebrew Immigration and Assistance Service, the International Rescue Committee, the American Funds for Czechoslovak Refugees, the United States Catholic Conference, the Travelers Aid International Social Service, World Relief, and the Council for Nationalities Service.

The primary task of the agencies was to find sponsors possessing the capacity to fulfill both financial and moral responsibilities and to match these sponsors with the refugee families. In short, the sponsors were to introduce the Vietnamese refugees into the new society while also helping them to become economically self-supporting. Sponsors included churches, affiliates, individual families, corporations, and companies with former Vietnamese employees.

Growth of Protestantism Among Vietnamese Americans

Protestantism officially came to Vietnam in 1911 by way of Dr. Robert Alexander Jaffray (1873–1945), a missionary commissioned by the Christian and Missionary Alliance (C&MA). During the presence of the US forces in Vietnam during the 1960s–1970s, American Protestant missionaries from different denominations such as Baptists, Presbyterians, Reformed, Church of Christ, and Methodists came. About half of Christians in Vietnam are members of ethnic minority groups.

Around 2 percent of Vietnamese are evangelical Christians. Many Vietnamese Christian churches have been established in the United States, and Southern Baptists represent the fastest growing denomination among Vietnamese American Christians. The two largest Protestant denominations among Vietnamese Americans are the Christian and Missionary Alliance (about 100 churches) and Southern Baptists (about 150 churches). The Vietnamese National Baptist Fellowship, US was established in 1984, and Christianity is one of the fastest expanding religions among Vietnamese Americans.

Vietnamese refugees and immigrants were influenced by American Christians during their resettlement process. Many churches and Christian believers opened their arms in welcoming the Vietnamese people. Among these American churches and groups, Southern Baptists made a significant impact in helping and sharing the Gospel to Vietnamese people.

Vietnamese Americans are much more likely to be Christians than Vietnamese who are residing in Vietnam. While Christians (mainly Roman Catholics) make up about 6 percent of Vietnam's total population, they comprise as much as 23 percent of the total Vietnamese American population.[33]

Opportunities for Evangelism

Existing agencies and organizational structures are already in place to provide opportunities to expand Christ's kingdom among Vietnamese Americans. These include the opportunity to:

- Expand beyond the 150 Vietnamese Southern Baptist churches in the United States. Many Vietnamese Baptist churches have been established in Vietnam since 2000. In 2006, Agape Baptist Church was established in Vietnam.
- Send more short-term US volunteer missionaries who are willing to go to Vietnam.
- Vietnamese Baptist Fellowship of North America has the Vietnamese Baptist Theological School (Education & Training), headquartered in Dallas, Texas, with five additional satellite centers in Vietnam.
- Vietnamese Mission Board (Evangelism & Mission).
- A network among Vietnamese Baptists around the world.

Challenges for Partnership

- Better Connections. SBC representatives can join the annual Vietnamese Baptist Conference to share information and show support.
- Better Missions Acts. The SBC can encourage local Baptist churches to send more short-term volunteer missionaries, and the IMB to send more permanent missionaries, to Vietnamese populations around the world.
- Better Network. The SBC can encourage local churches to sponsor Vietnamese church starters and church planters. The VBF can help to coordinate this network.
- Better Mentality. Leading Vietnamese Americans can be engaged to reach other people groups.

CONCLUSION

Asian American churches in the SBC face common challenges and share common recommendations with the SBC entities to assist them in Gospel ministry at home and abroad. We are part of the SBC family whom God has called from Asia to this land in the twentieth and twenty-first centuries, just as He brought European immigrants from many countries to build America over the past four centuries. Still, new immigrants arrive from both continents.

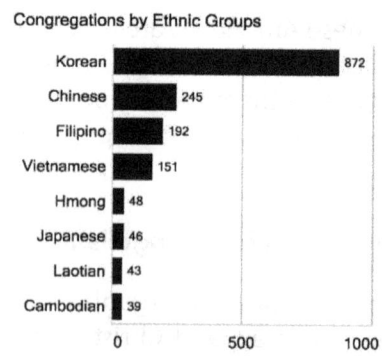

Congregations by Ethnic Groups

Korean	872
Chinese	245
Filipino	192
Vietnamese	151
Hmong	48
Japanese	46
Laotian	43
Cambodian	39

We desire to leave a legacy for the next generations showing how we worked together as equal partners in the Gospel. We have the same theological agreements and ministerial viewpoints to reach the world with the Gospel of our Lord Jesus Christ through our cooperative efforts and the Cooperative Program. Thus, we seek to work together in prayer and communication as equal partners in the Gospel.

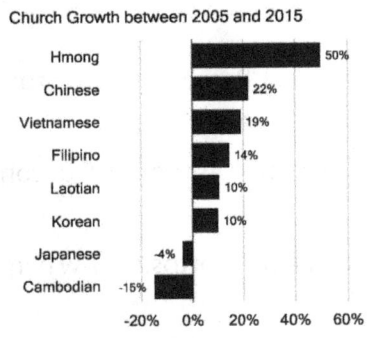

Asian American Baptist churches can contribute much in information and consultation regarding church planting and international missions. These eight Asian American fellowships and churches can work with the International Mission Board in those Asian countries. We speak both our native language and English. We know the culture and our people. Regarding the North American Mission Board, these Asian American pastors and leaders can reach out to our people groups. We can reach more people with NAMB's help, mobilizing more churches to plant new churches targeted toward Asian Americans. We are to work together, but as it stands today there are only a few denominational workers for these people groups. Both IMB and NAMB should consider hiring more workers to help the 1,900 Asian American Baptist churches in the SBC.

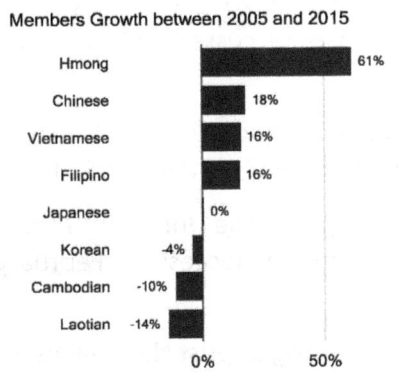

Asian American Southern Baptists can serve as trustees on the national boards and on the state Baptist convention boards, as well as in associational ministries and many other shared ministries to build the SBC stronger. Now is the time to see full reconciliation through the Gospel, serving as equal partners in ministry. Asians are not mission objects but rather partners in the Gospel, as Apostle Paul writes of Jews and Gentiles in his epistles.

We live in a new day, not as past generations. Our future will be brighter if we work together in equal partnership for the Great Commission. Many Asian Americans are highly educated from top-notch universities in America and in many top-paid professional fields. The next generation will be the minority group that experiences the most significant population growth in the US. Thus, we must prepare the next generations for the Great Commission, until the return of Christ for His Church![34]

BIBLIOGRAPHY

2015 American Community Survey. US Census Bureau. https://www.census.gov/programs-surveys/acs (accessed February 12, 2017).

"2015 Annual Church Profile." LifeWay Christian Resources. http://www.lifeway.com (accessed February 12, 2017).

"2015 Global Status of Evangelical Christianity." Global Research, IMB. http://grd.imb.org (accessed February 12, 2017).

"2015 Philippine Statistical Yearbook." Philippine Statistics Authority. Quezon City: Philippine Statistics Authority, 2015.

"2015 Racial Ethnic Counts." North American Mission Board. https://www.namb.net (accessed February 12, 2017).

"Chinese Baptists." *SBC Asian Advisory Council Report 2013–2015*. http://www.sbc.net/AdvisoryCouncilReports/asian.asp (accessed February 12, 2017).

"Chronology of US–Vietnam Relations." US Department of State. https://vn.usembassy.gov/our-relationship/policy-history/chronology-of-us-vietnam-relations (accessed February 12, 2017).

"Facts and Figures 2011 — Immigration Overview: Permanent and Temporary Residents." Government of Canada. Last modified October 16, 2012. http://www.cic.gc.ca/English/resources/statistics/facts2011/index.asp (accessed February 16, 2017).

"Filipino Southern Baptists." *SBC Asian Advisory Council Report 2013–2015*. http://www.sbc.net/AdvisoryCouncilReports/asian.asp (accessed February 12, 2017).

"Genocide Studies Program: Cambodian Genocide Program." Yale University. http://gsp.yale.edu/case-studies/cambodian-genocide-program (accessed February 12, 2017).

"History of the Hmong Baptist National Association." Hmong Baptist National Association. http://www.hbna.org/history (accessed February 12, 2017).

"Hmong Baptists." SBC Asian Advisory Council Report 2013–2015. http://www.sbc.net/AdvisoryCouncilReports/asian.asp (accessed February 12, 2017).

"Japanese Church Planting Network." *SBC Asian Advisory Council Report 2013–2015*. http://www.sbc.net/AdvisoryCouncilReports/asian.asp (accessed February 12, 2017).

"Korean Baptists." SBC Asian Advisory Council Report 2013–2015. http://www.sbc.net/AdvisoryCouncilReports/asian.asp (accessed February 12, 2017).

"Laotian Immigration." North American Immigration. http://www.northamericanimmigration.org/179-laotian-immigration.html (accessed February 17, 2015).

"Mapping Project." Documentation Center of Cambodia. http://www.d.dccam.org/Projects/Maps/Mapping.htm (accessed February 12, 2017).

"National Household Survey (NHS) Profile: Canada 2011." Statistics Canada. Last modified September 11, 2013. http://www12.statcan.gc.ca/nhs-enm/2011/dp-pd/prof/index.cfm?Lang=E (accessed February 16, 2017).

"Philippines Takes over China as Number One Source of Canadian Immigrants." Canadian Visa Bureau. Last modified December 31, 2008. http://www.visabureau.com/canada/default.aspx (accessed February 16, 2017).

"The Spaniards as Colonial Masters." Philippine History. http://www.philippine-history.org/spanish-colonial-masters.htm (accessed February 16, 2017).

"Thai Army's Atrocity at Mount Dangrek: Khmer Refugees' Tragic Stories." Cambodia Watch. http://camwatchblogs.blogspot.com/2011/05/thai-armys-atrocity-at-mount-dangrek.html (accessed February 12, 2017).

"US – Vietnam Relations." US Department of State. https://vn.usembassy.gov/our-relationship/policy-history/us-vietnam-relations (accessed February 12, 2017).

Bankston, Carl. "Vietnamese-American Catholicism: Transplanted and Flourishing." In *US Catholic Historian* 18, no. 1 (2000): 36–53.

Berman, Larry and Jason Newman. "The Vietnam War and Its Impact." In *Encyclopedia of the New American Nation*. http://www.americanforeignrelations.com/O-W/The-Vietnam-War-and-Its-Impact.html (accessed February 12, 2017).

Coker, Matt. "New PBS Show Explores Why Cambodians in Long Beach Don't Graduate from High School." *OC Weekly*. http://www.ocweekly.com/news/new-pbs-show-explores-why-cambodians-in-long-beach-dont-graduate-from-high-school-6460047 (accessed February 12, 2017).

Cu, Diane Duyen. "Generation Gaps." *Viet Q (Viet Kieu) News Blog*. Last modified April 9, 2008. http://vietq.wordpress.com/category/generation-gap (accessed February 12, 2017).

Deats, Richard. *Nationalism and Christianity in the Philippines*. Dallas: Southern Methodist University Press, 1967.

Do, Anh, Tran Phan, and Eugene Garcia. "Camp Z30-D: The Survivors." Dart Center for Journalism and Trauma. Last modified March 1, 2002. http://dartcenter.org/content/camp-z30-d-survivors (accessed February 12, 2017).

Do, Hien Duc. "The New Migrants from Asia: Vietnamese in the United States." *OAH Magazine of History* 10, no. 4 (1996): 61–66. http://www.jstor.org/stable/25163102 (accessed February 12, 2017).

Espiritu, Yen. *Filipino American Lives*. Philadelphia: Temple University Press, 1995.

Hardison, Ricky. "Korean Baptists Celebrate Missions; 450 Commit to Overseas Service." *Baptist Press*. Last modified May 29, 2003. http://www.bpnews.net/15990/korean-baptists-celebrate-missions-450-commit-to-overseas-service (accessed February 12, 2017).

Hoeffel, Elizabeth, Sonya Rastogi, Myoung Ouk Kim, and Hasan Shahid. "The Asian Population: 2010 Census Briefs." US Census Bureau March 2012. https://www.census.gov/prod/cen2010/briefs/c2010br-11.pdf (accessed February 12, 2017).

McNamara, Keith and Jeanne Batalova. "Filipino Immigrants in the United States." Migration Policy Institute. Last modified July 21, 2015. http://www.migrationpolicy.org/article/filipino-immigrants-united-states (accessed February 17, 2017).

Penfold, Helen. *Remember Cambodia*. Seven Oaks, England: OMF Books, 1980.

Pfeiter, Mark. "Hmong Americans." In *The Face of Asian Pacific American: Numbers, Diversity, and Changes in the 21st Century*, edited by Eric Lai and Dennis Arguelles. San Francisco: AsianWeek, 2003.

Phan, Phuoc Christian. "Recognizing the Effects of Comprehension Language Barriers and Adaptability Cultural Barriers on Selected First Generation Undergraduate Vietnamese Students." EdD dissertation, Argosy University, 2009.

_____. Vietnamese Americans: Understanding Vietnamese People in the United States 1975–2010. Maitland: Xulon Press, 2010.

Phan, Shandon. "Vietnamese Amerasians in America Asian-Nation: The Landscape of Asian America." Last modified 2003. http://www.asian-nation.org/amerasians.shtml (accessed August 11, 2009).

Phapphayboun, Toon. "Laotian Americans." In *The Face of Asian Pacific American: Numbers, Diversity, and Changes in the 21st Century*, edited by Eric Lai and Dennis Arguelles, 93–104. San Francisco: AsianWeek, 2003.

Ponchaud, Francois. *Cambodia: Year Zero*. New York: Holt, Rinehart and Winston, 1978.

The Killing Fields. Directed by Roland Joffe. 1984. Warner Bros, 2016. DVD.

Willoughby, Karen. "Korean Fellowship Vote Echoes SBC Annual Meeting." Baptist Press. Last modified June 30, 2016. http://www.bpnews.net/47147/korean-fellowship-vote-echoes-sbc-annual-meeting (accessed February 12, 2017).

Wright, Wayne E. "Khmer as a Heritage Language in the United States: Historical Sketch, Current Realities, and Future Prospects." *Heritage Language Journal* 7, no. 1 (Winter 2010), 117–147.

Hispanics in the SBC

Daniel Sanchez and Bob Sena

As the largest cultural minority, Hispanics are a significant part of America's population that can be seen as a mission field and a mission force simultaneously. The Hispanic American population has experienced rapid growth in the past four decades. Since 1980, the number of Hispanics living in the United States has increased from 15 million in 1980 to 55.4 million in 2014. While Hispanics currently constitute 17 percent of the total population in the US they are projected to become almost one third of the US population by 2050. We rejoice over the fact that today 23 percent of the Hispanics identify themselves as Evangelical/Protestant. An understanding of the history, culture, and religious orientation of Hispanics is crucial in reaching many more for Christ.

Socio-Historical Overview of Hispanics in the United States

A historical overview of Hispanics in the United States begins with the arrival of Spanish explorers and colonizers who became the first Spanish Americans. Other groups that joined America's mosaic of ethnicities were Mexican Americans, Puerto Ricans, Cubans, and Central and South Americans, as well as those who were placed in the Census Bureau category of "Other Hispanics."

Spanish Americans

The presence of Hispanics in what is now the southwestern United States can be traced to the early 1600s. In 1528, explorations of New Mexico, Texas, and California began.[1] Also in that year, Juan de Oñate (who married explorer Hernán Cortéz's niece) established the first colony in what is now New Mexico.² Subsequently villas (provincial towns) were established in Santa Fe, Santa Cruz (Española valley), and San Felipe de Neri, which is now Albuquerque. In California, the famous Franciscan missionary Fray Junípero Serra founded twenty-one missions along the California coast (the mission of San Diego was founded in 1769 and Monterrey in 1770). By 1821, four principal areas of settlement had developed in New Mexico, California, Texas, and Arizona.

Mexican Americans

Due to a variety of historical factors, significant numbers of Hispanics were added to the colonial Spanish Americans living in California, Colorado, Arizona, New Mexico, and Texas.³ The largest of these groups are Mexican Americans, some of whom already resided in these territories when they became a part of the United States. Others arrived through the ongoing process of immigration. Today Mexican Americans constitute 66.9 percent of the US Hispanic population. While initially concentrated in the southwestern states, Mexican Americans now have significant numbers throughout the country.

Puerto Ricans

Puerto Ricans gained legal status in 1889, when their island became an unincorporated territory of the United States. They officially became US citizens in 1917. The first large wave of migration to the continental US occurred during the 1920s and 1930s, driven by high rates of unemployment on the island. The sharp drop in job opportunities was caused in part by severe hurricane systems in 1928 and 1932 that devastated the coffee plantations, the primary source of income at the time. Following World War II, large numbers of Puerto Rican migrants who came as contract farm workers, as well as those who had served in the US armed forces, became permanent mainland residents. The advent of affordable airfare dramatically increased the numbers traveling to and from the island. "The movement can best be understood in terms of a continuous internal migration within the United States."⁴ Puerto Ricans constitute 8.6 percent of the Hispanic population in the US.

Cuban Americans

As early as 1830, Cubans were living in Key West, Florida. Toward the end of the nineteenth century, in the waning years of Spanish colonial rule, other Cuban political refugees settled in the Tampa area. Still other Cubans came during the 1930s when

Cuba came under the dictatorship of Flugencio Batista. Then, in 1959, when Fidel Castro overthrew Batista, and it became evident that he intended to establish a communist government, large numbers of people sought asylum in the United States. Between 1959 and 1962 more than 155,000 Cubans immigrated to the US. The Mariel boatlift movement in the 1980s, as well as ongoing arrivals of political refugees, has contributed to the continuous increase of the Cuban population. Today Cubans constitute 3.9 percent of the Hispanic American population.

Central and South Americans

Central and South Americans constitute a variety of national and ethnic groups, representing eighteen different countries. Immigration from Central America began in the 1830s and continued at a slow rate. Following World War II the number of immigrants from Central America increased rapidly. In the 1980s, this number increased at an even faster rate due to political turmoil in such countries as Nicaragua, El Salvador, Honduras, and Guatemala. Today Central and South Americans make up 14.3 percent of the Hispanic population.

Other Hispanic Americans

The US Census Bureau uses the category "other Hispanics" to identify Hispanics of other national and regional origins that are not represented in sufficiently large numbers that require a separate designation. This category includes Hispanic people who trace their origins to Spain, Germany, Portugal, Jamaica, Trinidad/Caribbean Islands, Italy, or "other countries."[5] These people, therefore, may come from a wide variety of places where the Spanish language and culture are predominant. The fact that they come from a Spanish-speaking area means that they have some things in common with other Hispanic Americans. "Other Hispanics" constitute 6.5 percent of the Hispanic population. Since the presence of Hispanics in the US dates back to the early 1600s, the various other Hispanic groups listed above migrated at different periods and through a variety of circumstances.

Socio-Cultural Characteristics of Hispanics

While the term "Hispanic" is used as an overarching term, the people within this group represent significant variety in terms of national origin as well as generational status. As seen in the opening overview, Hispanics migrated to the United States from Spain and Latin America, and from other countries and territories and as well. Nonetheless, their commonalities relative to language and culture make it possible for us to view them as a socio-cultural group with characteristics that need to be considered in the development of evangelistic and church planting strategies.

Generational Diversity

In addition to Hispanic American diversity relative to national origin, there is significant variety in generational status due to the assimilation process. In *Hispanic Realities Impacting America*, Dr. Bobby Sena outlines the various levels of assimilation among Hispanics[6]:

1. Traditional (First Generation: Immigrants) — They arrive in this country speaking only Spanish. Their social contacts (close friends) are primarily confined to their own cultural group.

2. Bi-Cultural (Second Generation: US born, or arrived as children) — These migrants are bilingual (perhaps a bit more fluent in Spanish than in English) and have social contacts in both their cultural group and the predominant society.

3. Marginal (Third Generation: US born) — These Hispanics are more proficient in English than in Spanish and have more social contacts in the predominant (Anglo) society than within the Hispanic American community.[7]

4. Acculturated (Fourth Generation: US Born). They basically speak only English and have the majority of their social contacts outside of the Hispanic American community.

These stages of assimilation need to be considered in determining language and methodologies to employ in leading Hispanics to a personal faith in Jesus Christ. It needs to be pointed out, however, that some Hispanic sub-groups will progress more rapidly along the assimilation ladder than others. Educational, economic, and even residential patterns will either accelerate or delay the assimilation.

Linguistic Diversity

An additional factor that needs to be taken into account in reaching Hispanics is their linguistic diversity. As can be seen in the following chart, first generation Hispanics overwhelmingly utilize the Spanish language, while third generation Hispanics are mostly English speakers. Only the second generation is able to utilize both languages with reasonable fluency.

Spanish Language by Generations

Language is a critical and often pivotal factor in ministry among Hispanic people groups. The Spanish language is essential for reaching most first-generation Hispanics; however, 60 percent of Hispanics can be engaged through witnessing and ministry using the English language.

Language by Generations[8]

Generation	Percent of Population	Spanish	Bilingual	English
First	40 percent	72 percent	24 percent	4 percent
Second	28 percent	7 percent	47 percent	46 percent
Third	32 percent	0 percent	22 percent	78 percent

Overview of SBC Work Among Hispanics

Evangelistic efforts initiated by individuals from Latin America and from the United States have taken place in the Southwestern region for decades, and the establishment of constituted Baptist churches can be traced to the early 1880s.[9]

Starting in the 1950s, intentional, coordinated efforts on the part of the Home Mission Board and several Baptist state conventions (utilizing sponsoring churches) contributed to significant growth in the establishment of Hispanic congregations.

The period between the 1970s and 1980s realized a marked increase in the number of Hispanic Southern Baptist congregations across the country. Since then there has been continued growth in the number of churches started. Several factors contributed to this.

Visionary Leadership

While other leaders had contributed to the expansion of Hispanic Baptist work in the United States[10], the arrival of Dr. Oscar Romo at the Home Mission Board in the early 1970s resulted in the implementation of strategies that were both missiologically correct and culturally appropriate.

Spanish Language Congregations

During the early 1970s many mainline denominations (Methodist, Presbyterian, etc.) determined that integration was the best strategy—merge Hispanic congregations into Anglo congregations—in order to foster better relations between these two groups. While the intention was sincere, at that time ethnic groups in United States wanted to establish their own identity and to find cultural expression within the context of worship.

With a profound understanding of the times, Dr. Romo led the Home Mission Board, and thus Southern Baptists, to focus on establishing Spanish-speaking Hispanic congregations. While not opposed to churches utilizing bilingual approaches for younger generations, Dr. Romo understood that more Hispanics would respond to the Gospel when presented in their heart language. Further, they needed the opportunity to express their Christian faith in terms that were consistent with their culture.

Today there is a need for Hispanic churches that offer some services in Spanish, some bilingual, and some in English. The principle, however, remains the same—one must take into account where people are spiritually and culturally in order to be more effective in leading them to faith in Christ and empowering them to start congregations in their communities.

Refugee Resettlement Ministries

Southern Baptist efforts in Cuban resettlement in the United States resulted in the establishment of Hispanic congregations along the eastern seaboard as well as in states outside of the Southwest region. Deeply concerned about the communist takeover of their country, many Cubans asked for political asylum in the United States. Having left their homes and possessions behind, Cubans received some assistance from the US government, but still needed help and encouragement as they started their lives in this country. Led by the Home Mission Board, and with the cooperation of state conventions, many Baptist churches ministered to them by opening their homes and their congregations to feed them, teach them English, and help them adjust to life in this country.

The fact that a significant number of Cubans were already Baptist led to the establishment of congregations in Miami and numerous other areas, including the Carolinas, Georgia, New Jersey, New York, and California. The love expressed by these American congregations led to the conversion of many Cubans, who then joined the church starts. The experience gained from the Cuban resettlement effort helped Southern Baptists to be very effective in resettling Vietnamese and other Southeast Asian refugees years later. This, in turn, aided the establishment of many churches among them.

Leadership Training

An additional factor that has led to the growth of Hispanic Baptist work has been the emphasis on leadership training. The Home Mission Board and some Baptist state conventions were aware that Hispanic congregations needed well-trained pastors and leaders and made provisions for Hispanic students to receive college scholarships. The earliest recipients of these higher education resources included Joshua Grijalva, Carlos Paredes, Mike Mojica, Rudy Hernandez, and Oscar Romo. All of these men became outstanding leaders in Baptist work in SBC entities.[11]

The Home Mission Board developed the Ethnic Leadership Development Program to assist Hispanic Baptists who had no opportunity to obtain a college education. The program continues to offer courses in numerous states to this day. Other entities, such as the seminary extension program and some of the Southern Baptist seminaries, also make it possible for Hispanics to further their formal education in ministry.

Many other factors have contributed to the expansion of Hispanic Baptist work throughout the years; however, those mentioned stand out as being among the most significant. The result of these combined efforts throughout the decades is that today there are more than 3,200 Hispanic Baptist congregations across the country. This figure does not include the increasing number of Hispanic congregations that are meeting within Anglo churches.

Current Status of Hispanic Americans

This segment will explore current population trends among Hispanics, and review the status of Hispanic churches and current needs among Hispanic Americans related to evangelism, church planting, and leadership training.

Population Trends

The Hispanic population in the United States has tripled since 1980 to a total of 55.4 million by 2014.[12] Middle baseline projections estimate that Hispanics in the US will reach 128 million by the 2050[13], or 29 percent of the total population. Even with these expanding numbers, immigration among Hispanics has hit a dramatic decline. The increase is attributable primarily to an annual birth rate among Hispanic Americans of approximately one million.[14] In light of the large number of births annually, the Hispanic population is projected to become a majority in the state of Texas by 2027[15] and in other states (such as California) shortly afterward.

States with the largest concentrations of Hispanics are: California (14.4 million), Texas (9.8 million), Florida (4.4 million), New York (3.5 million), and Illinois (2.1 million).[16] The states with the largest percentage growth since 2000 are: South Carolina (145 percent), Kentucky (132 percent), Arkansas (123 percent), Minnesota (120 percent), and North Carolina (120 percent). Further, Hispanic populations grew by more than 100 percent in South Dakota, Nebraska, Mississippi, Iowa, Louisiana, Maryland, West Virginia, Georgia, and Tennessee.[17] The Hispanic population has grown in 3,000 of the nation's 3,141 counties.[18] In ten counties, the Hispanic population grew by over 400 percent in the past decade.[19]

As statistics indicate, the Hispanic population has grown and has spread throughout the country. In light of this trend, the late Harry Pachon, Latino scholar, advocate, and former director of the Tomas Rivera Policy Institute, observed: "The major significance is that it's a national presence."[20] This national presence has significant implications for evangelism and church planting among Hispanic Americans. Hispanic churches are desperately needed in these areas of growth.

Status of Hispanic Evangelism

Keeping up with the pace of growth is challenging; however, the Hispanic population is more receptive to the Gospel message than at any other time in the history of this country. A recent survey by the Pew Research Center discovered that 23 percent of Hispanic adults identify as "Protestants/Evangelicals."[21] Taking into consideration that there is a greater percentage of Hispanic young people who have a similar identity, one can safely assert that one-fourth of Hispanics in America today are Protestants/evangelicals. Interestingly, the number of Hispanics identifying themselves as Catholics has decreased from 67 percent in 2010 to 55 percent in 2013.[22] While there is cause for rejoicing over the fact that more Hispanics are responding to the evangelical message, there is also room for deep concern over the 18 percent who identified themselves as "unaffiliated"[23] with any faith community.

The Pew survey offers reasons why Hispanics change their religious affiliation and sheds light on the factors they considered in decision making, which has implications for Southern Baptist outreach ministries. The survey reveals: 45 percent simply strayed; 52 percent quit believing the teachings of their church; 31 percent found a congregation that reaches out and helps members; 23 percent experienced a deep personal crisis; 19 percent moved to another community; and 9 percent married someone practicing a different religion.[24] It is apparent from the survey's findings that compassionate ministries can be effective in reaching people who are experiencing confusion in their beliefs, who are going through personal crises, and who are in transition, as they can be very receptive to the Gospel message.

Status of Hispanic Churches

The Hispanic population expansion has impacted the number of Southern Baptist Hispanic churches, which increased from 1,235 in 1998 to 3,206 in 2011. This is a net gain of 1,235 Hispanic churches, or 67 percent growth.[25] This is certainly cause for rejoicing! The deep concern we have, however, is that the Hispanic population has been growing at a faster rate than the Hispanic church planting rate. Whereas in 2002 the Hispanic church to Hispanic population ratio was 1:13,856, the 2011 ratio was 1:16,181.[26] We are not keeping up with the population growth.

Another area of concern is that the Hispanic population-to-church ratio lags significantly behind that of the SBC in general. For Hispanics nationwide, one Hispanic church exists for every 16,181 Hispanics. The general ratio for the SBC is 1:6,000.[27] In some states the church-to-population ratio is much more challenging, ranging from one Hispanic Baptist church for every 30,000 Hispanics to one for every 174,000 Hispanics.[28] In addition, there are 19 counties with a Hispanic population ranging from 48,000 to 748,000 but with no Hispanic Baptist church.[29] Given the high receptivity of Hispanics to the Gospel message, this field is truly ripe unto harvest.

Status of Hispanic Leadership Training

The Hispanic population has made significant strides in the area of education. The percent of high school graduates among Hispanics (ages 18–24) increased from 52 percent in 1991 to 76.3 percent in 2011.[30] While we are still concerned about those who did not finish school (and recommendations are offered in a subsequent section), there is rejoicing that many more Hispanics are completing their high school education. The same applies to the marked increase in the number enrolling in college, which increased from 35 percent in 1993 to 49 percent in 2012.[31] The university graduation rate among Hispanics has also increased. The overall college attainment percentage among Hispanics (ages 18–24) increased from 20 percent in 2000 to 33 percent in 2011.[32]

Hispanics Enrolled in Universities[33]

Educational attainment among Hispanics (ages 25 and older)—many of whom were born abroad—lags significantly behind the group that is 18 to 24 years old. While there are several contributing factors, including finances,[34] proficiency in English is one of the major challenges. As seen in the chart, 52 percent of Hispanics over age 18 speak English "less than very well."

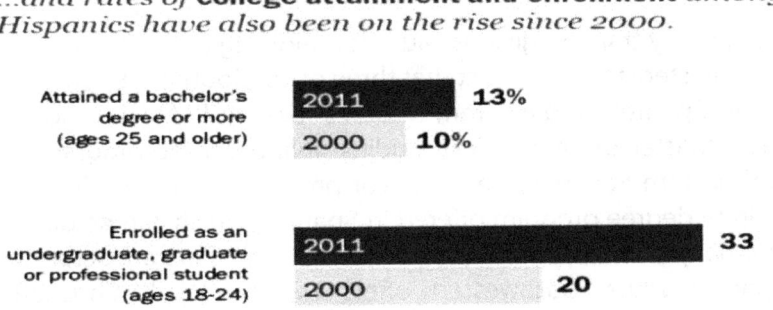

...and rates of **college attainment and enrollment** among Hispanics have also been on the rise since 2000.

Pew Research Hispanic Center tabulations of 2000 Census (5 percent IPUMS) and 2011 American Community Survey (1 percent IPUMS)

Language Proficiency

The educational panorama among Hispanics is a tale of two cities. Native-born Hispanics and those who came to this country at a very early age are in a position to plug in to existing institutions and obtain an education. Those who are older, and mainly those born abroad, should start their training in Spanish while they learn English in order to continue their journey to higher levels of education. There are two ministries that can be offered by churches to address this challenge. One is English as a Second Language (ESL). The other ministry is GED (general education development) exam preparation courses. Students who pass the GED exam may qualify to take college level courses. While the initial interest of these ministries is

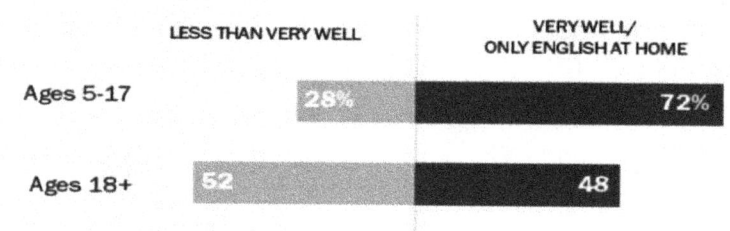

educational, in many instances people have been won to the Lord after they have seen the love and concern manifested by those who are ministering to them in those areas. Furthermore, this is a vital area in which lay people can be involved.

The trends in ministry training give us cause for rejoicing as well as reason for concern. The rejoicing stems from the fact that three of our Southern Baptist Seminaries have degrees in Spanish ranging from Master's level to PhD level. Southwestern Seminary has a Master of Theological Studies online degree program offered in Spanish. Southeastern Seminary has a similar program. Southern Seminary has a Master of Divinity degree program offered in Spanish, which can be done partially online and partially on campus. Midwestern Seminary offers a Doctor of Ministry degree in Spanish, while Southwestern offers a PhD in World Christian Studies, which can be done in Spanish with three weeks on campus each year. These excellent degree programs are meeting many urgent needs among Hispanics training for ministry.

One of the major unmet needs is that of an undergraduate degree program that begins at an entry level. Such a program would provide a ramp for students to obtain credit for courses taken in Spanish, with the goal to fully engage in a bachelor's degree. This would open the way for Spanish-speaking ministry leaders to move on to a Master's degree and beyond.

In addressing the status of the Hispanic population in this country, the status of Hispanic evangelism, the status of Hispanic churches, and the status of Hispanic leadership training, there is definitely cause for rejoicing over the marvelous progress that has taken place. At the same time, all of us are aware of the fact that the Hispanic population continues to grow, thus presenting us with the challenge of developing strategies that will enable us to lead significant numbers of them to a personal experience of salvation and then on to start many more churches among them.

Strategies for Significant Advance Among Hispanics

In its work, the SBC Executive Committee's Hispanic Advisory Council gave special attention to discover best practices in the areas of Evangelism, Church Planting, and Leadership Training. These will be shared along with some recommendations for greater effectiveness in implementing the Great Commission among Hispanic Americans.

An analysis of evangelistic methodologies reported by church leaders revealed that the following are the most effective ones among Hispanics.

Relational Evangelism

A survey conducted by LifeWay indicates that 77 percent of Hispanics who are now evangelical Christians first heard the Gospel message from a family member or a friend.[35]

The same survey sheds light on the willingness of Hispanic persons to receive information through personal conversation with a friend or neighbor from the church.[36]

Heard for the first time	percent of Converted Hispanics
Family Member	45 percent
A Friend	32 percent
A Church Member	11 percent
Own Effort or Declined Comment	10 percent

The survey conducted by the PEW Hispanic Center affirms the importance of relational evangelism in the Hispanic setting:

Family members and acquaintances emerge as important factors in the conversion process. Frequently they are the ones who introduce the new religion. That personal

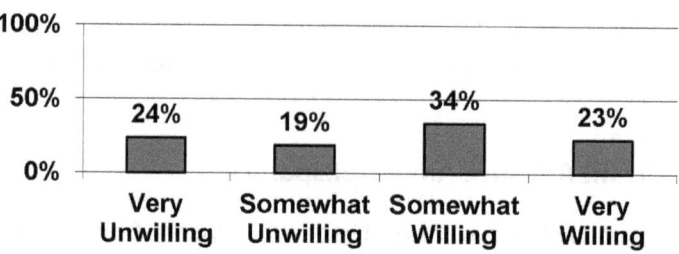

relationship is far more important in impacting conversion than the influence of the media or personal contacts with other members of the church.[37]

Therefore, close church members of other cultural groups can be very effective in leading Hispanics to Christ if they make an effort to establish meaningful friendships with them.

Ministry-Based Evangelism

Ministry-Based Evangelism is proving to be one of the most effective ways to share the Good News of salvation. Ministering to the felt needs of Hispanics establishes relationships that open many doors to evangelism.

A recent survey conducted by the George Barna Institute revealed that the most pressing needs among Hispanics centered on issues related to family, education, occupation, economy, and immigration.[38] These issues and concerns provide meaningful opportunities for ministries that open doors and foster the types of relationships that are instrumental in leading Hispanic people to a salvation experience through Jesus Christ. Among these, the most time sensitive are those related to immigration.

Excellent resources have been developed and are being utilized to minister to those needing counseling on immigration issues.[39] This ministry can open countless doors for the sharing of the Gospel message.

Ministry with Adults

The Hispanic Advisory Council fully supports the resolution "On Immigration and the Gospel," adopted by the Southern Baptist Convention on June 15, 2011. In efforts to minister to undocumented Hispanics and lead them to a saving knowledge of Jesus Christ, the resolution calls "on all churches to be the presence of Christ in both proclamation and ministry to all persons regardless of country of origin or immigrant status."[40]

Thousands of Hispanic adults will benefit greatly from ministries related to English as a Second Language (ESL) and citizenship classes. These ministries have the potential of establishing relationships with untold numbers of Hispanics who will become receptive to the Gospel message. Churches, associations, and state conventions that have these ministries will see unprecedented opportunities to lead Hispanics to Christ.

Ministry to Hispanic Young People

Of the 1.7 million children of undocumented parents who now qualify for the Deferred Action Program, 1.3 million are Hispanic. In order to qualify for this program, candidates need to have enrolled in high school, have a high school diploma or a GED or have been honorably discharged by the military, not convicted of a felony, and enrolled in school by their application date if they have not finished high school.[41]

Ministries that address these needs among young people will open an untold number of doors to lead them to a saving faith in Jesus Christ.

Target "Event" Evangelism

A LifeWay survey found that Hispanics are more open to consider matters of faith during certain holiday seasons or life experiences. Christmas and Easter provide marvelous opportunities to host special events (dramas, cantatas, films, videos, dinners, block parties, celebrations, etc.) that can help cultivate friendships and invite Hispanics to participate in Bible studies. The other events also represent further opportunities to open doors and share the Gospel message.[42]

Cell Group Evangelism

In light of the fact that Hispanics are so relational, small group gatherings lend themselves to the establishment of personal communication that can offer a non-threatening presentation of the Gospel message. Cell groups in homes are especially effective in sharing the message of salvation with Hispanics. The saying: *"Mi casa es su casa"* ("My home is your home") expresses the type of hospitality that opens doors to evangelization. Home cell groups overcome many of the

Periods of Greater Openness to Matters of Faith

During Christmas Season	**49 percent**
During Easter Season	38 percent
After a national crisis (e.g., 9/11)	**41 percent**
After a natural disaster	38 percent
After the birth of a baby	**34 percent**
At the start of a war	26 percent
During economic crisis	**28 percent**
In the Fall – start of school year	12 percent
During summer vacations	**12 percent**

apprehensions that non-evangelical Hispanics have initially associated with attending evangelical churches.

Gospel in the Rosary (Evangelio en el Rosario) is an evangelistic Bible study resource that is being used very effectively as a bridge to lead Hispanics to a personal experience of salvation in Jesus Christ.[43] In preparation for these types of Bible studies, and in light of the religious background of many Hispanics, the book, *Sharing The Good News with Roman Catholic Friends* can be an excellent resource as well.[44]

Children and Youth Evangelism

Hispanics have the largest percentage of children and young people of any socio-cultural group in this country. The median age of Hispanics is 27. For native-born Hispanics, the median age is 18. In light of the fact that half of the Hispanic population is under age 27, it is imperative that churches and SBC entities focus as never before on evangelistic strategies to reach them with the Gospel message. In its survey of key Hispanic pastors, the Hispanic Advisory Council learned that tutoring programs and youth ministries are among the most effective tools to led Hispanic children and youth to faith in Christ. In these types of efforts, members of churches from other cultural groups can partner with Hispanic congregations in reaching this highly receptive group.

Vacation Bible School

As a result of its long years of involvement in children's ministries, LifeWay has found Vacation Bible School to be the most effective evangelistic tool to reach this population segment among Hispanics, as well as the other cultural groups.[45] LifeWay is to be commended for making Vacation Bible School resources available in Spanish.

While numerous other outreach activities are proving to be effective in leading Hispanics to a personal faith in Jesus Christ, those named here are among those the Lord is blessing in a greater manner for His honor and for the implementation of the Great Commission.

Hispanic Church Planting Strategic Considerations

The following considerations are based on the extensive study and experience of this author as well as on the input received from the Hispanic Advisory Council.

Necessity of Concerted Prayer

Reaching Hispanics (with their socio-religious background) is a challenging task, but one we must undertake without ceasing. Many will face pressure or alienation from their families. There are many obstacles; therefore, prayer is essential.

If we are going to reach this growing and diverse people, it is incumbent upon Hispanic leaders to bathe everything in prayer. This has been the weak link for many in the past. Our calling and our purpose come from God—not from human beings, not from a denomination, nor from an agency. Let us call for solemn assemblies of prayer. Let us call for times of fasting and prayer. Let us call for confession and repentance as a Hispanic people. Then let us stand back and watch what God does in our midst!

Need for Culturally Relevant and Informed Strategies

Research scholar Miguel de la Torre makes the observation that a clear understanding of the generational and socio-cultural variations among Hispanics is essential in the development of effective strategies to reach them with the Gospel. Regarding strategies, he affirms, "one size does not fit all."[46] He explains the concern of some scholars with regard to the exit of significant numbers of Hispanics from the Catholic Church:

> Catholic scholars maintain that a principal cause for defection of Hispanics from the Catholic Church is that the church is not equipped or structured to meet the diverse needs of the growing number of Hispanic believers. They insist that the church lacks sufficient numbers of Spanish-speaking clergy who understand and appreciate the Latino/a community's diverse cultural and religious idiosyncrasies…. They note that there is a lack of awareness of ethnic and social class distinctions. Instead, an undifferentiated "option for the poor" on the part of socially active clergy reveals a tendency to conceive of Hispanics only in terms of deficits or dysfunctions, which can lead Hispanics who happen to be upwardly mobile to regard themselves as outside the church's pastoral concerns.[47]

We must not repeat the mistakes others have made. Taking into account the social and generational differences among Hispanics, developing appropriate strategies will result in their responsiveness and willingness to be involved in the culturally contextualized congregations. The Pew Foundation report underscores the fact that a significant segment of the Hispanic population prefers Hispanic-oriented congregations:

> The houses of worship most frequented by Latinos have distinctly ethnic characteristics. Foreign-born Latinos are most likely to attend Hispanic-oriented churches and to comprise the largest share of Hispanics who worship at such churches…. While 77 percent of the foreign born Latinos attend Hispanic-oriented worship services the phenomenon is also widespread among the native born, with 48 percent saying they attend ethnic churches.[48]

These findings underscore the fact that language is only one factor in reaching Hispanics with the Gospel message and starting churches among them. There are cultural factors that lead many Hispanics to look for churches that reflect their heritage and values. The PEW report also underscores this:

> Indeed, a great many Latinos who speak only English were born in the US and trace their ancestry in the US for several generations attend churches that are characterized by a Hispanic orientation.[49] The willingness and ability of Evangelical denominations to make provision for the establishment of Hispanic-oriented congregations will greatly enhance their effectiveness in reaching unprecedented numbers of Hispanics with the Gospel message. Conversely, the assumption that all Hispanics are the same and that they are all assimilating into the predominant society at the same rate will lead them to make the types of strategic mistakes that De La Torre describes as being made by some Roman Catholic leaders.[50]

THE NEED FOR SPECIALIZED TYPES OF CHURCHES TO REACH ALL SEGMENTS OF HISPANIC POPULATION

Spanish Language, Hispanic Culture Churches

An estimated 77 percent of foreign-born and 48 percent of native-born Hispanics attend Hispanic oriented churches where: (1) A majority of those in the congregation are Hispanic; (2) Some Hispanics serve as clergy; (3) Liturgies are available in Spanish.[51] The Spanish language and culturally relevant approaches are essential to reaching large segments of the Hispanic population. Of the Hispanic Catholics who always attend a Spanish-language mass, 74 percent are immigrant and 24 percent are native born.[52]

Spanish-speaking congregations are essential to outreach efforts in states with large percentages of foreign-born Hispanics. There are fifteen states in which foreign-born Hispanics exceed 40 percent (Maryland, Florida, Georgia, North Carolina, Virginia, Alabama, Louisiana, South Carolina, Mississippi, Arkansas, Nevada, Illinois, New York, Utah), and nine states in which they exceed 30 percent of the Hispanic population (Nebraska, Indiana, Kansas, Iowa, South Dakota, Kentucky, Washington, Kansas, Wisconsin, and Texas).

Churches and ministries among Spanish language congregations need to recognize that their children and young people are rapidly becoming more proficient in the English language and are absorbing some of the cultural values of the predominant society. If they ignore this fact, these churches risk losing their children and young people—not only to their local congregation but to church itself.[53] The mission of the Hispanic church must be to evangelize and disciple all segments of the Hispanic community, not merely to preserve the culture.[54] Nevertheless, cultural sensitivity can empower the Hispanic church to "reach beyond the barrio" to cultural groups in their communities, in this country, and in other countries as well.

English Language Hispanic Culture Churches

Due to selective acculturation, native-born Hispanics are fluent in the English language, yet they retain socio-cultural elements that motivate them to worship in these types of churches. Therefore, church planting strategies should include the following options: (1) English language services; (2) Bilingual Services; (3) Two services—English and Spanish.

Some of the largest Hispanic congregations in North America are those that are bridging linguistic and generational barriers by employing a variety of worship services that have a "Latin flavor." These Hispanic congregations are characterized by: (1) High level of relational warmth—emphasis on love and friendliness; (2) Latino flavor in their music; (3) Events for the entire family (some have as many people on Mother's Day as on Easter; Christmas Eve services attract many families as well); (4) Messages that are relevant to their life experiences (identity: "Who we are in Christ, not second class"; hope: "A better future in Christ"); (5) Relational outreach—life groups for ministry and discipleship.

English-Speaking, Anglo-Cultural Churches with Hispanic Culture Sensitivity

While the more acculturated Hispanics may be more attracted to English-speaking, predominantly Anglo culture churches, the greater the cultural sensitivity of these churches, the more effective their ministries will be.

Some of the suggestions made by Hispanics to Anglo culture churches with Hispanic visitors or members are:[55]

- Don't give us the impression that we are welcome but that we have to check our culture at the door.
- Don't stereotype." If we visit you it is because we are comfortable with the English language.
- Have people on your staff (and praise team) that are representative of our cultural group.
- Remember, we have more things in common in our daily struggles than we have differences.
- Have a high level of relational warmth.
- Honor the family in your services and ministries.
- Do a survey of Hispanics in your community.[56]
- Above all, speak the language of love.

The Necessity for Exponential Church Planting Methodologies

The Hispanic population is growing exponentially and our church planting initiatives are not keeping pace with their growth. Church starts with the resources to have their own building (even with the initial help of partnership churches) are to be commended. The fact remains that there are literally thousands of communities where Hispanic churches are needed and traditional modes of funding are not available. New and innovative church multiplication strategies must be employed.

The underlying concern is that the Hispanic population is multiplying exponentially while our church planting methodologies are incremental at best.

Small Groups in Church Planting

The Hispanic congregations that are reaching the largest numbers of people are those utilizing small groups (home cells) or in house churches.[57]

Hispanics are very relational. In Hispanic culture, establishing a relationship of trust is often necessary before they respond positively to the presentation of the Gospel message. Bible studies in homes often become a bridge between Hispanics and evangelical churches. Small groups meeting in homes provide a nonthreatening environment where Hispanics can hear the Good News of salvation.

House Churches

The house church approach is useful to overcome geographical and relational barriers. This approach will also appeal to many first generation Hispanics, those who come from a Catholic background and who tend to stay away from the traditional "Protestant" churches. These individuals may feel more comfortable worshiping and studying the Bible in a home ("a safe zone") than at a church building.[58]

House churches can be catalysts in helping believers to mature spiritually and to be what God has called them to be as they live the Great Commission. House churches can also help to solve many of the financial struggles of more traditional churches and freeing up funds for other Great Commission ministries that would not normally be possible due to operational costs. House churches can be a vital part of raising, training, and multiplying many servant leaders.

The Total Effort Needed

Hispanic churches need to plant more churches at a faster rate than ever before. Hispanics have come to North America from diverse backgrounds and for a myriad of reasons. In their journey, seeking the American dream, numerous Hispanics have come to faith in Christ. For many years the Hispanic Church has been on the receiving end of Southern Baptist work in North America. Today, however, as a result of the investment of faithful Southern Baptist leaders, the Hispanic Church is strong, visionary, and poised to lead in cross-cultural evangelism and ministry among the nations in North America. Established Hispanic church planting and evangelism networks can provide the necessary avenues for mobilization of the largest ethnic group in North America.

Then, churches of other cultures need to start Hispanic churches. We are seeing instances where African American and Korean churches are starting Hispanic churches. Churches of other cultures and Hispanic churches need to partner to start churches. Hispanic congregations need to start churches of other cultures within their buildings as a strategy to launch churches with relevant cultural and language worship experiences. English-speaking churches need to start churches of other cultures within their buildings to function as a multi-congregational church. Examples of these are: (1) Prestonwood en Español in Plano, Texas; (2) Champion Forrest en Español in Houston, Texas; and (3) Shadow Mountain en Español in El Cajón, California.[59]

The growth of the Hispanic population is about more than just statistics. It's a reality that poses both challenges and opportunities for NAMB as a national denominational agency assigned the task of reaching the peoples of North America. This challenge extends to state conventions, associations and established churches as well.

There continues to be a need to mobilize Hispanic and non-Hispanic congregations for a church planting movement within the Hispanic population that extends to all the generational levels of Hispanic work.

A Critical Need for Partner Churches

In discussing "best practices," one must take into account the new paradigm being implemented at the NAMB. New church plants are being initiated with the assistance of partner churches throughout North America. The majority of these are traditional church plants in one of the thirty-two Send North America cities. Churches are clustering their resources for church planting, including a number of Hispanic churches. Many of these clustered Hispanic churches are planting outside the Send Cities where resources are limited. An increasing number of Hispanic churches are being identified as churches that are raising their own planters through an intentional process.

Hispanic Leadership Training Recommendations

The advances of Hispanics in the area of education as well as the challenges they face have been presented in the introductory segment. In this segment we want to make some recommendations to parents, to churches, and to Baptist agencies to enhance the attainment of unprecedented goals in this strategic area of Hispanic work.

Recommendations for Parents of Hispanic Students

We encourage parents to get more training themselves. This will enable them not only to become more efficient, but also to assist their children in their educational tasks. This can be done by taking special classes, such as ESL and GED. Parents need to partner with schools and teachers to be better informed on ways to guide their children in their educational process. Parents need to help their children with homework or find someone who can help tutor their children. It is important for parents to sacrifice time and resources to make an investment in their children. Families need to clarify and solidify their values between helping the family financially (thus dropping out of school) and sacrificing to attain an education that will bring greater long-range benefits to the student and the family. Above all, parents need to catch a vision of what the future can hold for their children if they attain a higher education.

Recommendations for Churches

Churches need to help parents and reinforce to children of the value of getting an education. At the dedication of babies at the altar, the church can give the parents a Bible and take up an offering (or purchase savings bonds) to assist in the establishment of an educational fund for the child. Churches need to encourage their young people to stay in school. Churches can provide tutors (some churches do this on Wednesday nights, during Sunday school, or at other times). Churches can have a recognition service for graduates to emphasize the importance of educational achievements and reward their efforts. Churches need to invest financially in education by partnering with colleges to provide scholarships or by establishing a church scholarship fund. Churches need to have ministers of youth who encourage their young people to pursue higher education. Churches can declare their community a "no dropout zone" and partner with the schools to address the issues that cause students to drop out. Churches can get official training to function as a community-based accredited organization and give legal advice to undocumented children and parents on how to qualify for deferred action, thus enabling the young people to attend college.[60]

Recommendations for Baptist Agencies

There is much that the entities of the Southern Baptist Convention can to enhance educational endeavors among Hispanics. They can write articles that include success stories of young people from different ethnic backgrounds and stress the value of obtaining an education. They can address this topic in literature (e.g., Sunday school lessons). They can provide conferences that emphasize education and provide information on Baptist colleges/universities. They can include this topic in brochures (e.g., IMB and NAMB including educational qualifications for appointment). These are a few of the things that Baptist entities can do in their effort to undergird the work that parents and churches are doing to enhance the education of Hispanics.

Recommendations for Southern Baptist Seminaries

While there is cause for rejoicing over the bold and visionary actions that SBC seminaries and colleges have taken to recruit and train more Hispanics, there is serious concern about those who have not attained a college education. This is especially true of the Hispanic immigrant generation. There is a gap between the graduate-level courses that our seminaries offer and the Hispanics who have not attained a baccalaureate degree. Entry-level courses offering theological training are desperately needed.

A number of Hispanics are getting enrolled in training centers sponsored by churches and associations. Some of these take Seminary Extension courses. In the past, a number of Baptist colleges and seminaries granted credit for these courses in light of the fact that Seminary Extension was accredited through adult education. Since courses offered in Spanish are no longer accredited, this prevents Hispanic students from receiving credit that could help them obtain a college degree. A partnership among SBC seminaries and colleges could provide entry-level (basic) courses to Hispanics in Spanish.

As the Hispanic population continues to grow and expand, the ability to evangelize and congregationalize Hispanics will continue to depend on the ability to provide theological education for the leaders of these congregations. As it stands now, significant percentages of the pastors of Hispanic congregations have little or no formal theological education.

In light of this we make the following recommendations:

- SBC seminaries redouble their efforts to recruit and train Hispanics for ministry.
- Find ways to coordinate the work of the institutions and centers providing entry-level training so that the necessary access routes to higher education are established.
- Employ the use technology as a delivery methodology (e.g., online courses) for theological education in order to train the largest numbers of Hispanics possible.
- Seminaries continue to be intentional in the employment and recruitment of Spanish-speaking professors to teach courses in a manner that takes linguistic and cultural factors into account.

- In light of the severe financial limitations of many Hispanic pastors and leaders, the cost of seminary courses should offered should be made as affordable as possible.
- Churches with sufficient financial resources should consider providing scholarships for Hispanic pastors and leaders desiring to obtain a theological education.

CONCLUSION

The Hispanic population continues to grow at such a rapid pace that they are predicted to constitute one-third of the United States population by the year 2050. Their diversity in terms of national origin, generational assimilation, and linguistic skills requires that these factors be taken into account in reaching Hispanics for Christ. It is indeed encouraging to know that nearly one-fourth of Hispanics identify as "Protestant or evangelical." Their receptivity to the Gospel message challenges all of us (pastors, lay people, mission leaders) to make bold plans in evangelism, church planting, and leadership training so that the Lord will be pleased and future generations will say "This was their finest hour."

Native Americans in the SBC

Gary W. Hawkins

When a people group must deny who they are to become acceptable to others in order to become acceptable to God, a major barrier arises. Therefore, in order to effectively reach the 5.2 million people who identify as American Indian or Alaska Native, Southern Baptists must understand their various subcultures to develop and implement effective outreach strategies.

According to the 2010 Census[1], the US population totaled 308.7 million. Of that total, 2.9 million people (0.9 percent) identified themselves as American Indian or Alaska Native. In addition, another 0.7 percent, or 2.3 million people, reported American Indian or Alaska Native ethnicity in combination with one or more other races. Together, these groups totaled 5.2 million people. Thus, slightly less than 2 percent of United States residents identify as American Indian or Alaska Native, either alone or in combination with one or more other races.[2]

SOCIO-CULTURAL CHARACTERISTICS OF THE NATIVE AMERICAN

Social Challenges[3]

Both within and outside reservations, Native Americans often deal with a plethora of social challenges. Of all ethnic groups in the USA, American Indians have the highest rates of the following conditions:

- Highest rate of school drop outs (54 percent)
- Highest rate of child mortality

- Highest rate of suicide
- Highest rate of teenage suicide (18.5 per 100,000)
- Highest rate of teenage pregnancy
- Lowest life expectancy (55 years)

Exacerbating these conditions are unemployment, environmental destruction, and the decay of the reservations. There is a dearth of positive prospects or leisure time activities to distract them from their circumstances, which undoubtedly makes their harsh living conditions harder to bear. Substance abuse is a common form of escape. Drug abuse and alcoholism are massive problems among American Indians. On some reservations, eight out of ten families have problems with alcoholism; unfortunately, these numbers include children.

Place	American Indian and Alaska Native Populations					
	Alone or in Combination		Alone		In Combination	
	Rank	Number	Rank	Number	Rank	Number
New York, NY	1	111749	1	57512	1	54237
Los Angeles, CA	2	54236	3	28215	2	26021
Phoenix, AZ	3	43724	2	32366	7	11358
Oklahoma City, Ok	4	36572	7	20533	3	16039
Anchorage, AK	5	36062	5	23130	6	12932
Tulsa, OK	6	35990	6	20817	4	15173
Albuquerque, NM	7	32571	4	25087	16	7484
Chicago, IL	8	26933	10	13337	5	13596
Houston, TX	9	25521	8	14997	8	10524
San Antonio, TX	10	20137	11	11800	11	8337
Tucson, AZ	11	19903	9	14154	24	5749
Philadelphia, PA	12	17495	25	6996	9	10499
San Diego, CA	13	17865	23	7696	10	10169

Cultures

Native Americans are not monolithic; there are many subcultures within this people group. Additionally, these cultures are in a constant state of fluctuation. Native Americans value the past and we visualize the future through that lens; although, just as all other cultures are changing, so is ours.

Four generic groups can be identified to describe the diverse world views of Native Americans. These groups are actually continuums, with distinctives within and among each group.

Group One: Traditional/Ceremonial[4]

- This group of Native Americans has been reared in their traditional culture, to the extent that it survives.
- They resist the dominant culture and its attempts to acculturate them. For the most-part this group views Christianity as the "White man's Religion."
- Traditional/Ceremonial Native Americans usually are bilingual, yet prefer to speak in their heart language. Even when they come to faith in Christ, they prefer worship, teaching, and preaching in their heart language.

Group Two: Artisans
(Traditional Singing and Drumming Groups, Pow Wow Dancers, Etc.)

- These are Native Americans who have a primarily traditional Native world view, but function proficiently in the dominant culture. They are not satisfied with the dominant culture's world view and have a feeling of incompleteness.
- They are interested in anything about their people's history, mythology, customs, and culture. They are attempting to better understand who they are by returning to their roots.
- This group identifies more with Native religious practices rather than with Christianity.

Group Three: "Pan Indians"
(Found Mostly in Larger Metropolitan Areas)

- These Native people are active in Pow Wows (Native gatherings that celebrate "Indian-ness"), which began to spread in the early twentieth century.

- Pow wows cross intertribal lines, advancing pan-Indianism through song, dance, regalia, honoring ceremonies, giveaways, prayers, and speeches in native languages and English.
- These persons are proud to identify as Native American, yet some may be predominantly of another race.

Group Four: Acculturated
(This group often lacks knowledge of their heritage, language, customs, and culture and have incorporated a "generic identification" to validate their "Indian-ness.")

- They have accepted the dominant culture's world view. In so doing, they have rejected their Nation's traditional world view.
- They primarily speak only English and the majority of their social contacts lie outside of the Native American community.
- They are referred to as "card carrying" Native Americans, meaning they are enrolled tribal citizens who utilize tribal entitlements (health care, educational programs, housing, etc.).
- These are people who may or may not be distinguishable by appearance and have little involvement with cultural or spiritual activities.

These descriptions are not all inclusive; rather, they are offered to illustrate that a "one-size-fits-all" approach does not have extensive success among Natives. An effort must first be made to learn how Christ can impact their lives at their given time and place.

Non-Native or tribal people unfamiliar with another tribe would do well to seek out a "Person of Peace" (a person who serves as a bridge to the community) in advance of mission endeavors to individual groups. This will prove beneficial and will help them to better understand bridges and barriers to ministry entry points. What worked in New Mexico may have little or no impact among tribes in Montana.

The following graph[5] demonstrates why the ministry approach to and among the 567 tribes of the United States has, in many instances, failed. When churches and ministry groups fail to learn the basic culture of the Indigenous People they are seeking to reach, it is viewed as gross negligence and creates significant resistance to the Gospel.

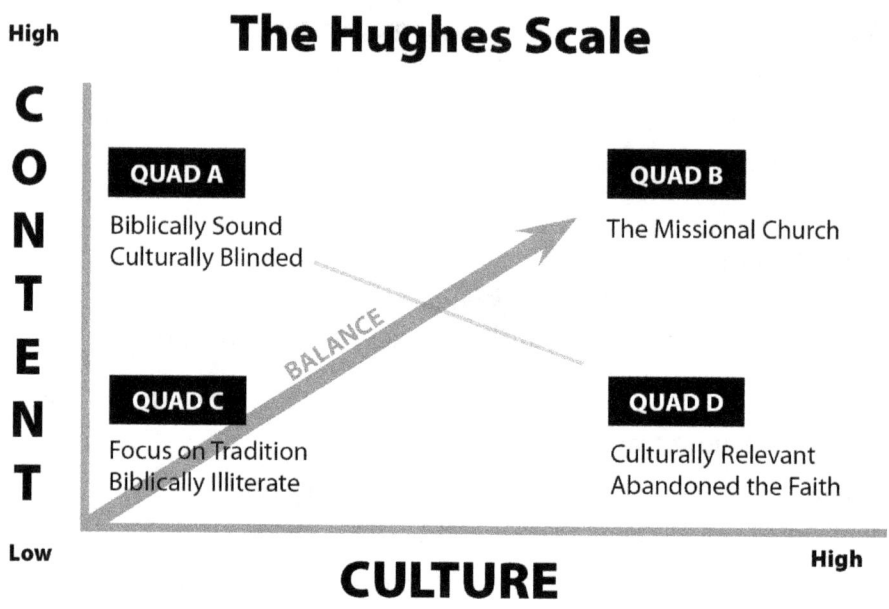

Understandably, all cultures are challenged by the Word of God, yet the philosophy of "kill the Indian, save the man," was what the Native people grew to understand as the "White man's gospel."[6]

Beginning in 1887, the federal government attempted to "Americanize" Native Americans, largely through the education of Native youth. By 1900, thousands of Native Americans were studying at almost 150 boarding schools across the United States. The US Training and Industrial School founded in 1879 at Carlisle Barracks, Pennsylvania, was the model for most of these schools. Boarding schools like Carlisle provided vocational and manual training and sought to systematically strip away tribal culture. They insisted that students drop their Indian names, forbade the speaking of native languages, and cut off their long hair. Not surprisingly, such schools often met fierce resistance from Native American parents and youth. But the schools also fostered a sense of shared Indian identity that transcended tribal boundaries. The following excerpt (from a paper read by Carlisle founder Capt. Richard H. Pratt at an 1892 convention) spotlights Pratt's pragmatic and frequently brutal methods for "civilizing" the "savages," including his analogies to the education and "civilizing" of African Americans.

It is a sad day for the Indians when they fall under the assaults of our troops, as in the Piegan massacre, the massacre of Old Black Kettle and his Cheyennes at what is termed "the battle of the Washita," and hundreds of other like places in the history of our dealings with them; but a far sadder day is it for them when they fall under the baneful influences of a treaty agreement with the United States whereby they are to receive large annuities, and to be protected on reservations, and held apart from all association with the best of our civilization. The destruction is not so speedy, but it is far more general.[7]

Visionary Leadership of Annie Armstrong[8]

In 1880, in her first prominent leadership position, Annie Armstrong served as the first president of the Woman's Baptist Home Mission Society of Maryland, which involved women in supporting the Home Mission Board (now North American Mission Board) of the Southern Baptist Convention. The society's first priority locally was forming an Indian school and ministering to Chinese immigrants. The organization also provided support for work in Cuba and New Orleans. One of Armstrong quotes still inspires: "The future lies all before us . . . shall it only be a slight advance upon what we usually do? Ought it not to be a bound, a leap forward, to altitudes of endeavor and success undreamed of before?"

Visionary Leadership of David Brainerd[9]

When Brainerd was twenty-four years of age, he entered upon his missionary career among the Indians. The Apostle Paul was his great hero as he carried on his missionary endeavors. He was deeply influenced by the ministry of John Elliot. Brainerd was sent to the Stockbridge Indians in Massachusetts in the year 1743 under the auspices of the Scottish Propagation Society. He established a school for Indian children, and, with the aid of an interpreter, preached to the adults. There was no English family within many miles and his dwelling was a room made of logs. There was no floor other than the hard-packed earth, and his bed was a heap of straw. His principal food was boiled corn and bread baked in the ashes. After about a year, Brainerd was asked by his mission director to begin work among the Delaware Fork Indians. About the same time, he received a call to the pastorate of the largest and wealthiest church on Long Island, but he deemed that the will of God was not always found where comfort, ease, and wealth are offered. He determined to continue as a missionary to the neglected red-skinned people of America.

HISTORICAL OVERVIEW OF SBC WORK AMONG NATIVE AMERICANS

Domestic Mission Board—Native Americans and New Orleans Slaves

When the Southern Baptist Convention was formed in 1845, the constitution adopted by this body established two distinct mission boards—Domestic and Foreign. Initially, the Domestic Board of Missions focused on evangelism and church planting exclusively in Southern (slaveholding) states. In these early years, much of their missions efforts were dedicated to ministry among the African American enslaved population.

During the 1850s, the mission board turned its interests westward. Missionaries were sent to California and to the Native peoples living in western territories. In 1855, the Domestic Board merged with the American Indian Mission Association to become the Domestic and Indian Mission Board of the Southern Baptists.[10]

Language Missionaries

There have been some great men who served as national missionaries for the Native Americans of the Home Mission Board and the North American Mission Board, and some who have worked in conjunction with the mission boards to advance God's Kingdom to the Native Nations of the United States of America.

Dr. B. Frank Belvin[11], a Choctaw Indian from Oklahoma was chosen by the Baptist Home Mission Board to serve as a missionary to Apache, Creek, Kiowa, and Seminole Indians. During his forty years with the Board, he was responsible for building over sixty mission churches and for the conversion of countless numbers of Native Americans to Christianity.

Jimmy Anderson (Muscogee Creek) from Oklahoma is perhaps the most well-known and beloved Native minister. He dedicated his entire life to ministry among Native Americans. "Bro. Jimmy," as he was called, followed Dr. Belvin as the appointed Native National Missionary for the Home Mission Board. He helped organize Native mission teams that assisted missionaries across the United States. Bro. Jimmy has been retired as a national missionary for quite some time. However, he had continued to lead teams as recently as 2016, when he led a team to the Northwest Territory to assist a missionary to the First Nations People.

Russell Begaye (Navajo) from New Mexico served as Native national missionary for the Home Mission Board. Russell entered the political arena in public service to the Navajo Nation in 2011, after serving four years as director of missions for the San Juan Baptist Association in Farmington, New Mexico. Previously, he retired from a thirty-year career as a missionary, church planter, and foreign language outreach director with the North American Mission Board, and had served as a preacher while earning a Master of Divinity degree from Southwestern Baptist Theological Seminary. He is now president of the Navajo Nation[12], the nation's largest Native Tribe.

Mark Custalow (Mattaponi) from Virginia followed Russell Begaye as the national missionary for Native Americans at NAMB. Mark presently serves as the church planting specialist for the Southern Baptist Conservatives of Virginia and continues to be an advocate for presenting the Gospel to Native People of North America. Mark is a progressive thinker in developing strategies and approaches to reaching Native communities.

Ledtkey (Lit) McIntosh (Muscogee Creek) followed Mark Custalow as the national missionary for NAMB, and pastors Oklahoma's largest Native church, Glorieta Baptist Church in Oklahoma City, Oklahoma. Lit is chairman of the FoNAC (Fellowship of Native American Christians) executive board, established in 2012. While Lit served as the national missionary for NAMB, he saw the value of having an advisory council to aid him in formulating plans and strategies directly affecting Native ministry.

Dr. Emerson Falls (Sac and Fox and Choctaw) served as FoNAC (Fellowship of Native American Christians) chairman. Dr. Falls was very instrumental in forming FoNAC in 2012, and served as president until June 2016. Dr. Falls has a long list of personal accomplishments. He was founder (1989) and director of the Rocky Mountain Campus of Golden Gate Seminary, in Denver, Colorado. He has served as president of Cook College and Theological School. Dr. Falls also became the first elected Native American to serve as president of the Baptist General Convention of Oklahoma. He currently serves as president of the Gathering and campaign chairman for Indian Falls Creek.

Dr. Mike Cummings (Lumbee) from North Carolina, was an integral part of the development of the FoNAC, encouraging Native congregations to support prayerfully and financially the origination and development of the organization. Dr. Cummings served the North Carolina Baptist State Convention as president in 1999, the first Native American ever elected to that office. The Burnt Swamp Association of Lumbee Indians in North Carolina has led and been involved in missions across many areas of Native America as well as some mission endeavors internationally.

Early Native American Language Congregations

The Indian Removal Act was passed by Congress on May 28, 1830. The law authorized President Andrew Jackson to negotiate with Indian tribes in the southern United States for their migration to federal territory west of the Mississippi River in exchange for their ancestral homelands. The relocation of tribes spanned from east of the Mississippi River to Oklahoma Indian Territory, which became the state of Oklahoma in 1907. "Oklahoma" is a Choctaw word that means "Red People."

Between 1898 until 1907, names were accepted from the Choctaw, Cherokee, Creek, Chickasaw, and Seminole tribes that were allotted land grants[13] that were used to build homes, plant crops, and to build places of worship. The traditionalists built ceremonial grounds, while those who were believers in Christ built churches. Many of these churches are still in existence; yet sadly, many have disbanded, no longer have a pastor, or have very few members.

Leadership Training

The greatest church planting movement among Native people in Oklahoma occurred as a result of indigenous men and women who were forcibly removed from their homelands to Indian Territory. These were remarkable people of faith, in spite of very difficult circumstances. The churches trained leaders from within their own families and congregations. They sang and preached in their Native tongue, but as time progressed the people were forced to speak English in order to function in the dominant society. Eventually, fewer and fewer could speak their heart language fluently. As a result—during the transitional period from these Natives being fluent speakers to being limited in their understanding of their native tongue—many lost connection with their spiritual heritage. The growing younger population moved to urban areas in search of employment, education, and housing. Upon leaving their family's allotted lands, many only returned for special occasions.

Population Trends

The Indian Relocation Act of 1956[14] (also known as Public Law 959 or the Adult Vocational Training Program) is not to be confused with the Indian Removal Act.

The Public Law 959 was a United States law intended to encourage Native Americans in the United States to leave Indian reservations, acquire vocational skills, and assimilate into the general population. Part of the Indian termination policy of that era, which terminated the tribal status of numerous groups, it played a significant role in increasing the population of urban Indians in succeeding decades.

In 1960, it was reported that in excess of 31,000 people had moved from the reservation and to urban areas since 1952, with about 70 percent of them becoming self-sufficient in their new cities.[15] It is estimated that between the 1950s and 1980s, as many as 750,000 Native Americans migrated to the cities, some as part of the relocation program; others on their own. By the time of the 2000 census, the urban Native population was 64 percent higher than it had been in the pre-termination era of the 1940s.

Overall, the Relocation Act had devastating long-term effects. Transplanted tribe members became isolated from their communities and faced racial discrimination and segregation. Many found only low-paying jobs with little advancement potential. They also suffered from a lack of community support and were economically challenged by the higher living expenses that are typical for urban areas; but they could not return to dissolved reservations.

Given the rapid urban expansion of the period, Native Americans found that lower-cost housing was often in areas most likely to be targeted for urban renewal and replaced with office buildings, freeways, and commercial developments. This added to the instability of their lives. Further, the practice of redlining[16] by financial institutions made it nearly impossible for Natives and other people of color to find homes near their employment or to afford desirable housing. Children of relocated workers had difficulty enrolling in segregated public schools and faced the same social discrimination as their parents.[17]

The American Indian and Alaska Native population grew in every region between 2000 and 2010. The American Indian and Alaska Native alone-or-in-combination population also grew in every region between 2000 and 2010, led by 36 percent growth in the South and 35 percent growth in the Northeast (see Table 2). In the West and Midwest, the American Indian and Alaska Native alone-or-in-combination population increased as well, but at slower rates. The American Indian and Alaska Native alone population also increased in every region, but at slower rates than the alone-or in-combination population. The American Indian and Alaska Native alone population grew most in the Northeast, increasing by 31 percent.

Education and Poverty by Race in the US

The American Indian/Alaska Native, Black, and Asian racial groups include mixed-race populations among their numbers, and all of them have high percentages of poverty and lack of education. Regardless of their origin, Hispanics can be of any race/color, but they also have high dropout numbers. Whites, however, include only single-race, non-Hispanic Whites.

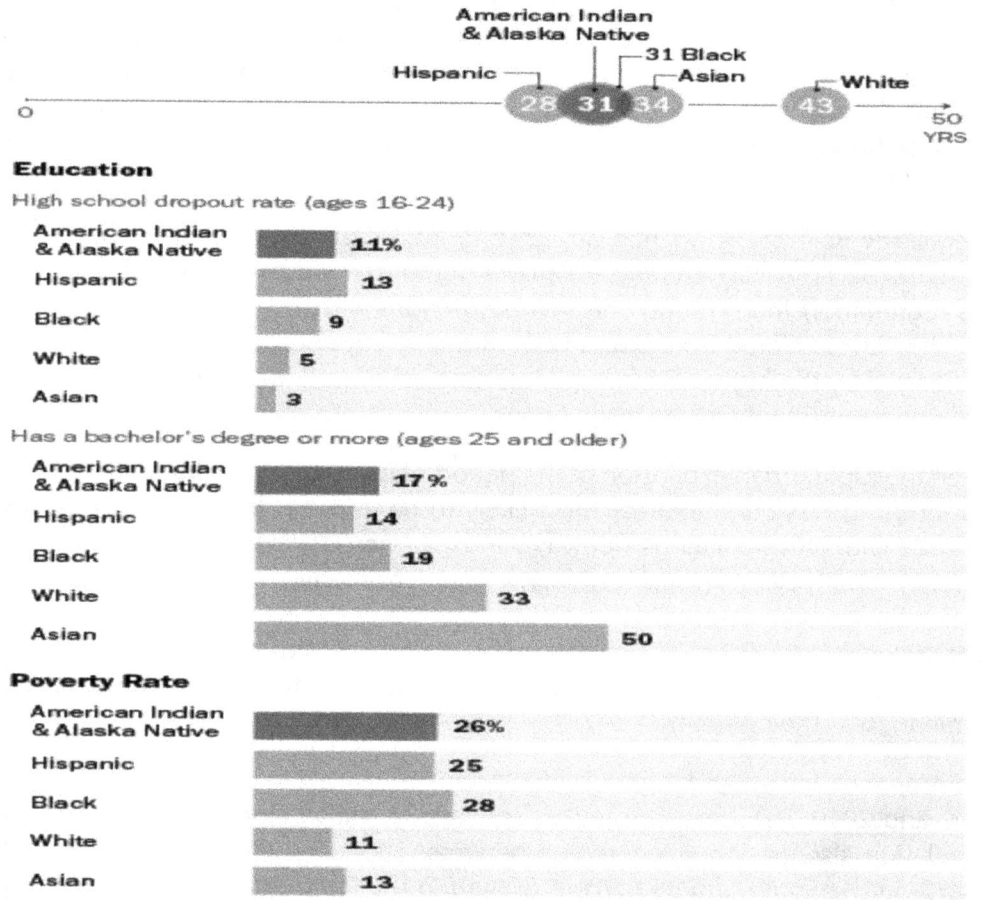

Dropouts are defined as people ages 16–24 who are not enrolled in school and who have not attained a high school diploma or equivalent credential, such as a General Educational Development (GED) certificate.[18]

Status of Native American Southern Baptist Churches

The number of Native churches affiliated with the SBC has not increased significantly in the last several years. The vast majority of churches whose ministry focus group is Native Americans exists in two states—North Carolina and Oklahoma. More than 70 percent of the Native population is located in the larger cities of the US, yet less than 25 percent of the churches are located in these cities. Many factors contribute to this lack of church plants in the cities, such as lack of planters/pastors, the high cost of meeting places, and the lack of primary churches willing to serve as a sponsoring church.

Status of Native American Leadership Training

Strides are being made in leadership training, small in comparison to need, yet not insignificant. Training schools are being designed to develop leaders among the indigenous peoples of the United States. Minnesota, New Mexico, Oklahoma, Arizona, North Carolina are among states that are partnering with state conventions, associations, or other mission sending organizations to take on this God-sized task.

Ministry-Based Evangelism

Ministry-based evangelism is proving to be one of the most effective ways to share the Good News of salvation. Ministering to the felt needs of Native Americans establishes relationships, which opens many doors for evangelism. Native People are among the most economically depressed in America. Offering a "hand up" without developing a need for dependency can be very rewarding for people who sometimes feel neglected or those engulfed with a sense of hopelessness. The most pressing needs among Native Americans are centered on issues related to family, education, occupation, economy, and health issues.

Children and Youth Evangelism

Vacation Bible School has been a very effective tool of reaching into communities, reservations, and urban areas. Native children are very artistic and love using their creative ability. Storytelling about Bible characters has always intrigued children of all ages. Learning songs and following active movements become an exciting learning time for kids of all walks.

- Our Native people as a general observation are oral learners.
- The idea of enlisting workers from within the particular focus group to serve alongside mission volunteers, doing the teaching or instruction, can be a positive mentoring tool.
- For many years, Native people have felt that they had to have outside help to conduct VBS. This could be attributed to two distinctive factors: (1) The zeal of

volunteers having a set way of doing things and little willingness to share responsibilities; (2) The reality of having others do something that they have never felt comfortable attempting, and thus drawing the false conclusion that their attempts would never be as effective as others.

Native American Church Planting Strategic Considerations

- Prayer is the absolute first step in planting new works to unreached and underreached people, especially as it relates to different ethnicities.
- Enlist teams to do prayer walking.
- Pray for a "Person of Peace" who will add validity and credibility to those mission volunteers and agencies.
- Develop a ministry profile, an essential element in finding out key information to aid in strategy building.
- Enlist ministry partners who can financially lend support to assist volunteers from other states or regions.
- Locate a meeting place, whether in homes, community centers, schools, churches, or any place affording a place of gathering.
- Gather small groups and identify and develop leaders.

Need for Culturally-Informed Strategies

All cultures have practices that are challenged by the Word of God, but Native Americans have long felt that their entire culture was condemned. They have often felt that in order for them to have a right relationship with God, they had to abandon who they were to become acceptable to God.

Today, there is a movement to become so culturally relevant that some well-intentioned ministries have presented a syncretistic message (the blending of traditional religion with Christianity), which does little, if anything, to rescue sin-sick souls for Jesus. Missional churches walk a razor's edge—if they fall to the left, they fall into syncretism; if they fall to the right, they fall into obscurantism.

The Strategic Importance of Partner Churches

New church plants are in desperate need of partnerships that will help enable them to become successful without dependency. Beginning with and never excluding prayer, the Lord said it best: "The harvest truly is plenteous, but the laborers are few;

Pray ye therefore the Lord of the harvest, that He will send forth labourers into His harvest" (Matthew 9:37–38, KJV).

Laborers are people without any particular skill set but are people with a willingness to do whatever they can with whatever they have, working together to accomplish a common goal.

Partnerships can offer workers, facilities, resources, and financial support. Each of these will aid in facilitating a stand-alone new healthy church plant with indigenous leadership.

Recommendations for Churches

Churches can adopt a church or mission pastor that is serving in a repressed area. I know personally the feelings of being displaced among a people who possess a world view that was quite foreign to what I was accustomed to in Oklahoma. It was always a blessing to receive letters of encouragement or for my children to receive small gifts from a church on special occasions.

Many churches could offer surplus items (not junk) to aid in carrying out ministry to children and youth. Adults could receive items that help promote discipleship and books that address the needs and growth of new believers (Bibles, DVDs, Christian literature, Christian computer software, and Christian worship resources).

Recommendations for SBC Entities

- There is much that the entities of the Southern Baptist Convention can do to enhance educational endeavors among Native Americans. They can begin by enlisting writers to craft articles that include success stories of young people from local and different tribal backgrounds.
- Recognizing and realizing the life difficulties of poverty, high school drop-outs, alcohol abuse, teen suicides, and a host of other social issues, Baptist entities can partner with Native ministries that may be lacking in resources, workers, and finances to deal with such hard issues and offer assistance to support those in the heat of the battle.
- Provide conferences that emphasize education and provide information on Baptist colleges/universities. They can include this topic in brochures (e.g., IMB, NAMB), including educational qualifications for appointment.

- Prayerfully and financially partner with SBC Native organizations and ministries whose sole purpose is ministry to Native Americans across North America, presenting a doctrinally-sound, culturally-relevant message of hope, care, love, encouragement, and instruction in the Christian life and its impact on the world.
- Establish partnerships with Native Americans. Native Christians are not seeking a handout from the Southern Baptist Convention. We know that too often Native Americans are viewed as a demographic that many people associate with entitlements and social programs. As God's children, we seek to partner with other Christian groups and organizations as an approach to bring the Gospel to Native people. We believe that we can accomplish more when we work together to reach the lost for Christ. We believe that partnerships with associations, state conventions, churches, and auxiliaries of the Convention can work to bring the Gospel message to Native people.

Recommendations to Baptists

- Develop world view resources that are culturally-relevant and doctrinally-sound. Culturally relevant resources that focus on Native Americans' particular worldview can help to bridge the gap that has for so long separated Native people from churches in their particular region. The perception of Native people used to be, "How will I be accepted by the church?" The perception today among many Native people is, "How will I be accepted among my peers?"
- Adopt a missionary, church planter, existing pastor, or people group.
- Provide resources: the need for resources can at times can be overwhelming.
- Prayerful support when ministering is the key to effective ministry.
- Financial support in light of a partnership that includes accountability and responsibility.
- Join in praying for a "Person of Peace," which can help open doors to the community, tribal leaders, and denominational leaders.
- Assist leader development by providing training resources, office equipment, books, resource kits, video series, etc.
- Provide financial assistance for Native mission teams. Many volunteers have very limited resources yet they are sent to areas of the most pressing needs.
- Serve with compassion, remembering that Native Americans lead the nation in many disturbing areas such as teen suicides, accidental deaths, alcoholism, and diabetes.

CONCLUSION

The Indigenous people of the United States and Canada are unreached or mostly under-reached people. The ministry to these proud people has been considered difficult at best. Many factors contribute to this—history of the government, forced removal from their homelands, forced acculturation, boarding schools (government and religious), job relocations, addictions, suicides, and suspicions of those asking too many questions.

The great Apostle Paul once said, "For a great door and effectual is opened unto me, and there are many adversaries" (1 Corinthians 16:9, KJV). Partnerships are vital, networking is key, understanding world view is essential, and total reliance upon God is without question!

Multi-Ethnic Ministries in the SBC

Lennox Zamore

Race can be a determining factor for people when they decide where to worship. Research cited in this report shows that approximately 92.5 percent of both Catholic and Protestant churches throughout the United States can be classified as "mono-racial," where 80 percent or more of the individuals who attend are of the same ethnicity or race.

In 1998, the number of non-Anglo Southern Baptist congregations totaled 6,044. By 2014, 10,709 congregations (out of 51,636 total SBC congregations) identified themselves by an ethnicity other than Anglo, an increase of 77.18 percent. (The SBC disparity is depicted by the chart.)

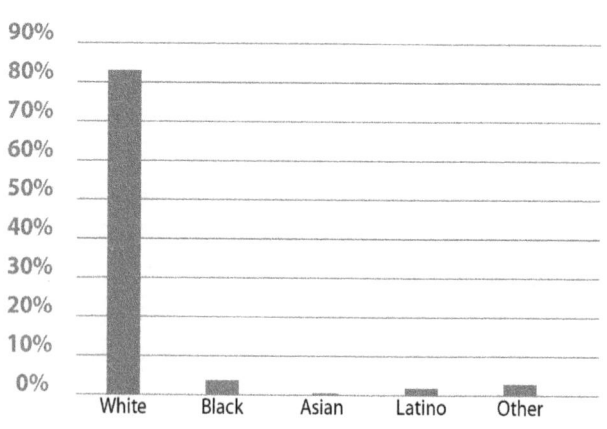

A similar disparity exists for Deaf Christians in the US. There are roughly 26,228,529 Deaf people living in this country, and only eighty-four uniquely Deaf Southern Baptist churches. This means there is approximately one church per every 312,244 Deaf people.

Southern Baptists are not strangers to multi-ethnic missiology. However, the rapidly changing demographics of America presents an unprecedented opportunity for the SBC to chart a broader course on multi-cultural missiology. To that end, President Frank Page has proactively seized the opportunity to address the ethnic divide in SBC by formulating a Multi-Ethnic Advisory Council comprised of twenty three individuals representing the following respective ethnic groups:

1. Arabic Baptist Fellowship
2. Caribbean Baptist Fellowship
3. Ghanaian North American Assembly
4. Haitian Baptist Fellowship
5. Intercultural Ch. Planting & Missions
6. Jamaican Baptist Fellowship
7. Multi-Ethnic Church
8. Native American
9. Central Eastern African Ministry
10. Native American
11. Nepali Baptists
12. Romanian (E. Euro.) Fellowship
13. Romanian Baptist Fellowship
14. Russian Fellowship
15. SBC Conference of the Deaf
16. SBC Messianic Fellowship
17. All-Ukrainian Baptist Fellowship

Ethnic Groups Chart

The formulation of the Council was predicated on the biblical mandates of: the Great Commission (Matthew 28:19); the example of Jesus (Luke 8:25; 9:52; 10:25); the model of the Gentile church (Acts 13:47); and the eventual composition of heaven (Revelation 7:9). The Council served a three-year term and provided general and specific recommendations to the president on ways to bridge the ethnic gap in our local churches and convention.

General Recommendations

The council developed general and specific recommendations pertinent to the ethnic groups indicated above. The following are the general recommendations:

1. Partner with relational church networks, like Mosaix Global Network, that exist to establish healthy multi-ethnic and economically diverse churches throughout North America and beyond.
2. Appoint church leaders who will review and provide evidence-based best practices.
3. Continue to lay out the framework, which includes theology, sociology, our commitments, challenges, obstacles, and the need for models of multi-ethnic ministry.

4. Study healthy multi-ethnic churches that are flourishing in the US and beyond.
5. Adopt a set of recommended core values that promote unity and diversity.

The following were suggested core values.

SPECIFIC ETHNIC GROUP REPORT AND RECOMMENDATIONS

The Deaf Population

Demographics

The term "Deaf" is used in this report to refer to seven distinct groups: Hearing Impaired, Hard of Hearing, Congenitally Deaf, Adventitiously Deaf, Accidentally Deaf, Pre-lingually Deaf, and Post-lingually Deaf. The Deaf community is both a culture and a community, and they are often overlooked in both policy and practice, both within the faith and without. Therefore, in this report, they are considered an ethnic group.

Challenges

The first challenge in reaching persons in the Deaf community is that hearing people regard Deaf communities as monolithic. The second is that the models used for hearing ministries are not the most effective for reaching Deaf individuals. The third is that few hearing people are willing to immerse themselves that deeply into Deaf culture. The fourth challenge is that few Deaf are ready to take on the task of running or establishing a church. Finally, cookie-cutter methods of conventional "hearing culture" outreach are not effective in reaching Deaf persons.

Recommendations

The recommended missiology for reaching Deaf individuals is to establish ministries that are Deaf-led, or led by hearing people who are committed to affirming Deaf culture, supporting Deaf culture, and living "as Deaf as possible." Also, our outreach models need to be missiological rather than pathological. Deaf should be seen as people first, and not by their impairment. It involves waiting to be accepted, not imposing hearing values, but giving up the rights of our hearing culture just like we do for international missions. The Deaf language must be honored and learned fluently, and Deaf culture and values must be respected and followed, unless they violate Scripture.

The Caribbean

Demographics

The Caribbean comprises thirty-three major island nations and 7,000 smaller islands, with more than forty million people. Originally, the Caribbean was home to Caribs, Arawaks, and Tainos, some of whom still thrive on reservations today. Most of the Caribbean is now populated by the descendants of freed slaves, most of whom came from West Africa. They have lost all connections to their ethnic groups in Africa, however. Post-slavery indentured servitude also brought large numbers of East Indians to the Caribbean. As a result, the Caribbean is a confluence of diverse people groups that have blended through slavery, immigration, and tourism.

Languages of the Caribbean (in order of prevalence) are Spanish, French (including French Creole), English, Papiamento, and Dutch. The major religions of the Caribbean islands are Roman Catholicism, non-Catholic Christianity, Islam, Judaism, Hinduism, Obeah (Voodoo), and Rastafarianism.

Challenges

The primary challenge to evangelization of Caribbean people is the stigma and stain of colonialism. Religion was a major tool of colonization and, as a result, resistance to colonialism is transferred to religion.

The second is the very real geographic challenge of non-contiguous nation islands, separated by hundreds of miles of ocean, each with individual governments and residual European sovereignties. Another challenge is widespread poverty. When survival is the foremost concern, eternal salvation has little urgency. Another challenge is the rapid growth of the Rastafarian religion that seems to have swept over youth in various areas of the Caribbean for two generations. The fifth challenge to outreach and evangelism is two generations of ineffective and dying churches. Finally, the ancient African religion or cultural practice called Obeah, or voodoo, is a great challenge.

Recommendations

Following are some practical steps for outreach and evangelism in the Caribbean Islands:

- Revitalize dying churches and/or plant new multi-ethnic churches.
- Teach Caribbean people to be missional.

- Affirm Caribbean people and encourage them understand and appreciate their own ethnicity.
- Identify, train, and develop ethnic Christian leaders.
- Identify a strategic multi-ethnic Caribbean council.
- Address quality of life issues through the churches.
- Plant more Spanish, French, and Papiamento churches.
- Emphasize reaching the twenty largest cities.

Jewish People

Demographics

There are an estimated 5.6 to 6.7 million Jewish people in the US, with a only few of them affiliated with the 37 Southern Baptist Messianic congregations. The members of the Southern Baptist Messianic Fellowship (SBMF) are scattered across North America. The SBMF is a member of the International Organization of Jewish Evangelists called the Lausanne Consultation on Jewish Evangelism (LCJE).

CITIES/REGIONS	NO. OF SYNAGOGUES	NO. OF MESSIANIC CHURCHES	SBMF CHURCHES
NORTHEAST	262	20	0
SOUTH	370	32	2
MIDWEST	740	64	4
WEST	1,480	128	8
TOTAL	2,960	256	16

Challenges

- SBMF represents only a small portion (6.25 percent) of the Messianic congregations. Other factors should be considered with conducting outreach among American Jews.
- Only 33 percent of American Jews born after 1980 have two Jewish parents, which means they may have experiences with non-Jewish religions. Further, Messianic Jews tend to be more committed to Judaism than the general American Jewish community.
- Multi-ethnic evangelism efforts seldom target Jews, so Southern Baptists and most other non-Jewish believers are seldom taught how to reach Jews.
- The SBMF does not receive Cooperative Program support through NAMB, which has caused them to look outside the SBC for help.

Recommendations

- The SBMF needs to partner with other biblically-sound groups that engage in the same type of evangelism and teaching as do the members of the SBMF.
- Do not target Jewish people with tract evangelism strategies.
- Learn about this people group and engage in prior planning, training, and research before doing outreach.
- Contact SBMF for recommendations on best approaches and other suggestions.
- The SBMF should recommend speakers/instructors on Jewish evangelism, Jewish feasts, and prophecies about the Messiah Jesus.
- Jewish people have been instructed, for generations, against recognizing Christ as Messiah and need teaching in understanding Messianic prophecies.

Native American People

Demographics

Native Americans once numbered about fifty million in North America, but were reduced in numbers by disease, genocide, war, government oppression, and relocation by European settlers. They now comprise about 5.2 million people native to the United States.

In order to keep track of these diverse groups, anthropologists and geographers divided them into ten separate culture groups as they are today. There are an unprecedented 567 federally recognized tribes, most, residing on 617 Native American reservations. Native Americans are a younger population than other American groups, with a median age 29 compared to the national average of 37.2.

Challenges

The biggest challenge, yet one of the biggest opportunities, is that Native Americans fare significantly below average on wellness scales. They have a 28.4 percent poverty rate, compared to the nation's 15.3 percent. Native Americans die at higher rates: 600 percent higher for tuberculosis; 510 percent higher for alcoholism; 189 percent higher for diabetes; 229 percent higher for vehicular accidents; 152 percent higher for injuries; and 62 percent higher for suicide.

The second challenge is a composite of historic calamities imposed upon Natives—the many wars during which even our women and children were massacred; the broken treaties that led to broken trust; the reservations being located on the worst land available, which led to despair and anger; and, the establishment of boarding schools that were produced for the purpose of taking the "Indian out of the Indian."

The third is a challenge we all share. After two hundred years of evangelizing, fewer than 2 percent of Natives are Christians. This should be deemed unacceptable.

Recommendations

The SBC has been working with Native Americans since its inception, and remains the best entity to help Native people. The following are recommendations for SBC:

- Pray the Lord of the Harvest to call Native Americans to the ministry.
- Work in partnerships with Native Americans.
- Develop world views that are culturally relevant and doctrinally sound.
- Implement an "Adopt a Missionary, Church Planter, or Pastor" program for Native Americans, financially supporting those who are being effective.
- Pray for a liaison—a "person of peace"—to work between the cultures.
- Focus heavily on urban areas (an estimated 70 percent or more of the Native population live in urban areas).
- Address health and wellness matters.

Russian Church Report

Demographics

Russian immigration to America dates back to Alaska in 1784. Russian people in America are identified both by ethnicity and by language. The language policies of the Soviet Union forced all citizens to learn the Russian language, so, it is common to meet Ukrainians and Moldovans, Uzbeks, and Georgians who speak Russian. However, not all people who speak Russian are ethnic Russians. What we call Russian congregations in US are Russian-speaking congregations, which may include representatives from many ethnicities. The Russian population in America is about 2.9 million, up from less than one million in 2010.

Challenges

More than one-half of Russians in America cannot speak conversational English.

Currently, there is no single entity uniting Russian-speaking Baptists in the United States. There are about five different unions, of which the SBC is partnering with only one—the Pacific Coast Slavic Baptist Association.

A significant segment of Russian-speaking immigration comprises Jewish people, who should be reached primarily as Jewish immigrants, not just as Russians.

Recommendations

Southern Baptist churches should be intentional in reaching and partnering with Russian-speaking people and churches.

- Southern Baptists need to discover, and fund theological education for, prospective Russian-language church planters.
- Southern Baptists can offer buildings, support, expertise, and resources to new church plants on a long-term basis.
- Southern Baptists can reach out to Russian-speaking immigrants who enter established immigrant communities and offer help in finding housing and jobs, teach them English, distribute Russian language Bibles, celebrate their heritage, and, most importantly, share the Gospel with them.
- Ministering to the second generation of immigrants in the same congregation is a challenge. So, it is increasingly important that immigrant churches serve the needs of the new English-speaking generation.

For communities with a small number of Russian-speaking individuals, Southern Baptist churches can:

- Help find housing and work for new immigrants.
- Offer individual English language lessons.
- Offer evangelism literature and Bibles in Russian.
- Offer translation in Russian during worship services.
- Encourage Russian-speaking individuals to find other Russian-speaking families and share the Gospel with them.
- Grow and train Russian-speaking ministry leaders.

For communities with a dense population of Russian-speaking people, Southern Baptist churches can:

- Organize an ESL (English as a Second Language) ministry.
- Reach out to a Russian-speaking seminary student or encourage gifted Russians-speaking believers to go to seminary, then hire them as part of the pastoral staff and provide them with a building and necessary resources to start a ministry.

Middle Eastern Report

Demographics

Arab immigrants began coming to the US in sizable numbers during the 1880s. Today, it is estimated that nearly 3.6 million Americans trace their roots to an Arab country. Arab Americans are found in every state, but more than two-thirds of them live in just ten states: California, Michigan, New York, Florida, Texas, New Jersey, Illinois, Ohio, Pennsylvania, and Virginia. Metropolitan Los Angeles, Detroit, and New York are home to one-third of the population. American Muslims represent the fastest growing segment of the Arab American community.

Contrary to popular assumptions or stereotypes, the majority of Arab Americans are US-born, and nearly 82 percent of Arabs in the US are citizens. The Pew Research Center estimates that there were about 3.3 million Muslims of all ages living in the United States in 2015. This means that Muslims made up about 1 percent of the total US population, the majority of which has ancestral ties to Lebanon, Syria, Palestine, Egypt, and Iraq.

Challenges

By 2040, Muslims are projected to become the second-largest religious group in the US. By 2050, the American Muslim population is projected to reach 8.1 million people or 2.1 percent. Therefore, evangelizing them is critical. The various religions among the Middle Easterners are Greek Orthodox, Roman Catholic, Assyrian Catholic, Chaldean Catholic, Sabian, Yazidi, and Muslims Their understanding of God will not lead to salvation unless there is a church community of believers that will patiently work with them and be supportive of them.

Their beliefs make it complicated for scholars and historians to pin down the nuances of their religion.

Recommendations

- Study Arab religions and understand where they are coming from. Ask them to share with you what they believe and why they follow their religion.
- Find theological ground that you agree on, such as the belief in one God, and then explain the reason why you follow Christ.
- Understand your own doctrine of God, Trinity, sin, atonement of salvation, and judgment.
- Middle Eastern churches are traditional in their format, and the majority of the people who attend have no idea what the Bible says about their religion. They follow different traditions with significant variants of Christian beliefs and call it Christianity.
- Most Middle-Easterners are newcomers to your neighborhood and came to the US as refugees. Welcome them into the neighborhood.
- Some foods are forbidden by their Arab religions. Avoid them in their presence so you don't risk offending anyone.
- Invite them to come with you to your church. Ask their youth and kids to participate with your church youth/children's group.
- Love them truly and sincerely. Attend their wedding, their funerals, and their festivals. As neighbors, be available when they need you.
- Learn not to have boys and girls together in Arab functions, and do not offer to shake the hands of their women.
- Volunteer at a refugee relief organization in your city.
- Let them see what Christ has done in your life by your conduct, dress, eating, prayer, and church attendance.

Central-Eastern Africa Report

Demographics

Central-Eastern Africa comprises people originally from Burundi, Congo, Rwanda, Kenya, Uganda, Tanzania, and Sudan.

Most of these people came to the US as refugees, international students, diplomats, or seeking jobs. In addition to their native language, most of them speak up to eight different languages, including English.

Challenges

The Central-Eastern Africans are not monolithic. In fact, they have different backgrounds, beliefs, cultures, and behaviors.

Also, they have many different languages, which poses a challenge to translators.

Recommendations

We give thanks to the SBC for the leadership and hard work reaching this generation and recommend that Southern Baptists continue providing assistance.

- Because 90 percent of Central-Eastern Africans came into this country as refugees, they need help overcoming the challenges of acclimating to their new home.
- Central-Eastern Africans need financial support in the ministry to be able to evangelize, mentor and teach leaders, and plant new churches and help them to grow.
- Central-Eastern African believers need help in making fliers and creating websites to reach their fellow countrymen in their native languages.

Women in the SBC

Rhonda Kelley and Candi Finch, Compilers

Southern Baptists determined one of the best ways to increase the involvement of women in the SBC was to start a conversation. In January 2016, Frank Page, president and CEO of the SBC Executive Committee, appointed a Women's Advisory Council to gather information concerning the involvement of women's ministry leaders and ministry wives in their churches. The task force is comprised of eighteen ladies from fourteen states representing different age groups, stages of life, ethnic backgrounds, and ministry positions.

The task force was hosted on three on occasions (January 7–8, 2016, August 11–12, 2016, and March 30–31, 2017) by officers of the Executive Committee of the SBC including: Frank Page, president and CEO of the SBC Executive Committee; Ken Weathersby, vice president for Convention advancement; and Roger S. (Sing) Oldham, vice president for Convention communications and relations. During the meetings, the purposes of the task force were defined:

- To determine if and how women are involved in the SBC;
- To discuss how the SBC can serve women as they minister to other women in and through the local church; and
- To recommend a variety of ways for Southern Baptist women to be involved at all levels in Convention life according to biblical guidelines.

Rhonda Kelley, president's wife at the New Orleans Baptist Theological Seminary and a leader in women's ministry, served as chairwoman of the Women's Ministry Advisory Council and facilitated the discussion of the following:

- What ministries, training, and resources are provided at this time for women in the SBC?

- What evangelistic methods and resources are effective in reaching women with the Gospel of Jesus Christ?
- What additional support is needed by the women of the SBC?
- What recommendations should be made to the SBC Executive Committee for consideration to increase involvement of women in Southern Baptist life, according to biblical guidelines?

Following the meetings, press releases were published announcing the work of the committee.

A survey was developed for distribution to Southern Baptist women, and areas of ministry were identified for individual committee members to investigate. Survey Monkey was used to conduct the survey which was composed of twenty questions, both quantitative and qualitative. A link to the survey was published through Baptist Press and social media. Results were digitally compiled and immediately available to task force members. In order to gather data, the group created a shared document to post input and findings about resources and ministries specifically for women.

Historical Findings

The Bible teaches that women are created in God's image, equal in worth and value, and have unique roles in ministry based on their gender (Genesis 1:26–28, 2:8–25; 1 Corinthians 11:2–16, 12:7–11; 1 Timothy 2:11–15; Titus 2:3–5). Southern Baptists follow a complementarian perspective of gender roles in the local church and across denominational entities. (See *Baptist Faith and Message*, Article VI on The Church and Article XVIII on The Family for additional information.) Throughout history and in the Southern Baptist Convention, women have played important roles in the local church and denominational life.

For more than one hundred years, Southern Baptist women have been involved in mission education through the capable leadership of the Woman's Missionary Union. This mission organization was begun in 1888 with a three-fold purpose: to learn about missions, to do missions, and to support missions. Southern Baptist churches have organized missions for women in different ways. During the 20th century, women within many local churches recognized the need for more than missions and began to organize a variety of other ministries.

At several times in more recent years, SBC leadership has considered how to involve and support women more effectively. In 1992, SBC President Ed Young appointed a task force to consider how the denomination could support women's ministry. Then, in 1993, the Baptist Sunday School Board (now LifeWay Christian Resources) created the Women's Enrichment Ministry to provide resources, leadership, and field services specifically for women's ministry. In 1996, a research proposal summarized the historical, biblical, philosophical, and ministry perspectives in order to recommend increased involvement and support of women in the SBC. Other entities of the SBC have also appointed staff to specifically serve women of the SBC.

Current Findings

National – Several entities of the Southern Baptist Convention provide specialists in women's missions and ministry.

- International Mission Board – Global Mission Catalyst, Women, and Non-Traditional Churches.
- LifeWay Christian Resources – Women's Ministry Specialist.
- North American Mission Board – Consultant for Pastors'/Ministers' Wives.
- Woman's Missionary Union – Consultants for myMISSION, Women on Mission, and Adults on Mission.

Regional – The six Southern Baptist seminaries are located in different geographic areas of the country to focus on ministry training in their areas. Women are enrolled in all Southern Baptist seminaries for training in ministry. All six Southern Baptist seminaries have programs for student wives and several have academic training for women's ministry students.

- Gateway Seminary of the SBC (Ontario, CA) – www.gs.edu.
- Midwestern Baptist Theological Seminary (Kansas City, MO) – www.mbts.edu.
- New Orleans Baptist Theological Seminary (New Orleans, LA) – www.nobts.edu.
- Southeastern Baptist Theological Seminary (Wake Forest, NC) – www.sebts.edu.
- The Southern Baptist Theological Seminary (Louisville, KY) – www.sbts.edu.
- Southwestern Baptist Theological Seminary (Fort Worth, TX) – www.swbts.edu.

State – Most Southern Baptist state conventions have a staff position for women's missions and ministries and/or ministry wives, often requiring seminary training. Several states have consultants working with specific ethnic groups, such as Hispanic women in Arizona and Texas and Asian women in North Carolina.

Associational – Many associations of Southern Baptist churches have lay leaders serving in women's ministry as mission leaders, and as ministry wives.

Local Church – An increasing number of Southern Baptist churches have organized women's ministry and missions programs, each varying according to the local church context.

Survey Findings

An electronic survey was conducted in order to gather information from women across the SBC. It was distributed through *Baptist Press* and social media channels and was available from March to November of 2016. In total, 3,617 women responded. The survey was composed of twenty questions, soliciting both quantitative and qualitative responses. The following questions were included in the survey. Also noted are the percentage of responses and a sample of additional comments:

1. **Does your church have an organized women's ministry or other programs specifically for women?**

   81.31% Yes, 18.69% No

The significant majority of respondents indicated their churches have an organized program for women though the types of programs seem to vary significantly. Some comments indicated a formal organization like women's ministry or Woman's Missionary Union, while others noted individual components like Bible studies, special events, or exercise classes. Several explained that their programs were "struggling" or "under reconstruction."

2. **Is there a woman on your paid church staff whose focus is ministry to women?**

   9.29% Part-time, 9.40% Full-time, 81.31% No

Fewer than 20 percent of the respondents reported a full-time or part-time paid staff position for women's ministry. Most leaders of women serve as lay leaders in local churches, although most state Baptist conventions have paid positions for women's missions/ministry, as do some associations of churches.

3. **Do you serve as a leader of women in your church?**

   34.81% Lay Leader, 3.68% Paid Staff, 61.52% No

The majority of the respondents do not serve in positions of leadership with women. The women are active in church and serve in a variety of ways. However, they were familiar with all programs and ministries for women in their churches.

Survey Respondents by Age

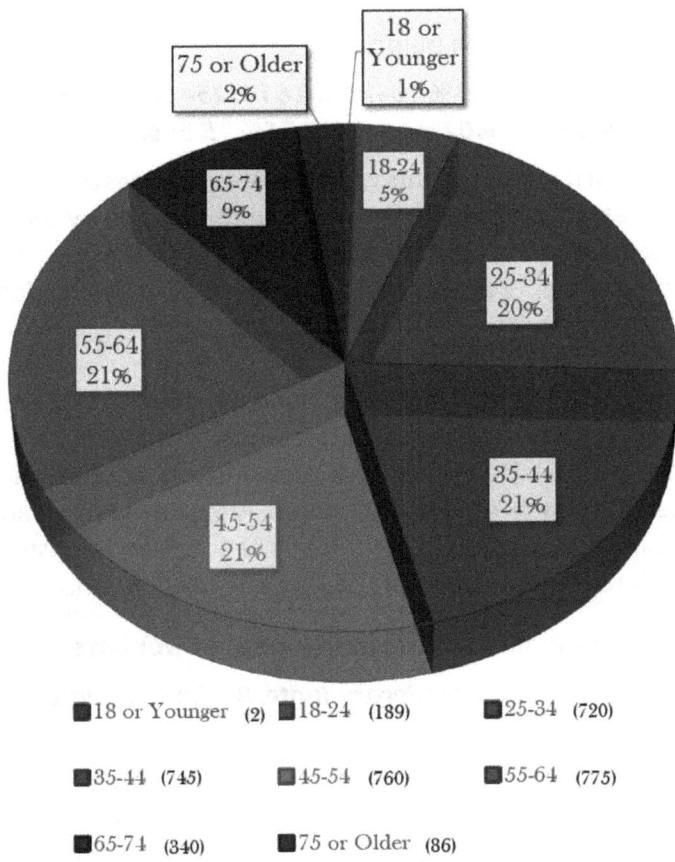

- 18 or Younger (2)
- 18-24 (189)
- 25-34 (720)
- 35-44 (745)
- 45-54 (760)
- 55-64 (775)
- 65-74 (340)
- 75 or Older (86)

4. **Are you involved in Woman's Missionary Union, Women's Ministry, or another group of women?**

   56.51% Yes, 43.49% No

Just over one-half of the respondents are involved in women's organizations. Many women participate in one specific ministry (Bible study or prayer group) but do not consider themselves to be a part of a women's organization.

5. **Are you the wife of a minister?**

   28.61% Yes, 71.39% No

Twenty-eight percent of the respondents are ministry wives—wives of pastors, youth ministry, and education ministers. Several noted their husbands serve as deacons.

While some ministry wives serve in positions of leadership for women, most leaders are lay women.

6. **In what age group do you belong?**

   0.06% 18 or younger, 5.31% 18–24, 20.61% 25– 34, 20.98% 35–44, 21.07% 45–54, 20.70% 55–64, 9.02% 65–74, 2.25% 75 or older

Sixty-three percent of the respondents were between the ages of 35 and 65. Attempts were made to increase the respondents from younger women by submitting the survey to collegiate ministers to distribute and to increase the respondents of older women by printing copies of the survey for distributions to senior adult groups.

7. **In which state or territory do you live?**

A larger number of responses came from Florida, Kentucky, Louisiana, Oklahoma, and Texas. Fewer responses came from states with a smaller number of Southern Baptist churches (such as Delaware, Iowa, New Mexico, and Hawaii). At least one response came from each of the fifty states. Attempts were made to increase participation from states with smaller numbers of Southern Baptists through social media and emails to the state directors of women's missions and ministry.

8. **Do you have academic training in the areas of women's leadership?**

   4.62% Certificate, 4.23%, Undergraduate, 8.46% Graduate/Seminary, 82.69% No

The overwhelming majority of respondents have no academic training in the areas of women's leadership. About 17 percent reported certificates, undergraduate, or graduate degrees in women's leadership.

9. **Have you received specific leadership training for your work with women (i.e. LifeWay Women's Leadership Forum, WMU training conferences)?**

   24.99% Yes, 75.01% No

The majority of respondents do not have leadership training in any of the given areas. For the 25 percent who said yes, comments were given that training was received through various leadership conferences, Women's Leadership Forum, and WMU trainings. Those who attended some form of training event commented of attending between one and three a year.

10. **Does your church provide training opportunities for women in leadership positions?**

    19.41% Yes, 80.59% No

The vast majority of respondents indicated that their churches do not provide training opportunities for women in leadership positions. The 20 percent who said yes commented that trainings held in their churches were for VBS, Sunday school, Bible studies, Precept, and various other leadership trainings offered through LifeWay, local associations, or state conventions.

11. **Does your church utilize online resources specifically for women?**

    22.20% Yes, 77.80% No

The majority of respondents responded that their churches do not utilize online resources for women. Several that said yes commented that LifeWay and WMU were where they received their online resources.

12. **Does your church utilize Southern Baptist Convention printed resources for women (LifeWay, WMU, New Hope, Broadman-Holman)?**

    58.09% Yes, 41.91% No

The results indicate that nearly one-half use SBC printed resources for women and that the other half does not. The majority of those who said that their churches did use SBC printed resources commented that the resources came from LifeWay.

13. **Does your church utilize non-Southern Baptist Convention printed resources specifically for women?**

    27.90% Yes, 72.10% No

The majority of respondents indicated that their churches do not use a non-SBC printed resource. Non-SBC printed resources included Precepts, Group Publishing, and a variety of other Bible studies by authors such as Lysa Terkeurst and Kelly Mintor.

14. **Does your church offer Bible studies specifically for women?**

    82.80% Yes, 17.20% No

The significant majority of respondents replied that their churches offered Bible studies specifically for women. A comment box was not given for respondents to elaborate their answers.

15. **Does your church provide missions and community ministry opportunities specifically for women?**

    54.27% Yes, 45.73% No

About one-half of the respondents indicated that their churches provided missions and community ministry opportunities specifically for women. A little less than half responded no. A comment box was not given for respondents to elaborate their answers as to where or what capacity the missions/community ministry opportunities took place.

16. Does your church provide evangelism and discipleship training specifically for women?

29.08% Yes, 70.92% No

A significant majority of respondents said that their church does not provide evangelism or discipleship training specifically for women. Respondents who said yes were not given the opportunity to comment on the types of training their churches offer for women.

17. Does your church host special events specifically for women?

80.56% Yes, 19.44% No

A significant amount of respondents replied that their churches host special events specifically for women, with only 20 percent of churches who do not. A comment section was not given for respondents who said yes to elaborate on the type of events the churches host for women.

18. In your opinion, are women adequately involved across Southern Baptist life?

42.24% Yes, 57.76% No

About 42 percent of respondents believed that women were adequately involved across Southern Baptist life, whereas a little more than one-half disagreed with the question. Several explained that women are "disconnected from SBC life," or "majority of women are involved within the church, but not with overall SBC life." Others were concerned with the exclusion of women in their own ministries and with SBC life.

19. Could women be more involved in Southern Baptist life?

91.07% Yes, 8.93% No

The vast majority of respondents believed that women could be more involved in Southern Baptist life. Even those who think there's good involvement think there should be more. Respondents suggested that women should be more involved in all levels of the SBC life through trainings and mentorships, and should become more aware of resources for women provided by the SBC.

20. Do you have any additional comments about women in the SBC?

15.68% Yes, 84.32% No

The majority of respondents did not leave any additional comments about women in the SBC. Sixteen percent said yes, and comments suggested further education to equip women at all stages of life, apps for women, and Bible studies that cover various forms of mental illness.

Research Findings

In order to gather data, the group created a shared document to share input and findings about resources and ministries specifically for women. Each committee member researched an area and provided findings in specific categories. A brief summary of the findings is listed below. More complete findings are included in the Council's report posted at SBC.net.

1. **Personal Evangelism Resources** — While numerous evangelism resources are available, few have been developed specifically to reach women and even fewer to reach minority women with the Gospel. Many present resources can be adapted for use with women as well as translated to specific languages and cultures. Resources to share the Gospel and engage the lost are cited in the Council's report posted at SBC.net. Additional personal evangelism resources developed by women and for women would be useful in spreading the Gospel to women of all backgrounds.

2. **Evangelism Training Resources** — Fewer evangelism training resources are available than general evangelism resources. Two evangelism training resources have been developed by women specifically to train women for evangelism: *HeartCall* by Jaye Martin and *Why Do You Believe That? Living in Truth,* by Mary Jo Sharp. These two resources are highly recommended for use in training women to reach other women with the Gospel. Additional evangelism training resources developed by women and for women would be useful in equipping women to spread the Gospel to women of all backgrounds.

3. **Evangelistic Events and Ministries** — Several entities of the SBC sponsor evangelistic events and ongoing ministries for women. The International Mission Board hosts service opportunities as well as giving opportunities throughout the year. The North American Mission Board encourages evangelism through movements, materials, events, and volunteer opportunities. LifeWay Christian Resources provides leadership training and resources as well as special events through LifeWay Women. The Woman's Missionary Union offers mission trips and Christian Women's Job Corps as well as leadership training and resources.

4. **Lay Leadership Training and Resources** — A wide variety of leadership training opportunities and resources are available to Southern Baptists. Some are specifically geared toward training women who are lay leaders in the church.

LifeWay Women hosts training conferences for women's ministry leaders and ministers' wives and produces books and webshows. The Woman's Missionary Union publishes training materials and hosts leadership conferences. Other evangelical ministries provide lay leadership training and resources as well.

5. **Academic Training at Colleges and Seminaries** — Women are enrolled in many different degree programs in secular and Christian colleges and seminaries. However, few schools offer accredited degrees specifically for women serving in the local church and other ministries. Several Christian colleges and SBC seminaries include academic programs to equip women. The seminaries offer other programs and degrees in a variety of fields that are open to both men and women, from degrees in education to theology to practical ministry to courses strategically aimed at preparing for woman-to-woman ministry. Many schools offer classes in several formats (on-campus, online, hybrid, weekend or week-long intensives) to enable women desiring more academic training with more options than ever before in the history of the SBC.

6. **Academic Training for Ministry Wives at Colleges and Seminaries** — Few colleges provide academic training for ministry wives due to the younger age of students and smaller percentage of married students. However, several seminaries provide academic training for student wives to equip them for ministry alongside their husbands. All six of our SBC seminaries offer certificate level training for ministry wives. While each program is unique, all combine practical ministry and biblical studies courses. In addition, several programs offer specific courses approved by the International Mission Board to fulfill seminary training requirement for wives. In addition, the six SBC seminaries host fellowship meetings for student wives on a regular basis. Non-student ministry wives are often invited to participate in academic courses and ministry fellowships as well.

7. **Ministry Wives Training, Resources, and Support (non-academic)** — Non-academic training, resources, and support are provided for Southern Baptist ministry wives. Connections on social media seem to be very popular, as ministry wives can share fellowship and counsel with more anonymity and no cost.

8. **Women and Culture** — Several Southern Baptist organizations provide helpful resources for women on the culture. There are some books specifically about navigating the culture as a Christian woman. Resources and training have begun to be offered to specific ethnic and language groups, though a great need continues as the SBC diversifies. Special attention is also being given to bivocational/smaller membership churches.

9. **Prayer Resources and Ministries for Women** — Many books are available through LifeWay and other publishers to equip women to learn how to pray for themselves, their families, their churches, and other ministries. Some resources are geared for individual study and growth while other materials help women gather with other believers to guide them in growing in the discipline of prayer as well as forming strategic and focused prayer groups. Prayer, one of the mightiest tools in the believers' spiritual armory, is often the most overlooked. However, our research showed that there are already many excellent resources to help teach and train women on the discipline of prayer.

10. **Missions Education and Resources** — Three organizations within the Southern Baptist Convention have missions as their central focus: the International Mission Board, the North American Mission Board, and the Woman's Missionary Union. Each provides a variety of missions' education and resources. WMU educates all ages about the importance of domestic and international missions. NAMB focuses on domestic missions and training, and IMB focuses on international missions and training.

11. **Mission Experiences and Opportunities** — There are many ways for women to be involved in missions, both short term and long term, in their own communities and overseas. These opportunities are planned each year, so the best way to find out about what is available is to check with local Southern Baptist churches, associations, state Baptist conventions, WMU organizations both the state and national level, NAMB, and IMB.

12. **Discipleship and Mentoring Resources and Training**— One of the blessings of Southern Baptist life is being a part of a denomination that has been faithfully producing and publishing discipleship and mentoring resources for many years. Through LifeWay Christian Resources, as well as through other publishing companies and through local churches, there is a wealth of materials available, many of which are geared specifically to women who are interested in discipling and training other women. Leadership training for women in the areas of discipleship and mentoring should be increased.

13. **Bible Study Resources and Training** — Similar to discipleship and mentoring resources, women have a plethora of Bible study resources available to them. In addition to the training provided by each of the six SBC seminaries on how to study the Bible, resources in a variety of categories are available today.

14. **Community Ministries** — The possibilities for community ministry are practically endless. On average, the target audience for the local church lives within a five-mile radius of the church. For this reason, the church must be sensitive to the needs of their local community and provide ministries that address those needs.

There are resources available within the state conventions and associations to help churches identify their community demographics. If the church is successfully reaching its community, then the needs of the congregation will be the same and the ministries and programs of the church should reflect those needs. As members are transformed and developed, then they are equipped and empowered to further evangelize their community through powerful, personal testimonies.

15. **Special Events for Women** — Many local Southern Baptist churches have special events for women throughout the year, targeting different ages and life stages of women. More than 80 percent of respondents said their church hosts special events for women throughout the year. Leaders should develop strategies and be more intentional about evangelizing the lost at special events.

16. **Involvement of Next Generation Women in the SBC** — The survey results showed that more than 90 percent of respondents felt that women could be more involved in SBC life. Leaders of women should train older adults to cultivate relationships with the younger generation. Biblically-based mentoring programs should be encouraged as well as involvement in ministry by younger women. In 2017, the Executive Committee of the Southern Baptist Convention appointed a Young Leaders Task Force to hear from those within the younger generation in the Convention. Hopefully this new task force can also discuss ways to involve the next generation of women in the SBC since there is work to be done in encouraging younger women in SBC involvement.

Recommendations

As a result of the survey results and the research findings, the following recommendations are made by the women's advisory council to increase involvement of women in the SBC:

Recommendation One — We affirm the many vital ways women are currently serving in local churches, associations, state conventions, and the denominational entities of the Southern Baptist Convention, and we encourage increased recognition of the spiritual gifts and leadership skills of women already serving in biblically appropriate ways in their churches and beyond.

Recommendation Two — We request a revision of the Annual Church Profile (ACP) to include new categories such as gender of church members and women in leadership positions. This addition and other measures will help identify more women in leadership positions in local churches, associations, state conventions, and denominational entities to help disperse information about existing resources, training, and support provided for women in the SBC.

Recommendation Three — We promote the development of vehicles to communicate more effectively with Southern Baptist women. New forms of communication could include:

- Email for Southern Baptist women (sbwomen@sbc.net).
- Southern Baptist Women page on sbc.net to include "Did You Know" and "How To" as well as "Best Practices in Women's Missions and Ministry" sections.
- Videos "I am a Southern Baptist Woman" to depict diversity in age, stage, race, etc.
- News articles and blogs.
- Social media (Facebook, Instagram, etc.).
- Hashtag - #sbwomen.
- Printed pieces.

Recommendation Four — We recommend that state conventions and local associations encourage churches to provide training for women's missions and ministry leadership as well as identify and network with lead churches in the area to offer support to smaller churches.

Recommendation Five — We propose the development of more resources and training materials as well as the use of all available technologies for Southern Baptist women especially in the areas of discipleship, evangelism, and mentoring. We encourage the production of leadership materials by women with seminary training and biblical studies backgrounds.

Recommendation Six — We recognize the need for support of women in leadership positions as well as ministry wives who struggle with personal crises or emotional health issues. Increased awareness of resources is needed as well as lay counseling by women and for women.

Recommendation Seven — We desire increased involvement of Southern Baptist women, representing the different ages and seasons of life as well as the diverse ethnic and cultural backgrounds, on state and national convention committees and boards.

Recommendation Eight — We suggest that several members of the Women's Advisory Council also serve as representatives on the Convention Advancement Advisory Council.

Recommendation Nine — We acknowledge the need for a follow-up meeting of this task force to discuss specific strategies for the implementation of the recommendations through the appropriate SBC entities.

Conclusion

The SBC Women's Advisory Council has been a valuable and productive task force not only to identify present resources for women in leadership and to reflect the involvement of women in the SBC but also to recommend ways to increase involvement of women at all levels in Convention life according to biblical guidelines. The group of eighteen ladies met on three occasions to develop strategies to accomplish the assigned task, distributed a survey to hear from Southern Baptist women, researched areas of training and resources for women by category, and delineated recommendations for action. Historical and current findings were identified, then survey and research findings were summarized in the report. Additional information is provided in five appendices at the end of the report posted at SBC.net.

A draft of the final report was compiled by Rhonda Kelley (chairwoman) and Candi Finch (council member) and emailed to all council members for review and input. Suggestions by the council members were incorporated into the report prior to the Council's third and final meeting, where the final report was completed. The final report was submitted to Drs. Page and Weathersby at the "Many Faces of the Southern Baptist Convention" booth in the exhibit hall on June 12, 2017, the Monday prior to the 2017 meeting of the Southern Baptist Convention in Phoenix, Arizona.

Members of the council express appreciation for the opportunity to serve Southern Baptists on this task force. Our prayers will continue for Southern Baptist women to use their spiritual gifts in ministry effectively and spread the Gospel of the Lord Jesus intentionally. We are available to assist in implementation of our recommendations and communication with Southern Baptist women. Our prayer is for Southern Baptist women to grow in their personal faith, disciple women in the faith, and lead others to salvation.

What the SBC Looked Like

Rodney Webb

What kinds of people comprised the Southern Baptist Convention at its inception in 1845? The predominantly Anglo American group encompassed various Caucasian people groups descended from England. Others were of European ancestry and enslaved Africans who worshiped in the church their owners attended. During this time, Baptists were also extending their evangelistic efforts to reach Native Americans. Many Southern Baptists desired to form their own mission agencies; however, some were not ready for this change.

Spanish philosopher George Santayana said, "Those who do not remember the past are condemned to repeat it."[1] It is prudent for Southern Baptists to remember our history so that we may move forward, not repeating missteps of the past.

History of SBC Formation

The Southern Baptist Convention was born into a highly charged atmosphere that was influenced by geopolitical, socio-economic and theological issues. The Convention has grown from 4,126 cooperating churches with 351,951 members in 1845 to 47,272 churches with 15,216,978 members in 2017. "Today the SBC is the largest non-Catholic, evangelical denomination in North America."[2]

To understand Southern Baptists, it is imperative to comprehend the world in which they lived at the time of formation. Their environment and culture evolved within each period of society. Dr. Robert A. Baker, in *The Southern Baptist Convention and Its People 1607–1972*, points out that the period between 1814 and 1845 was filled with turmoil and rapid change across the South.[3] The issues impacting change overlapped economic, social, political, and religious circles.

A major change agent in the South's socioeconomic trajectory was Eli Whitney's cotton gin invention in 1793. This innovation had enormous impact upon the southern economy, resulting in the expansion of the South's cotton industry. The cotton growing spread from the coastal regions to the South's interior. Whitney's invention allowed for a faster and more profitable production of a short-staple variety of cotton, which grew very well in inland southern soil.

The Industrial Revolution's ripple effects continued to impact the cotton trade and the southern economy. The invention of the spinning jenny, the power loom, and the development of the factory all enhanced the textile industry, which boosted the need for more cotton.

The negative consequence of these agricultural and industrial developments was the nagging problem of slavery. The capacity to produce more cotton faster had also invigorated the slave trade. The cotton industry's advancements had increased profits, but the need for more slaves had accelerated simultaneously.

Dr. Baker points out that the period from 1814 to 1845 was filled with turbulent events that impacted the expansion of Baptists in the South. The growth that took place in the southern region of the US represented an average annual membership gain of 5.25 percent:[4]

> When the Baptists from various parts of the South met in Augusta, [Georgia], on May 8, 1845, in response to the call issued by Virginia Baptist Foreign Mission Society, some of them had been giving considerable thought to the kind of denominational body or bodies that Baptists in the South should organize. The kind of structure finally adopted was, in fact, somewhat of a departure from the former practice of carrying on benevolent work through separate autonomous societies.[5]

There were major differences in the way northern Baptist churches supported their mission work to facilitate the distribution of designated funds needed to implement mission goals. These varying practices were contributing factors in the division between the Baptists in the North and the South.

> In its organizational meeting in Augusta, Georgia, in 1845, the Southern Baptist Convention established two mission boards to serve at home and abroad. The work of both foreign and home missions would be conducted by one convention, with a separate board for each rather than with a completely independent organization for each. The convention would determine assignments, elect directors, receive reports, give instructions, and make suggestions as it deemed wise. The then prevalent plan of

> working through societies provided membership in a society for the individual, church or group of churches which cared to contribute, apart from organic connection with a denominational body. The establishment and direction of the mission boards by the Convention itself identified the work of missions as a basic concern of the Convention. It emphasized that missionary work is not optional to the Christian or to the church. Nevertheless, it remained for these mission agencies, the Foreign Mission Board and the Domestic Mission Board, later known as the Home Mission Board, to gain the confidence and support of Southern Baptist churches. Support was especially a challenge for the Domestic Board located in Marion, Alabama, in the Southwestern part of the Convention territory. The Foreign Mission Board was located in Richmond, Virginia, in the northeastern section of the [Southern Baptist] churches.[6]

Southern Baptist churches in 1845 were concerned about God's work but they also had become victims of cultural captivity. Many in the emerging Convention had been against slavery until the economy changed with a rapid influx of money. The potential for increased revenue became a motivating factor for a number of Baptists inclined to support slavery.

Shaping a New Baptist Body

Early events in Baptist life shaped the Convention, and over the course of two centuries, various events (wars, financial crises, political crises, racial tension, and religious conflict) have molded our culture and impacted our churches. Negative influences have impacted who we are as a Convention, but good and positive events have shaped Southern Baptists as well.

> The single most dominant factor in the beginning of the Convention's growth was revivalism growing out of the two great awakenings. The first awakening will be shown to flow south into the coastal states. The second wave of revivalism spread west. The organized revival became a major mode of church extension. . . . A consequence of the camp meetings was the vitality which it poured into the participating churches.[7]

South Carolina Baptists had organized the first state convention on December 4, 1821. This body was built on a network of local associations, looked toward sponsoring multiple benevolences, and had other centralizing features. Other southern states adopted similar structures in succeeding years. The experience of Southern

Baptists with these bodies led them to feel that there was little to fear that any of these structures might ever become oppressive.

In addition to the previous measures, another strong safeguard for keeping such a new body from usurping the authority of the local church was the democratic nature of the Convention. The floor vote at the annual meeting was the final authority in the body, and this inhibited usurpation. The 1845 constituency felt that should there be any evidence of misplaced authority, the matter could be firmly and quickly settled through free discussion and decisive vote.[8]

In the earlier part of the 1870s, several Baptist leaders urged closer cooperation between the Home Mission Board, the state boards, and the Southern Baptist Convention board. These leaders recognized that if Southern Baptists did not give full support to the Home Mission Board, the mission agency's existence and the Convention itself were at stake. Unfortunately, this full support did not come until the next period in Baptist life.[9]

The Role the Cooperative Program

Historian Robert Baker helped Southern Baptists recognize how the economy and financial issues from the 1850s through the twentieth century influenced Southern Baptists both negatively and positively.

> Sensitiveness relative to centralization in the Convention began to disappear rapidly during the 1920s. [I]ncreasing financial stringency following the Seventy-five Million Campaign; . . . [and] the recognized need for a Convention "watchdog" to maintain the integrity of the body brought the appointment of a Committee on Correlation.... It became the fiduciary, fiscal, and executive agency of the Convention in all its affairs, not specifically committed to some other board or agency. It represented a *de facto* year-round corporate voice for the Convention.[10]

The SBC Executive Committee, formed in 1917 and restructured in 1927, continues this function today.

Cecil and Susan Ray wrote about the Cooperative Program (CP): "Before we as Southern Baptists could adopt a lifestyle of cooperation, we had to learn how to harmonize two great loves—love of freedom and love of missions."[11] Cecil Ray led Southern Baptists' Planned Growth in Giving stewardship emphasis during the 1980s and researched the CP's origins with his daughter, Susan. In their book they affirm that the Cooperative Program was not something merely created; but rather, it was a gift from God to enable Southern Baptists to accomplish His mission in the world. The CP has been a channel that has helped send missionaries both in our own country and to other countries.

Post-World War II

After World War II, Southern Baptists were geographically limited to work in seventeen Southern states in accordance with agreements established with Northern Baptists. In 1949, the Convention took action to assure that "the state conventions of Baptists may cooperate with whomever they will, irrespective of geographical location." Two years later in 1951, the Southern Baptist Convention passed a resolution instructing its agencies "to serve as a source to any community or any people, anywhere in the United States."[12]

Enormous industrial growth and massive migration continued in the post-war boom. In that process, the country was becoming more urbanized, and industrialization was postured to dictate much of America's future. Meanwhile, the SBC was preparing for a twenty-year era of its greatest numerical growth in churches and membership. The SBC realized a net gain of 7,197 new churches in that period. State conventions reported starting 9,955 churches during that time. However, as new churches were started, others were dissolved. The SBC had a loss of 2,758 churches that started but did not constitute during this same twenty-year period.[13]

The decisions coming out of the SBC's annual meetings after World War II prepared Southern Baptists for a movement of God through their churches, which was accomplished chiefly by the southerners who had migrated out of the south into all sections of the country. Encouraging the state conventions to work with Baptists wherever they were and whenever they asked for help was a major denominational breakthrough. The SBC was able to hold the allegiance of rural Baptists who relocated from the rural areas into the towns and cities. Many brought with them leadership skills that provided strong leaders in the churches they joined or helped start.[14] The migration from the southern region of the country led to the planting of new churches for several reasons.

The influx of rural residents into urban settings benefited those areas; however, the migratory pattern also resulted in the death or decline of many rural Southern Baptist churches. Those who migrated were not always fulfilled in the churches they were visiting. In many cases, they were uncomfortable with the theology and worship styles. In response to their frustration, they started new churches that replicated the worship experiences they had experienced in the South. They recruited pastors from the South, and soon the term Southern Baptist became equated with components like worship style, theology, and doctrine, and not just a geographical region. Adrian Lampkin Jr reflected: "Few denominations can tell a story equal to this." Border states in the middle of the northern and western migrations—Missouri, Tennessee, Kentucky, and Texas—benefited the least. Post-war industrialization brought growth to almost all the states. "This was not a planned challenge to the existing Baptist bodies in the North," Lampkin stated. As new state conventions were formed and churches and associations affiliated with existing state conventions, tremendous growth was literally thrust upon the Convention.[15]

In 1969, my wife and our baby daughter moved to the New York City metropolitan area. Dr. Maurice Fain, pastor of the newly-constituted Rockland Baptist Church, the only Southern Baptist church in a county of over 250,000, helped us find an apartment in New City. From there, I served as the missionary to the Deaf for a nine-state area in the Northeast. After we moved into our New City apartment, many of our neighbors would ask why we moved there. From these types of questions, my wife and I had the opportunity to share our faith. Our church was a plant started by Dr. Fain. The first time we attended a worship service, we discovered a congregation that consisted primarily of people from the South who had migrated to the region because of employment. A great thing about our church was that we had diversity among the thirty-five members. Several families in the church were native New Yorkers. The worship leader was a Chinese music professor. The church was greatly blessed and aided by churches from the South, the Baptist Convention of New York, the Metropolitan New York Baptist Association, and the Home Mission Board. Summer missionaries and mission teams came to assist with Vacation Bible School, provided inspirational speakers, and visiting choirs. The association offered a variety of training opportunities. Eventually, with the help of the Home Mission Board Church Loans Department, we were able to purchase property and modular units. Construction teams from southern churches provided assistance to help make the modular units usable.

Many pastors and lay people who served in new work areas came to the realization that their churches had unmet needs. Southern Baptist churches in the South believed the mission needs of new work areas were critical, and worked to help new churches and fledgling state conventions reach the lost in areas beyond the southern parameters. Congregations in the Bible Belt provided programs and promoted methods and literature they felt could be useful in any size church. However, they were not effective in all geographical regions or in churches with small numbers and limited resources.

There appeared to be no specific strategy to help plan and develop materials according to what new work churches needed. Basically, there was a continuation of their current programs that the long-established churches felt had always been effective for them.

Church layman William Diehl, sales manager at a major overseas steel corporation, wrote *Christianity and Real Life*, about the gap between the secular and the sacred in church circles:

> In the almost thirty years of my professional career, my church has never once suggested that there be any type of accounting of my on-the-job ministry to others. My church has never once offered to improve those skills which could make me a better minister, nor has it ever asked if I needed any kind of support in what I was doing. There has never been an inquiry into the types of ethical decisions I must face, or whether I seek to communicate the faith to my coworkers. I have never been in a congregation where there was any type of public affirmation of a ministry in my career. In short, I must conclude that my church really doesn't have the least interest whether or how I minister in my daily work.[16]

Diehl's statement about the gap between the secular and the sacred in church circles, as well as his church never holding him accountable,, caused me to think about the Monmouth Baptist Church near an Army base in Monmouth, New Jersey. When one of their members was moving away, the church would set aside a Sunday night service to celebrate the departure by sending them out as missionaries from their church to serve in their new location. This church empowered these people as they commissioned them to service in a different place.

Combine what William Diehl said with how the Monmouth Baptist Church lived their faith in community with members as well as with the SBC, reveals that this is possibly a missing piece in many of our churches. The local church needs to equip and empower members by sending them out as disciples where they live and work, while supporting those who feel called by God to serve vocationally as missionaries.

Douglas Beggs characterized the rapid expansion of Southern Baptist work across the United States:

> The growth was often lay-led and lay-initiated. The growth of the newer conventions was so strong that in the decade of the 1960s, they matched the number of churches gained by the old-line states. In the 1970s the newer conventions had a net gain of ninety-one more churches than the Old South with all its resources. The Convention led in the development of a new approach to evangelism that captured the imagination of the churches. The evangelistic fervor was matched by the development of specific events and short-term programs to facilitate church extension. Evangelistic and church extension emphases were continuous from 1950

until 1964. This effort resulted in the greatest number of new churches being constituted in any period in the Convention's history.

The exciting growth of churches, associations, and state conventions climaxed in 1964 with the culmination of the Thirty Thousand Movement. The goal was 10,000 new churches and 20,000 new missions. The HMB reported 4,703 new churches constituted and 11,796 missions established between 1956 and 1964. These new churches and missions fueled evangelism growth. In 1950 the United States was 36 percent rural and 64 percent urban, but [Southern Baptist] churches were 83 percent rural. The Convention would have to break out of its regional mold if it would respond to the cries for help from every corner of the nation.[17]

Expansion, Extension and Evangelism: 1950 through 1964

- The SBC promoted and planned emphases to challenge churches, associations, and state conventions to partner with HMB to start new churches and missions.
- Evangelism was the primary tool to reach people.
- Every church was asked to start at least one new work.
- During the first two years, 75 percent of the churches held revivals.
- By 1956, fifty-two cities were involved in the City Missions Program Ministry (CMPM).
- The HMB partnered with associations to accomplish the CMPM. Later, state conventions joined in the process.[18]

The Big Cities Program focused on six urban centers from 1957–1961: Chicago, Baltimore, New York City, San Francisco, Seattle, and Detroit. The mission funds were used for assistance with pastors' salaries and/or loans for purchasing building sites. The three most successful cities were Chicago, Seattle, and Detroit. This program was dropped in 1962 due to a drop in Cooperative Program receipts.[19]

Southern Baptists had no developed strategy in the two decades after WWII, but the Convention set goals tied to projects and emphases. In 1966, the HMB adopted a set of guidelines for the decade ahead for mission work in cities:

> The urban centers of the United States shall receive the major thrust of the Home Mission Board. With 70 percent of the population now in urban centers by AD 2000, it seems necessary that urban missions be given priority. Urban areas are the centers of political, economic, educational, and moral influence. Giving priority to urban areas will not mean we will neglect human needs in other areas.[20]

Southern Baptist Work in Areas that Are Part of Adjacent State Conventions, 1967

States	Churches	Total Members
Connecticut	4	746
Delaware	5	2,158
Iowa	12	2,243
Maine	3	391
Massachusetts	8	1015
Minnesota	10	1,100
Nebraska	22	4177
Nevada	29	5,529
New Hampshire	1	262
New Jersey	16	2,861
New York	28	5,991
Pennsylvania	29	3,070
Rhode Island	3	587
Vermont	1	165
West Virginia	57	15,542
Wisconsin	17	2,830

Tanner, p. 125, from the *Quarterly Review*, Handbook Issue, 1968 Vol.28, No. 3, p.13

In 1959 the Convention instructed the HMB to enlarge their work in areas where the state conventions were weak or emerging. They were to turn existing work over to the established states and give attention to the pioneer areas. This brought the Convention to the fifth major program of the period, developing cooperative agreements and strengthening relationships with the established states.[21]

The years from 1945 to 1964 were wonderful decades of expansion and extension in both evangelism and migration. The Home Mission Board continually sought to bring their work and the work of their missionaries into mainstream Convention life. Loyd Corder noted: "Though insisting on complete freedom to administer its direct mission work, the Home Mission Board seeks the closest possible understanding and cooperation with the state conventions. The Convention was trying to learn how to coordinate a national mission approach that would touch every level of SBC life.[22]

The decision to stop direct missions in the South was well received by state conventions. The established states were to assume more responsibility and negotiate joint projects with HMB personnel.

Arthur B. Rutledge said: "Direct mission efforts principally included language groups, good will centers, and rescue missions. Cooperative missions included city and pioneer missions, rural and mountain missions." This was designed to unify the mission plan inside the state and to allow the board to assist smaller, less developed states. Meanwhile, the state convention related to the association or the church. This was a positive move to restore responsibility to the two historic drivers of Convention church expansion—the local church and the association. There can never be a national strategy without full cooperation from all four partners in the fulfilling of the mission plan that is in the heart of God.[23]

Bold Mission Thrust (BMT)

The Home Mission Board's (HMB) initiative to help cooperating Southern Baptist churches focus on mission needs in the United States was a major effort to reach a nation that was growing more lost each year. The objectives, strategies, and guidelines for the HMB in implementing Bold Mission Thrust were adopted on March 16, 1983.

BMT Objectives

1. To lead Southern Baptists in evangelizing our land by presenting the Gospel to all persons and giving them an opportunity to respond.
2. To lead Southern Baptists in congregationalizing so every person will have the opportunity to share in the life of a New Testament church.
3. To challenge and equip all Southern Baptists to minister to meet the needs of persons.
4. To move into new frontiers where the need for evangelizing, congregationalizing, and ministering is more crucial.
5. To lead Southern Baptist to a greater awareness of missions and evangelism needs and opportunities for response.

BMT Strategies

1. The Home Mission Board will appoint, support, and equip missions personnel to serve in their vital role as a means to accomplish the purposes of the Board.
2. The Home Mission Board will look upon the service of short and long-term volunteers and bivocational ministers as an important resource in the work of missions and evangelism.
3. The Home Mission Board will lead in strengthening Baptist associations.

4. The Home Mission Board will work in cooperation with various Baptist state conventions according to mutually agreed upon plans.
5. The Home Mission Board will assist churches in the development and promotion of evangelism and missions with special emphasis on the Church Evangelism Committee and Church Missions Committee.
6. The Home Mission Board will lead in the development of an effective, comprehensive, and cohesive approach to the great cities of our land.
7. The Home Mission Board will lead in the enlistment and development of leaders from the people served, recognizing them as full participants in Southern Baptist life.

BMT Guidelines

1. State conventions, associations, and churches shall be encouraged to accept responsibility for evangelizing, congregationalizing, and ministering in their areas, freeing the Home Mission Board to do what churches, associations, and state conventions cannot do alone.
2. The Board's continuing emphasis will be placed on investment in personnel involved in missions and evangelism.
3. The Cooperative Program shall continue to be emphasized as the basic means of support of the Home Mission Board. The Board shall continue to assist the Woman's Missionary Union in the promotion of the Annie Armstrong Easter Offering and gladly receive other special gifts.
4. The principles of good stewardship of the funds entrusted to this agency shall permeate all of its operations.
5. The Home Mission Board will work in close cooperation and consultation with other Southern Baptist Convention agencies.
6. Communication and cooperation with other denominations shall be welcomed and initiated by the Home Mission Board where there is no sacrifice of principles or weakening of basic beliefs and practices.[23]

Under the umbrella of BMT, new state conventions were formed in the West and in the East. In the newer state conventions, "new work was the constant focus of each church.... Even the smallest and newest churches endeavored to start missions and new churches."[24]

Migration from the South and the decline of many churches there had convinced the leadership of the old-line state conventions that there was not a widespread need for new churches. During the 1960s, the old-line states had a net gain of 1,057 churches, while new work areas had a net gain of 1,052. In the 1970s, new work states gained 769 churches, while old-line states gained 678. The majority of new churches were in the newer conventions. This trend reversed in the 1980s, due to the influences of the HMB and its research division.[25]

Anglo Church Planting

The years leading to World War I and World War II were years of discovery for Southern Baptists. What does this mean for Baptists today? Southern Baptist churches in the South were rural and many had farmer-pastors or bivocational pastors. Some of these part-time pastors had seminary training, but many did not. Experienced pastors often served as mentors to bivocational leaders who were passionate about sharing the Gospel with their communities. These bivocational pastors were committed to living the Christian life and they understood the importance of making a church available to all people, even those in sparsely-populated areas.

The post-World War II years brought with them a new season in SBC life—a fresh wave of young adults strongly desired to worship with believers of like mind and faith. When younger, mobile Baptist southerners moved beyond the Mason-Dixon line and to the West, they searched for churches with familiar worship styles. When none could be found, they connected with others who desired the same type of worship experience they did. These lay people acted under God's guidance and would form a church and call a pastor. When the SBC become aware of this phenomenon, it began to move in the direction of starting new churches with people who felt called to start churches. One presumption that impacted outreach efforts in the Northeast, Midwest, Southwest and far West, was that whites, Anglos, and other Caucasians could be reached using the same methodologies used to reach southern whites. Despite this lack of regional cultural awareness, God blessed and prepared Southern Baptist leaders for the next stage of phenomenal growth.

Under Redford's leadership the HMB's Church Extension Division developed strategies that empowered churches to reach different Anglo cultures. The term "Anglo" originally referred to Anglo-Saxons, which represented the Germanic people and much of Western Europe, including England. They came to America from different countries and from different cultures within the same country.

Redford presented a vision and strategy for the future of Anglo Church Extension in reaching the diverse Caucasian people groups in the United States and Canada. He emphasized that church planting is primarily the task of the local church. Second, that flexibility is necessary to effectiveness in building bridges to others. And finally, it is foundational that priorities be defined and humans be committed to the church plant. Dr. Redford led his division to work with state conventions to develop strategies to reach various Anglo people groups. Church extension provided training conferences for the state missions directors, Anglo church extension missionaries, and new church planters to equip and strengthen them for planting churches.

> Language missions became a focus along with a continuing attempt to reach the cities. The board hired its first ethnic leader in 1965, Oscar Romo. He orchestrated major new thrusts to start the SBC on a new path of indigenous language leadership. Dr. Romo led Southern Baptists to become the most effective denomination in the nation in reaching ethnic-language culture people groups, representing more than 100 languages and 97 Native American tribes. Under his leadership there were over 7,000 language congregations. The Language Missions Division developed strategies and budgets based upon census data from the US government. Strong catalytic missionaries were hired to strengthen ethnic congregations to grow and plant new churches for their language groups. The annual Language Missions Conference provided speakers and conferences that included expert missiologists, anthropologists, sociologists, and urban planners. Cultural experiences created awareness and sharpened the skills of denominational leaders. This passionate strategist worked at the grassroots level to find ideal locations and leaders for church plants. "Contextualization" was his favorite word. Romo worked diligently to train pastors and church leaders in many languages.[26]

Refugee resettlement became another way to plant new ethnic congregations. The Language Missions Division established an Office of Refugee Resettlement that worked with state convention staff to find churches to train and equip in resettling refugee. Many language churches began to meet the spiritual needs of the refugees. Lewis Myers, a furloughing missionary with the Foreign Mission Board, volunteered to help with refugee resettlement when the United States experienced the great influx of Vietnamese refugees. Myers rejoiced that Baptists started more congregations for this people group in the US than in Vietnam.

The Home Mission Board's Christian Social Ministries Division trained missionaries, pastors, and lay people to become better equipped to witness through ministries that often provided a programmatic foundation for new churches. Literacy missions and conversational English classes taught immigrants to read and write the English language. Their teachings included biblical content in these lessons. Many Anglo and ethnic learners accepted Christ as a result of these classes. Ministry centers met the daily physical and spiritual needs of people, and several had worship services for their communities.

The HMB's Evangelism Division had the task of motivating and training people to share their faith personally. They assisted churches and associations in preparing for evangelistic events, such as block parties and revivals.

The Division of Chaplaincy organized chaplain ministry to equip them for service. This division also processed and approved new chaplains for the military, hospitals, and police departments, as well as to serve in various businesses and industries.

The Church Loans Division assisted churches by realistically assessing the church's building needs and financial strength.

Black Church Extension gave leadership to planting Black Southern Baptist churches. They built bridges with the National Baptist Convention.

The Associational Missions Division focused on assisting associations with meeting the needs of local churches. Support and training were given to the associational directors of missions.

Interfaith Witness helped Southern Baptists understand world religions. Training and educational resources helped Baptists understand how to witness to adherents of different faiths.

> The major influence on church planting should have been BMT, . . . launched in 1977 by the HMB and then adopted in 1978 by the whole Convention. The goal for 1977–82 was 5,800 new churches and missions, which was exceeded when 7,465 churches and missions were started. This number included approximately 1,000 language-culture units. The goals for 1982–85 included 1,500 new churches and ignored the need for church-type missions that would feed church growth and reach more new people. A total of 1,321 new churches reported starts during this time. The baptismal goal was missed again by a wider margin without the new missions to spur the reaching of people. Goals were set, but there was never a strategy to drive the process. Every agency in the Convention took what part they wanted and moved forward with their programs.[27]

The roots of the Convention needed to draw it back to the twin emphases of evangelization to start new churches and for new churches to reach people. A good beginning was starting to unravel early in the process.... The Convention had begun to drift into theological liberalism as evidenced by several controversies. Conservatives began to bring the SBC back to its biblical roots in 1979. By 1990 the conservatives were in control of the Convention and church planting would come back into national prominence.[28]

Where do we need to go?

As Southern Baptists move further into the twenty-first century, the Convention faces several issues that are critical to witnessing the Gospel effectively in North America. These issues revolve around the urbanization of North America with growing multicultural and pluralistic urban centers; the redefining of the White American—termed Anglos by Southern Baptists; the declining presence of white Southern Baptist churches in urban centers; and the need to plant churches in the urban core that recognize the non-homogeneity of the white or Caucasian population. The search for identity by the white population has led in many directions of redefining the role of the Anglo population currently known as European American.

Key Issues for Southern Baptists

- North America is an unevangelized continent. An unevangelized continent is one that lacks a multiplying movement of churches that could significantly impact major sections of that continent for Jesus Christ.
- The United States of America is today the largest mission field in the English-speaking world.
- Between 92 percent and 98 percent of Canadians are unchurched.
- Perhaps the most striking trend in American religion in recent years has been the growing percentage of adults who do not identify with a religious group. The vast majority of these religious "nones" (78 percent) say they were raised in a particular religion before shedding their religious identity in adulthood.
- One-half of all churches in the United States did not add one new member through conversion growth in the past year.
- North America is the only continent where Christianity is *not* growing.

Options for Invigorating Church Growth

Given the current religious and social climate in North America, Southern Baptist church and Convention leaders face a moment of decision:

1. They can continue to stand by and watch while Canada and the United States slide further into a Christless void.
2. They can chase quick fixes and fads that have proven to be ineffective. For example, in the 1980s, Baby Boomers returned to the church looking for purpose

and meaning. Many failed to find anything in the church that was different from what they had in the world. As a result, they left again.

3. Or, Southern Baptists can turn again to the Bible and learn how the Early Church lived, witnessed, ministered, and grew in a pre-Christian society. From the Bible lessons can be learned that are culturally relevant, contextually correct, and methodologically appropriate.

The third option is the only valid choice. It is crucial that Southern Baptists be honest with ourselves by recognizing there are key issues that need to be confronted. For Southern Baptists to turn a major corner requires facing the truth that our structures, programs, and attitudes are not accomplishing the task. The job cannot be hired out to ministry professionals alone. The Apostle Paul set the table for how the church will thrive: "And He personally gave some to be apostles, some prophets, some evangelists, some pastors and teachers, for the training of the saints in the work of ministry, to build up the body of Christ" (Ephesians 4:11–12, HCSB).

Our churches have to focus on equipping all believers in our Convention to be Christian witnesses in their daily lives. Then new believers must be empowered to continue the cycle.

How do we need to get there?

What would revolutionize the way we do business, enabling an accelerated pace of church planting? Making key adjustments is imperative!

- Raise the value of prayer movements inextricably linked to church planting movements.
- Participate in simultaneous decision-making with partners.
- Galvanize partners toward task accomplishment.
- Create an environment where churches are not threatened by competition.
- Develop the ultimate church planting search engine.
- Raise the value of multiplication in the local church through mass communication.
- Create a global learning environment that immediately improves church planting in North America.
- Provide our field-based partners an ongoing, world-class missiological education.
- Provide church planting leadership with ongoing skill development in key areas (resource development, strategic thinking, leadership development, systems design, worship).

- Enhance personal relationships with church planters and churches for peer learning/resourcing.

In recent years, many Southern Baptists churches downsized or dissolved. This is discouraging, because the need is great for people to hear the Gospel and to be discipled by a church.

What is the cause of this decline? Many different cultures make up the Anglo community. Baptists need to contextualize the communication of the Gospel message without compromising. The only way this need can be met is for believers to mobilize and start new churches. It takes more than just "professionals" to do the job. Every church member must be willing to adapt for the sake of proclaiming God's gift of salvation.

To reach North America effectively requires that Southern Baptists reevaluate how we communicate the Gospel. We must move from focusing on the different parts or saying one is better than the other—such as evangelism is more important, but church planting is second in importance; or learning the Bible is more important than evangelism. We need to move from a program approach to refocusing what we are doing.

You might ask, Why? Because the current view of the Christian church and how we present our message, how we deal with crises, and how we present the Gospel often make it seem like just another religion to pick and choose from.

We need to learn from Jesus, the disciples, and the Apostle Paul how to hear a secular society in how it searches for God. Surveys reveal that people have a high curiosity and interest in God. We should go back and study what Jesus modeled for us, as well as what the disciples, Paul, and the Early Church modeled in the early years of the Church's rapid expansion across the globe.

They demonstrated a relationship with God through personal acceptance of His Son by faith, coupled with fellowship and discipleship before, during, and after people received Jesus Christ to become a child of God . . . and then they repeated the discipling process all over again.

The major questions for us, as Southern Baptist followers of Christ, is: Can we move beyond our culture and our traditions? Can we go "back to the future" within the context of the world today. Can we do just as the Early Church did and what the Reformation almost saw happen.

The direction we choose will determine how effective we will be.

Bivocational and Smaller Church Ministry

Ray Gilder

In 2014, Frank Page, chief executive officer, SBC Executive Committee, appointed an Advisory Council to develop a report for the Executive Committee on how the Southern Baptist Convention and its entities can better understand and work with the vast number of smaller membership churches and those whose pastor is bivocational. This Council was formed through the leadership of Ken Weathersby, vice president for Convention advancement, SBC Executive Committee. Ray Gilder, pastor of First Baptist Church, Gordonsville, Tennessee, and executive director of the Bivocational and Small Church Leadership Network (BSCLN) was asked to serve as chairman. Mark Tolbert, director of the Caskey Center for Church Excellence at New Orleans Baptist Theological Seminary, was asked to serve as vice chairman. Other advisory council members were:

- Ira Antoine Jr,, director, Bivocational Pastors Ministry, Baptist General Convention of Texas, Houston.
- Vernon E. Beachum Jr, pastor, First Baptist Church, Fort Ashby, West Virginia.
- Paul Biswas, pastor, Cambridgeport Baptist Church, Cambridge, Massachusetts.
- Fredrick Brabson Sr, pastor, New Covenant Baptist Church, Knoxville, Tennessee.
- Bobby Clark, pastor, Abbot Baptist Church, Mansfield, Arkansas.
- Gordon Donahoe, pastor, Neely's Bend Baptist Church, Madison, Tennessee.
- Kenny Heath, director of missions, Western Baptist Association, La Vale, Maryland.
- Hal Hopkins, pastor, Lighthouse Baptist Church, Breinigsville, Pennsylvania.
- Stephen R. Jones, pastor, Central Baptist Church, Alameda, California.
- Pusey Losch, pastor, Mountain View Community Church, Richfield, Pennsylvania.
- Henry Luckel, regional consultant for the BSCLN, Colorado Springs, Colorado.
- Gary Mitchell, pastor, First Baptist Church, Chataignier, Louisiana.

- Joel Perez, pastor, Iglesia Bautista La Cosecha, Okeechobee, Florida.
- Michael Pigg, pastor, Philadelphia Baptist Church, Lithonia, Georgia.
- Chip Smith, bivocational ministry, Alabama Baptist State Board of Missions, Montgomery, Alabama.
- Shannon Smith, regional consultant for the BSCLN, Fremont, Nebraska.
- A. Scott Tafoya, pastor, Indian Nations Baptist Church, Albuquerque, New Mexico.
- Elizondo Marcos Villarreal, pastor, Iglesia Cristiana Bautista, Lufkin, Texas.
- Cliff Woodman, pastor, Emmanuel Baptist Church, Carlinville, Illinois.
- Joe Young, pastor, Calvary Chapel, Parchman, Mississippi.

SMALL IS THE ~~NEW~~ TRUE BIG

In a report published by Bill Day from the Leavell Center for Church Health and Mark Tolbert from the Caskey Center for Church Excellence, of New Orleans Baptist Theological Seminary, it was determined that small membership churches make up the largest portion of all Southern Baptist Churches. The following data describes cooperating Southern Baptist churches as reported in the 2015 Annual Church Profile. In 2015, New Orleans Baptist Theological Seminary prepared a study, "Small Is the True Big." With updated data, it still holds true.

The Southern Baptist Convention is a large convention of mostly smaller membership churches. The SBC has churches of every imaginable size. Some well-known Southern Baptist churches are numerically large. We are grateful for the large churches that are part of the SBC family. We praise God for them. It would be inaccurate, however to think of the large churches in the SBC as being typical. The opposite is actually the case. The vast majority of our churches are smaller membership in size and worship attendance (the current measurement standard).

Churches that are seeking to fulfill the Great Commission and the Great Commandments are significant churches performing significant ministry. Significance is not measured by numerical size alone. Neither is church health always reflected by numerical size. Healthy churches exist in all size categories.

Smaller membership churches are the truest reflection of who the SBC really is. This is reflected as one considers the size of Southern Baptist churches. As pertains to worship size, 66.49 percent of churches have 100 or less in Sunday morning worship; 89.07% of churches have 250 or less in Sunday morning worship. Only 1.43% of churches have 1,000 or more in Sunday morning worship attendance. The largest number of churches have 50 or less in Sunday morning worship (37.95%). One could say with accuracy, smaller membership churches are normative churches in the Convention.

Smaller membership churches also make up the largest portion of Cooperative Program giving. Churches averaging 100 or less in Sunday morning worship attendance fund 17.26 percent of the Cooperative Program, 43.7 percent of the CP is funded by churches of 250 or less, 66.27 percent of the CP is funded by churches 500 or less, and 82.3 percent of the CP is funded by churches of 1,000 or less. In 2013, $449,553,873 was given to the Cooperative Program, $195,699,100 was given by churches that averaged 250 or less in Sunday morning worship attendance.

The number of baptisms is an important numerical measurement in Southern Baptist life. Here again, the number of baptisms reported by the SBC is driven by the baptisms reported by the normative, smaller membership churches. Almost one-half, 49.32 percent of baptisms reported by all churches, were performed in smaller membership churches. Here is the breakdown by size: churches of 1–50 in worship attendance (9.02 percent); churches of 51–100 in worship (16.24 percent); worship size of 101–150 (10.9 percent); worship size of 151–200 (7.52 percent); worship size of 201–250 (5.64 percent); worship size of 251–500 (13.92 percent); worship size of 501–1,000 – 11.32 percent, over 1,000 in worship (25.44 percent). Baptism ratio (baptisms per worship attendance) also showed favorable ratios for smaller membership churches. In fact, churches averaging in the lowest two categories were among the highest ratios for baptisms. Churches of 1–50 in attendance had a ratio of 15.5 (one baptism per 15.5 in worship); churches of 51–100 had a ratio of 15.3; churches in almost every other category showed higher baptism ratios.

There are several conclusions that may be drawn from these reports. First, a normative size Southern Baptist Church is a smaller membership church. Secondly, almost half of the total Cooperative Program dollars comes from smaller membership churches. Similarly, smaller membership churches baptize almost half of those baptized in Southern Baptist churches, and a healthy baptism to worship total ratio is reflected in these churches. One could easily conclude that *small is the true big*.

SBC BIVOCATIONAL/SMALLER MEMBERSHIP CHURCH ADVISORY COUNCIL REPORT

The report is presented under five major headings:

1. Connect and Communicate Effectively.
2. Encourage and Involve.

3. Recognize the Importance of the Local Association.
4. Provide Practical Resources for Church Health.
5. Elevate Bivocational Models.

Connect and Communicate Effectively

The Bivocational and Smaller Membership Church Advisory Council was tasked by Frank S. Page with improving the connectivity of the Southern Baptist family with the leadership of smaller churches. Currently there exists a disconnect between the Convention leadership and church leadership. Many serving in the local church feel the Convention leadership is out of touch with the small church, or that the Convention leadership simply does not deem the small church important. There is a belief that the Convention leadership is solely focused on the larger churches.

A foundational belief of the Southern Baptist Convention is that together we can accomplish more for the kingdom of God. The lack of cohesiveness or connection causes fragmentation, distrust, and loss of focus. Bluntly, our enemy has caused division, which has kept us from fulfilling the Great Commission to the best of our ability. Increased and realistic connection should bring about a desired unity and trust among all churches and church leaders. If the connection brings about unity and trust, CP giving should also see incremental increases, bringing about greater ability to accomplish our Great Commission task. If the advisory council's recommendations are effective in fostering connection, churches should see the realization of why we are working together as a Convention, understanding that we are a team, no stronger than our weakest teammate.

We cannot afford to come together, rehash ineffective strategies and walk away without implementing a plan that would embrace connection in a real and measurable way. Connection can be the cry that will call us to rally together our resources and prayers to petition God to bring a Great Awakening.

Objective 1: Identify Misperceptions

Misperceptions (in parentheses) identified by team:

1. Size (smaller churches are not that plentiful in the SBC)
    - 90 percent of Southern Baptist churches have 250 or less in worship.
    - 44 percent of Cooperative Program funds come from these churches.

2. Leadership (leaders of smaller churches have limited ability) — Many feel they are looked upon as second-class pastors, considered lacking in faith for not being full time or not very good preachers since they are in a smaller church.
   - Paul's model of tentmaker is biblical and effective.
   - Many effective and dynamic preachers in the Southern Baptist family are either bivocational or lead a smaller membership church.
3. Significance (smaller churches have little impact on the Kingdom of God)
   - Many key leaders in SBC life come from smaller churches.
   - Many smaller churches are *the* church for their membership and community.
4. Health (most smaller churches must be unhealthy)
   - Church health is not determined by size.
   - Body life (volunteerism, fellowship) is often more evident in smaller churches.

Objective 2: Recognize and Affirm their Significance:

- Challenge and encourage local associations to help in identifying and recognizing special accomplishments through smaller churches.
- Celebrate these ministers and churches on local, state, and national levels.
- Embrace and promote spiritual health, and not simply size, as a standard of measurement.
- Intentionally include bivocational and smaller membership pastors in key leadership roles at local, state, and national levels.
- Provide a viable platform where Southern Baptists can hear *from* these pastors not just *about* them.
   1. Seriously consider restructuring the "meeting life" of state and national conventions for this to happen.
   2. Recognize that many associations are already a model for this.

Objective 3: Learn *From* and not Merely *About* Bivocational and Smaller Membership Church Pastors

- Identify successful bivocational/smaller church ministry models.
- Seek and provide ways for these pastors to be mentors and not always the mentees.
- Share what we have learned through our networks of communications.

Encourage and Involve Them

A. Encourage Them

1. Address issues of value and self-worth.
   - Promote the sharing of information about their vision and ministries.
   - Use social media to affirm them.
   - Share stories of impact through SBC communications.
2. Connect with resources.
3. Develop relationships.
   a. Association and cluster groups.
   b. Replicate pray4everyhome.com model with pray4everychurch.com.
4. Increase value and relevance.
5. Provide incentives for first-time attendees at the SBC Annual Meeting.

B. Involve Them

1. Associational
2. State
3. SBC annual meeting
   - Track attendance of these pastors over last few years.
   - Look at involvement in leadership roles as well.
   - Check for proportionate representation.
   - Provide special ways for them to participate in mission work.
   - Help them to see their connection to CP missionaries.

Recognize the Importance of the Local Association

Basic premise: The local Baptist association is the basic unit of denominational life among Baptists. Therefore, we conclude:

- It is imperative that our national and state entities and agencies recognize the primacy of the local association in denominational life.
- Every denominational entity needs to work with local associations to effectively complete its own assigned tasks.
- Every entity should have leadership which understands and appreciates the local association.
- The associational director of missions must be recognized as the best link the denominational entities and agencies can utilize in accomplishing their tasks.
- Baptist national and state agencies need to be proactive and intentional in the delivery of their products to the churches through the local association.

As representatives of bivocational/smaller membership churches across the SBC, we believe we represent them in offering the following insights and suggestions to SBC agencies:

GuideStone

The bivocational and smaller membership church leaders often feel left out of the denomination's retirement program.

- We recommend that GuideStone work with local directors of missions to develop a network of advocates who understand the smaller membership church.
- GuideStone might employ a full-time bivocational/smaller membership church specialist.
- GuideStone could enhance its ministry by providing training for directors of missions and these smaller church advocates.

North American Mission Board

Regrettably, we learned that leadership in many small churches and their associations feel alienated from the North American Mission Board in recent years.

- The leaders of bivocational and smaller membership churches would like NAMB leadership to understand that it is impossible to accomplish its assigned tasks without the local associations as a means to reach individual churches.
- One of the best ways NAMB can restore confidence in its entity would be to employ a full-time liaison between NAMB and the local association, with adequate budget for travel and training of associational leadership.

- NAMB needs to recognize that defunding directors of missions unless they are planting a number of churches at any given time is unreasonable. NAMB should work aggressively to restore confidence in itself by returning to a plan of funding associations in pioneer areas without the church start requirement.

LifeWay

Among bivocational/smaller churches, LifeWay is perceived as beginning to make a turn toward providing materials that meet their unique needs.

- LifeWay should be commended for its recognition of the association in the delivery of its products and information regarding those products.
- LifeWay should continue to acknowledge that the local association is the best place to provide training for Sunday school and discipleship programs.

The Six Seminaries

- It was noted that several seminaries are providing training that will prepare the unique leaders needed in bivocational/smaller churches. The Caskey Center at New Orleans Seminary is one example.
- The Contextualized Leadership Development programs of some seminaries are to be applauded.
- It would be productive for the seminaries to consider providing training of future directors of missions with special emphasis on working with bivocational and smaller church leaders.

International Mission Board

- IMB needs to continue its connection to local associations as an avenue to involve workers from bivocational and smaller membership churches.
- IMB should be commended for recognizing that sending a bivocational pastor/missionary to a limited access area is the most productive way to evangelize and plant churches.

Untapped Resources

It should be noted that the Bivocational and Small Church Leadership Network (BSCLN), headquartered in Nashville, is currently the best place to turn for help in learning about bivocational and smaller membership church needs, capabilities, and possibilities in ministry. It is not necessary for each state and national agency and entity to reinvent the wheel. Working with the BSCLN would prove productive in strengthening the work of this large portion of Southern Baptist churches.

Provide Practical Resources for Church Health

A variety of helpful resources are available for bivocational and smaller membership pastors and their churches. The following is a list of eight areas of concern for which practical resources would positively affect the health of a church.

1. Physical health of the pastor and his wife.
   - Stress in the pastor's family is a growing concern.
   - Bivocational ministers and wives retreats are greatly needed on the state level as well as the regional level.
   - Training for ministers who have little formal ministry preparation will help produce confidence in a job well done.
   - A training program for the pastor and his leadership team on a regional basis would be quite effective in producing health for the pastor and his church.
2. Marriage enrichment for the pastor and his wife.
   - These resources may be provided or sponsored by LifeWay, Baptist state conventions, or local Baptist associations.
   - Pastoral support is provided by NAMB at www.namb.net/pastor-support/.
3. Management of church conflict/conflict resolution.
   - Need may be greater in smaller churches because of the possibility that prominent members often have greater influence and control.
   - LifeWay and our seminaries could help provide these resources.
   - A practical strategy could be developed to minimize the possibility of a catastrophic conflict arising.
4. Time management for pastors.
   - This is the number one issue with bivocational pastors.
   - Help in planning, prioritizing, and organizing is desperately needed.

- A bivocational pastor needs help in accepting the fact that he cannot do everything he would like to do. He must be at peace with this fact. It is also imperative that he learn to equip and delegate effectively.

5. Leadership skills.
    - It should be noted that many bivocational and smaller membership church pastors have not had formal ministry training and will need help in developing these skills.
    - These resources must by practical and easily accessible.

6. Personal and church evangelism.
    - NAMB should develop and implement intentional training and strategies for evangelism in the smaller church.
    - The potential of increase in conversions and baptisms through bivocational and smaller membership churches in the SBC should not be underestimated.

7. Spiritual vitality.
    - The smaller church deals with a sense of inadequacy when confronted with the numerical success in the larger church.
    - Spiritual vitality involves authentic worship. These churches could benefit from training in leading and experiencing genuine worship.
    - Spiritual vitality emphasizes church health. Spiritual growth should be measured by other standards than a simple increase in numbers.

8. Secular side of a bivocational pastor's life.
    - They need help in finding balance.
    - They frequently need help in find secular employment which is compatible with the life of a minister.
    - They frequently need help in finding ways to increase their earnings through secular employment.

Elevate Bivocational Models

With 90 percent of all Southern Baptist churches labeled as smaller membership (250 or less in worship attendance) or led by a bivocational pastor, it is time to:

- See the SBC recognize and affirm this vast majority of its churches.

- Acknowledge that having a pastor who is bivocational is a biblical, proven, and acceptable model for church leadership.

- Make a paradigm shift from promoting primarily megachurch models to an increased focus on promoting marketplace/bivocational models.

- Promote bivocational status as possibly the most successful model of church planting.

This is not an attempt to discredit or criticize fully-funded or megachurch pastors. This is an attempt to promote greater the focus to the true base of the SBC.

In an effort to elevate bivocational models in the SBC, the Bivocational/Smaller Church Advisory Council offers the following suggestions:

- Encourage the SBC Exective Committee to continue the outstanding efforts to affirm and champion the work of the bivocational pastor.

- Challenge SBC leadership to continue and to escalate the celebration of the work of bivocational pastors.

- Encourage directors of missions, state convention staff, and others to identify and report significant work being done by bivocational pastors to state convention editors and other key leaders.

- Feature articles of outstanding accomplishments of bivocational pastors in state convention papers, *Baptist Press*, and *SBC LIFE*.

- Use outstanding bivocational leaders to speak at state conventions, the SBC annual meeting, and other major events in SBC life.

The Executive Committee Bivocational/Smaller Church Advisory Council humbly submits this report to the Executive Committee of the SBC in hopes that these efforts will produce greater unity and fruitfulness in the Southern Baptist family.

PART THREE
Conclusion

- **Where do we go from here? — Kenneth Weathersby**
- **Synergy, Cooperation, and Autonomy — Roger "Sing" Oldham**
- **Endnotes**
- **Contributing Writers**
- **Index**

Where do we go from here?

Kenneth Weathersby

It is our desire that in reading these pages you gain a greater understanding of how God has worked in the Southern Baptist Convention since its inception in 1845. Upon review of the various perspectives offered by our contributing writers, a good question may be: *Where do we go from here?*

God sets our direction and our future, as He has during the most joyous and the most tumultuous times. As we look toward our Convention's next chapter, the most important thing to remember is that our starting point is the same as the concluding point—we go back to the Great Commission. The Great Commission commands us to go and make disciples of all nations. This implies that we must get to know the various ethnic groups and their cultures and share the Gospel with them. The participle "go/as you go" means we take ourselves to them. Jesus has already set the model as He reached out to people, even going to unpopular places, to give them the hope of the Gospel.

If we are to be Christlike in our evangelism, we must seek to understand other cultures and ethnicities in order for us to then be understood when we present the Good News. The Gospel demands that we build relationships with people for the purpose of proclaiming Jesus' name.

Therefore, here are seven points I want you to consider:

1. We must repent of behaviors that do not reflect the love and character of Jesus Christ.

There are large numbers of people who have not lived outside of their culture or community. What they know about other ethnic groups is what they may have read in books or articles or have seen on television. In the absence of firsthand knowledge, false portrayals, assumptions, and opinions get embedded deep in the heart without knowledge of the facts. We may find ourselves saying things and forming opinions based on information that may not be true. When we discover that the attitudes in our hearts do not reflect the attitude and heart of Christ, then we must repent and ask God to show us His love for all people. We must have the courage to confront the prejudices that lie within our hearts when revealed by God.

2. We must double our commitment to make disciples of all the nations.

There are large numbers of Christians who say they do not see color. However, it is hard for me to believe that statement in a nation so defined by race. I know what the person is trying to say, that he or she is not a racist and accepts all ethnic groups. We need to see color so that we can identify the large numbers of ethnic people who have separated or isolated themselves in various communities. We must be willing to reach them with the Gospel, even though they have congregated or segregated themselves, living among themselves to sustain their people group and their culture. There is no reason why we should not share the Gospel with them, even if they have decided to relate only within their culture/people group.

3. We must continue to celebrate our ethnic leaders' participation and to encourage more participation from all the churches in our Convention.

The Lord has blessed Southern Baptists to become the largest and most diverse protestant denomination of congregations in the United States. Therefore, we recognize that we can do more together than what we can do alone. We must invite all congregations, whether they are Anglo, Black, ethnic, large, Deaf, small, or bivocational to be on mission for and with Jesus Christ.

4. We must intentionally build relationships with people who are different and value their opinions.

Frank Page, president and CEO of the Southern Baptist Convention Executive Committee, appointed advisory councils to assist him in the work of the Convention. These council members were comprised of leaders from various groups within the Southern Baptist family. It is important for us to consider the recommendations resulting from their efforts and work hard to implement the ideas that they believe will help us to reach more people with the Gospel.

5. We must identify and embrace passing the baton to the next generation to give leadership in making disciples of all the nations.

God has raised and is raising young leaders who are committed and who are making disciples in the United States and around the world. We must give them a platform and opportunity to carry out the vision that God has given them. They may have some ideas and strategies that we may not fully identify with or understand, but that is not a reason to prevent them from carrying out the vision and values God has given to them. So, it is my prayer that we would continue identify these leaders and call them out for the cause of Christ.

6. We must emphasize discipleship over membership enlistment.

The Lord has sent many different ethnic groups from around the world to the United States. It is imperative for us as Christians to do our best to share the Gospel among these groups in order for them to repent and believe in the Lord Jesus Christ. However, we must also embrace the idea that small groups are very important. It is in small groups that people are able to learn from one another, hear the Word of God, participate, fellowship, and put into action the things that they are learning.

We have seen baptisms decline across North America. One reason, I believe, is because many pastors and leaders emphasize the importance of attending a worship service over the importance of being involved in small group ministries. Discipleship must be a priority if we are going to reach the various people groups. Indigenous New Testament churches will be the result of making disciples and indigenous leaders will be called out to plant the Gospel in groups where there are language barriers. When we disciple people, evangelism will result.

7. We must emphasize that the Cooperative Program levels the playing field for all churches, regardless of size.

Frank Page always says that giving through the Cooperative Program is still the best way to level the playing field for all the churches. The Cooperative Program gives every Christian an opportunity to do missions around the world. Dr. Page also says that giving through the Cooperative Program gives every church an opportunity to do mission around the world. It is because of the Cooperative Program that many people around the world have come to know the Lord Jesus Christ and many New Testament churches are starting to share the Gospel around the world. The Apostle Paul reminds us that we must continue to press forward in doing the work of God. He said we must forget those things that are behind and reach forward to the things that lie ahead. We must press toward the goal for the prize of the upper call of God in Christ Jesus (see Philippians 3:14).

We serve a Savior who was very much engaged in the cultures of His day. He cared more about impacting people's lives for the Kingdom than He did about the opinions of His detractors. Building the Kingdom requires the boldness of Jesus (Matthew

21:12–13), the tenacity of Paul (Acts 14:19–28; 1 Corinthians 16:8), the humility of Stephen (Acts 6:5), the generous heart of Dorcas (Acts 9:36–42), the obedience of Phillip (Acts 8:26–40), and the willingness of Peter to let go of beliefs that do not align with our Father's (Acts 10:9–16). No one among us possesses all of these virtues, but collectively we can use our strengths to reach the nations and the neighborhoods where hope seems to have died because the love of Christ has not been demonstrated among them.

Southern Baptists, we can do this! Our history demonstrates that we are a people of boldness and tenacity, of generosity and obedience. Above all, perhaps, we have demonstrated—as the various reports in this book reveal—that we are a people capable of letting go of that which does not align with our heavenly Father.

We have a ways to go, but we have come far from the ways of our past. In our ongoing efforts, we have formed a permanent Convention Advancement Advisory Council to work consistently and effectively with all entities and leaderships across the Convention. The council is to assist in any way possible the making of more disciples to reach all people with the Gospel a reality. We will continue to enlist and rely upon their guidance to advance the Gospel among *Ta Ethnē* — all people.

Synergy, Cooperation, and Autonomy*

Roger S. ("Sing") Oldham

The collaborative missions and ministries of the Southern Baptist Convention rest foundationally on four pillars, forging what one writer called a denominational "consensus"[1] that has allowed the Convention to develop an impressive array of cooperative ministries.

The four pillars are: (1) a common missional purpose; (2) shared doctrinal beliefs; (3) mutual trust; and (4) voluntary cooperation.[2] To the extent that these four pillars have been broadly embraced by Southern Baptists, the Southern Baptist experiment has thrived. When Southern Baptists' collective commitment to one or more of these pillars has shown signs of decay, the entire enterprise has been imperiled.

For example, W. A. Criswell, long-time pastor of First Baptist Church Dallas, and SBC president in 1970, told messengers to that year's SBC annual meeting, "[I]f ever we lose [our] missionary passion we shall dissolve like a rope of sand."[3] He continued, "Our world-wide missions program holds us together with cables of steel. We may differ over many things, but we are one on this; namely, the desire to see men brought to Christ throughout the nations of the globe."[4]

Four years later, in preparation for the fiftieth anniversary celebration of the Cooperative Program, James L. Sullivan, Baptist Sunday School Board president, coupled Criswell's two analogies into a compelling image to describe Southern Baptist work funded through the Cooperative Program (CP) as a "rope of sand with strength of steel."[5] Begun in 1925, the CP is Southern Baptists' channel of giving, through which a local church can contribute to the ministries of its state convention and the missions and ministries of the SBC with a single monthly or weekly contribution.[6]

In 2004, Morris H. Chapman, former SBC president (1990–1992) and former SBC Executive Committee president (1992–2010), used Sullivan's metaphor at a conference on Baptist identity hosted by Union University in Jackson, Tennessee. He asked the question, "How important is the concept of cooperation to Southern Baptist identity?" After giving a terse, three-word answer—"It is foundational"[7]—he elaborated:

> The "Rope of Sand" is James L. Sullivan's description of our cooperative polity. Since the rope has been in existence, it has proven in many ways to be as strong as steel. Conversely, the material used to weave the rope obviously is fragile, and remains strong only as long as it remains tightly woven, even strengthening under stress. When Southern Baptists are not bound tightly together, there can be only one anticipated result, a dismantling of the rope. At first, a few grains of sand may drop from the rope without much notice, but once the sand begins to move, one grain against another, the entire rope will disintegrate at warp speed. This does not mean the bricks and mortar will fall as did the walls of Jericho. Like the cathedrals of Europe, some semblance of structure may stand for generations, but they no longer will house a mighty force of God's people who came together with stouthearted biblical convictions, determined obedience to the Great Commission, a passionate love for the lost, and a compassionate heart for the hurting.[8]

Two movements within Southern Baptist life over the past forty years underscore and illustrate the fragile yet resilient character of Southern Baptist work—the Convention's "battle for the Bible" over the past three decades, culminating with the adoption of the revised *Baptist Faith and Message* at the 2000 SBC annual meeting in Orlando, Florida,[9] and the Convention's adoption of the Great Commission Task Force (GCTF) report ten years later at the 2010 SBC annual meeting, also in Orlando.[10]

A Common Missional Purpose

From the Convention's founding in 1845, Southern Baptists have believed they have an important role to play in world evangelization, trusting they can accomplish more by working together than they can by working alone.[11] The Convention's inaugural Constitution stated:

> We, the delegates from missionary societies, churches and other religious bodies of the Baptist denomination in various parts of the United States, met in convention in the city of Augusta, Georgia, for the purpose of carrying into effect the benevolent intentions of our constituents, by *organizing a plan for eliciting, combining and directing the energies of the whole denomination in one sacred effort for the propagation of the gospel* (emphasis supplied).[12]

Article II of the Constitution further set forth the Convention's *raison d'etre*—to promote foreign and domestic missions in cooperation with like-minded brothers and sisters.[13]

Thirty-six years later, the Convention adopted its first set of bylaws. The "one sacred effort" phrase was restated in its preamble, amplifying the Convention's focus on world evangelization by calling itself "to endeavor *more energetically and systematically* to elicit, combine, and direct the energies of the whole denomination in one sacred effort for the propagation of the Gospel" (emphasis supplied).[14]

This missional thread is woven through annual mission board reports and major addresses preserved in the SBC *Annuals*. It is also the focus of Convention-wide movements such as "A Million More in '54," an effort to enroll one million individuals in small-group Bible study in a single year, followed thirty years later by the "8.5 [Million] by '85" and "Challenge 10/90" campaigns held in conjunction with "Bold Mission Thrust," an initiative during the last two decades of the twentieth century to reach the nations with the Gospel.[15]

More recently, the Great Commission Task Force called on Southern Baptists to "make an unconditional commitment to reach the nations for Christ, to plant and serve Gospel churches in North America and around the world, and to mobilize Southern Baptists as a Great Commission people."[16] Its first recommendation, adopted in 2010, is posted online at SBC.net and states: "As a convention of churches, our missional vision is to present the Gospel of Jesus Christ to every person in the world and to make disciples of all the nations."[17] This remains Southern Baptists' common missional vision.

Shared Doctrinal Beliefs

From its founding, Southern Baptists were firmly committed to the centrality of Scripture as the basis for the tenets of their faith and practice. During the nineteenth century, they found common ground through earlier Baptist confessions of faith, notably the 1833 New Hampshire Confession of Faith as modified and popularized by J. Newton Brown in his 1853 *Baptist Church Manual*.[18]

Theologian John L. Dagg's *Manual of Theology* (1857) and *Manual of Church Order* (1858) were also influential,[19] with Dagg being asked by the Convention in 1879 to develop a catechism containing "the substance of the Christian religion, for the instruction of children and servants."[20]

Cooperating churches were also heavily influenced by notable Baptist scholars such as Basil Manly Sr., Basil Manly Jr., John A. Broadus, J. B. Jeter, E. C. Dargan, William B.

Johnson, R. B. C. Howell, Richard Fuller, P. H. Mell, and James P. Boyce, founder of The Southern Baptist Theological Seminary. The latter five served as presidents of the SBC from 1845–1888, imbuing the Convention with a strong doctrinal heritage.

In 1925, facing new theological and social pressures, Southern Baptists felt it prudent to adopt their own confessional *Statement on Baptist Faith and Message* to provide doctrinal guidance for the churches and institutions of the Convention.[21] Thirty-eight years later, with burgeoning controversy over the historicity of the first eleven chapters of Genesis, a new edition of *The Baptist Faith and Message* (*BF&M*) was adopted by the Convention in 1963.[22]

By 1971, messengers were expressing dissatisfaction with Article I of the 1963 *BF&M* through motions at SBC annual meetings, seeking to clarify that the Bible in its entirety was (and is) the Word of God.[23] After almost thirty years of Convention-wide debate, messengers addressed the inerrancy of Scripture through another edition of *The Baptist Faith and Message*.[24] The 1963 edition of *The Baptist Faith and Message* stated that the Bible is the "*record* of God's revelation of Himself to man"; the 2000 revision stipulated that the Bible "*is* God's revelation of Himself to man" (emphases supplied).[25] The 2000 *BF&M* also issued clear statements on pressing social issues such as racism, pornography, homosexuality, and other challenges to the Christian life.[26]

Three articles in *The Baptist Faith and Message* represent significant contributions Baptists have made to the stream of Christian thought—distinctively Baptist positions on the Church as an autonomous body of baptized believers, banded together under the Lordship of Jesus Christ, serving the Lord and one another with covenantal love (Article VI); the nature of Christian baptism and the Lord's supper in Christian worship (Article VII); and the personal responsibility "of every follower of Christ and of every church of the Lord Jesus Christ" to be fully engaged in evangelism and missions (Article XI).

Mutual Trust

During the Conservative Resurgence, Southern Baptists were convinced that the recovery of biblical inerrancy as a core theological commitment would secure the Lord's continued blessings for numerical and spiritual growth.[27]

By 2006, however, SBC statistical indicators were raising alarms. The SBC solicits an annual statistical snapshot from its cooperating churches through an instrument called the Annual Church Profile (ACP). For six successive years, beginning in 2000, annual reports showed that year-to-year membership was growing at less than 1 percent per year.[28] The number of reported baptisms declined by fifty thousand over the same six-year period.[29]

When the 2007 ACP report was released in April 2008, it sent shock-waves across the Convention. Total membership in Southern Baptist churches had declined. Even more alarming, baptisms hit their lowest point since 1987.[30] Both measures have continued this downward trend. Baptism numbers in 2016 were lower than any time since 1946, and total membership had fallen by more than one million since 2006.[31]

The 2007 report triggered hand-wringing and finger-pointing about potential causes for these declines.[32] Mistrust over how Convention funds had been spent and distrust about the theological, organizational, and personal motives of fellow Southern Baptists escalated.

The following year, this sense of discontent was fanned into flame when the sitting SBC president, following the lead of an SBC entity leader, declared the Convention was "bloated" and "bureaucratic" and in need of renewal, with a resultant call for a Great Commission Resurgence modeled after gains of the Conservative Resurgence.[33]

Though the 2009 SBC annual meeting exposed numerous flash points of acrimony and debate,[34] the meeting proved catalytic for a pivotal transition of the Convention. Over the next twenty-four months, the Convention adopted the Great Commission Task Force report authorized at the 2009 meeting (June 2010); adopted sweeping recommendations flowing out of the GCTF report (June 2011); saw changes in presidential leadership at its two missions entities and its Executive Committee (all in 2010); adopted twelve recommendations of a report designed to increase participation of ethnic church leaders in response to a referred motion at the 2009 meeting (June 2011); and reduced the percentage of Cooperative Program funds going to the SBC Executive Committee, shifting the difference to the International Mission Board (June 2011).

With so many dramatic changes in such a short time, new SBC Executive Committee (EC) President Frank S. Page set out to "rebuild trust by reducing bureaucracy" in preparation for the 2011 SBC annual meeting.[35] He reduced EC staff by 19 percent, cut the EC budget by 14 percent, and presented SBC messengers a Cooperative Program allocation budget that directed "95 percent of Cooperative Program dollars to international missions, North American church planting and evangelism, and seminary education."[36]

Page invited the SBC president, the eleven SBC entity presidents, the executive director of Woman's Missionary Union, executive directors of the forty-two state Baptist conventions that cooperate with the SBC, and leaders of numerous Southern Baptist ethnic and racial fellowships to join him in signing a historic document called "Affirmation of Unity and Cooperation." More than sixty Southern Baptist leaders joined him on the platform at the 2011 SBC annual meeting to demonstrate unity among and between these key Southern Baptist leaders.[37]

Two of the Affirmation's pledges addressed the fragile nature of cooperative relationships—"We pledge to maintain a relationship of mutual trust, behaving ourselves trustworthily before one another and trusting one another as brothers and sisters indwelt by the Holy Spirit of God (Philippians 4:8; Ephesians 4:20–32; 2 Peter 1:3–8)," and "We pledge to attribute the highest motives to those engaged in local church ministries and those engaged in denominational service in any level of Convention life—motives that originate within hearts truly desiring to serve the Lord Jesus Christ, whom we also serve (1 Samuel 2:3; 1 Corinthians 4:1–5; Matthew 7:1–5)."[38]

Page has since appointed a Calvinism Advisory Group, whose 2013 report helped calm rising theological tensions,[39] four ethnic and racial advisory councils, a mental health advisory group, a smaller church/bivocational ministry advisory council, a women's advisory council, and a young leaders advisory council, all with the goal of building bridges and rebuilding trust across the Southern Baptist landscape.[40]

Voluntary Cooperation

The final section of the Great Commission Task Force report opened with these words: "Southern Baptists hold to an ecclesiology that honors and affirms both autonomy and cooperation."[41] It continued: "[W]e cannot direct individual Christians, local churches, associations, or state conventions to take any particular or specific action. . . . However, our doctrine of the church does not prevent us from challenging, encouraging, admonishing, and advising one another at all levels of SBC life for greater passion and effectiveness in pursuing the Great Commission."[42]

This local church independence was enshrined in the Convention's 1845 constitution. The final clause of its Article II acknowledged that the Convention "shall fully respect the independence and equal rights of the Churches."[43] Article IV of the current SBC constitution is equally clear: "While independent and sovereign in its own sphere, the Convention does not claim and will never attempt to exercise any authority over any other Baptist body, whether church, auxiliary organizations, associations, or convention."[44]

This principle of non-coercive cooperation is amply illustrated in Scripture. In their 2005 book *One Sacred Effort*, Chad Owen Brand and David Hankins posited a "theology of cooperation,"[45] drawing special attention to the collaborative nature of the Jerusalem Conference and the resultant letters sent to the Gentile churches (Acts 15)[46] and Paul's encouragement for Gentile churches across the realm to contribute financially to the ministry needs of their Jewish brothers in Christ in the church at Jerusalem.[47]

The Old Testament also provides examples of cooperative service. When Israel entered the land of promise, the tribes of Reuben and Gad and half-tribe of Manasseh had already received their inheritance on the east of Jordan (Numbers 34:15). Nevertheless, they fulfilled their promise to help Joshua in the conquest of the Promised Land (Joshua 1:12–18; 22:1–6).

During the post-exilic era, the people worked cooperatively to rebuild the walls around Jerusalem. Apportioned along the wall according to their tribes and their families, each worked in support of the others for the benefit of the whole (Nehemiah 3–4).

Other Old Testament examples describe voluntary (freewill) offerings for the service of God's House:

- In preparation for the construction of the Tabernacle, the people presented freewill offerings to Moses (Exodus 35), bringing their offerings every morning throughout its construction (Exodus 36).
- Anticipating the Temple to be built by his son, David challenged the people to offer gifts for Solomon to use when he began its construction (1 Chronicles 29).
- During Hezekiah's reform, freewill gifts for the service of the Lord were encouraged, received, and disbursed for daily service in the house of God (2 Chronicles 31).
- Following the Exile, people voluntarily gave to construct the house for God's glory (Ezra 1) and for the day-to-day ministry of the rebuilt Temple (Ezra 3).
- When Ezra later led a group to return to Jerusalem, the people gave cooperatively for the service of the House of God (Ezra 7— 8).

In 2015, more than 42,600 of the Convention's 46,793 cooperating churches[48] had 250 or fewer persons in Sunday worship.[49] These churches contributed 42 percent of all Cooperative Program gifts.[50] On the other end of the spectrum, only 167 churches ran two thousand or more in Sunday worship.[51] In regard to the Convention's diversity, 10,665 congregations (churches and church-type missions with weekly services) are predominately non-Anglo.[52]

When churches work in collaboration, churches of all sizes and every ethnic composition have a seat at the table and are empowered to participate in the Kingdom initiatives they believe in so strongly. They are able to address national and international ministry goals that would otherwise be out of the reach of the majority of individual churches. Pooling their resources levels the playing field. Every church can play a vital role in reaching beyond its own Jerusalem with the Gospel of Jesus Christ.[53]

Conclusion

In 1973, Elmer Towns predicted that collaborative ministries of denominations would be replaced by what he called "super-aggressive churches" with no need of a denominational apparatus to accomplish bold Kingdom purposes.[54] While there will always be a certain number of strong churches that can do mighty ministries on their own, there is still a place for a network of churches of every size and economic status to impact the world with the Gospel. Despite current challenges of declining evangelistic effectiveness and church membership at the local church level, SBC ministries continue to flourish.

At the end of the most recent reporting year, the six SBC seminaries reported more than twenty thousand students enrolled for at least one course through their various degree programs, with a full-time equivalency of 7,976 Southern Baptist students in training for ministry.[55] The North American Mission Board (NAMB) reported 926 new church plants, bringing the five-year total of new churches to more than 4,700.[56] NAMB reported more than one-half of these new churches have been planted in some of the most culturally-diverse areas of America's major cities.[57]

Following a year-long financial reset, the International Mission Board (IMB) reported in November 2016 that its trustees celebrated a balanced budget for the first time in two decades. The mission agency also reported the appointment of fifty new fully-funded missionaries, stating its goal to appoint an additional 451 field personnel in 2017 to replace the estimated 350 missionaries who will retire from service or otherwise transition to other ministries. The agency projects a net increase of 3 percent to its overseas missions force.[58]

The Southern Baptist Convention is not a perfect organization. It has experienced many times of testing and will be tested in the future. Trust will be strained. A group of churches will believe it has a better plan for reaching the nations with the Gospel. Voluntary cooperation will seem a poor investment. Some churches will deviate from their founding orthodoxy.

The beauty of denominational synergy is that the long-term vitality and sustainability of the Convention's ministries, supported by a network of churches, are not dependent on the continued viability of any single church. By pooling their resources to "establish and advance Great Commission work," the SBC provides an opportunity to "create a synergy in which the impact of the whole can be greater than the sum of the individual parts, giving churches a way collectively to express their convictions and realize their vision."[59]

---

*This article was originally published in *The Journal of Mid-America Baptist Theological Seminary*, Volume 4, (Spring 2017).

Endnotes

Foreword

1. Richard (Richie) Stanley in The Many Faces of the Southern Baptist Convention, Nashville: The Southern Baptist Executive Committee, 2018, 26
2. PEW Hispanic Center Population Estimates & Projections (2008). Due to the fact that the Native American population of this country is less than 1 percent, they often do not appear in demographic analyses. Their presence, which predates the formation of the United States of America, continues to have significance in the social, political and religious life of this country.
3. Richard (Richie) Stanley, in *Many Faces of the Southern Baptist Convention*, Nashville: The Southern Baptist Executive Committee, 2018, 28
4. While the latter two are not necessarily ethnic/cultural entities, these were included in an effort to seek broader participation in SBC life.

Ta Ethnē: **The Biblical Mandate**

1. A. T Robertson, *Word Pictures of the New Testament, Volume 1: Matthew and Mark*, Nashville: Broadman Press, 1930, 246.
2. Campbell Morgan, cited in Hay, *op. cit.*, p. 63.

A Demographics Review

1. The source of all population data is the US Census Bureau.
2. White Not Hispanic is used interchangeably with Anglo. Both Anglo and Hispanic are better thought of as ethnicities than races. Rows in the racial ethnic tables cannot be added to yield the total population.
3. The Asian racial group in this chapter includes Pacific Islanders.
4. The source of all SBC congregation data is Annual Church Profile data from LifeWay Christian Resources.
5. Racial/ethnic groups for congregations are primarily self-selected as the majority group among members.
6. SBC congregations include churches as well as church-type missions.
7. The Other category identifies those that do not fit another of the categories, such as Haitian and multi-ethnic.

A Progress Overview

1. "Proceedings of the SBC Annual Meeting, 138th Session, 150th Year, June 20–22, 1995: Item 82," 1995 *SBC Annual*, 80–81.
2. *Ibid.*
3. "Proceedings of the SBC Annual Meeting, 157th Session, 169th Year, June 10–11, 2014: Items 15 and 55," 2014 *SBC Annual*, 59, 78.
4. "Proceedings of the SBC Annual Meeting, 152nd Session, 164th Year, June 23–24, 2009: Items 15 and 50," 2009 *SBC Annual*, 57, 74.
5. "Executive Committee Ministry Report to the Southern Baptist Convention," Matters Referred by the Convention, "Item 14: Directing the Executive Committee to Study Greater SBC Involvement for Ethnic Churches and Leaders," 2011 *SBC Annual*, 138–142.
6. "Proceedings of the SBC Annual Meeting, 154th Session, 166th Year, June 14–15, 2011: Item 38," 2011 *SBC Annual*, 70–71.
7. "Minutes," Inter-Agency Council, 5 March 1996, 8–9; and "SBC Inter-Agency Council Names Racial Reconciliation Task Force," *SBC Life*, May 1996, www.sbclife.net/Articles/1996/05/sla7.
8. See "SBC Inter-Agency Council Names" in Endnote 7.
9. *Ibid.*
10. "Minutes," Racial Reconciliation Task Force, May 23, 1996.
11. Herb Hollinger, "Arson fund disbursement to states tops $700,000," *Baptist Press*, January 16, 1997.
12. Herb Hollinger, "ITF hears NAMB concerns from racial task force," *Baptist Press*, April 7, 1997.
13. Art Toalston, "Unspent Arson Fund could boost training for African Americans," *Baptist Press*, May 29, 1997.
14. Dwayne Hastings, "SBC task force calls for increased emphasis on racial reconciliation," *Baptist Press*, February 16, 1999.
15. *Ibid.*
16. Lonnie Wilkey, "Election of vice presidents gives diversity to SBC posts," *Baptist Press*, June 15, 1994.
17. David Winfrey, "SBC President Jim Henry re-elected to second term," *Baptist Press*, June 21, 1995.
18. "Minutes," Racial Reconciliation Task Force, May 23, 1996.
19. Lonnie Wilkey, "Okla. Pastor Tom Elliff elected SBC president without opposition," *Baptist Press*, June 12, 1996.
20. Barbara Denman, "Fred Luter elected as SBC 1st VP," *Baptist Press*, June 15, 2011.
21. Karen Willoughby. "Historic: Fred Luter elected SBC president," *Baptist Press*, June 19, 2012.
22. John Evans, "Luter sails to second term as SBC president," *Baptist Press*, June 11, 2013.

23. Michael Foust, "WRAP-UP: Messengers elect Johnny Hunt president, launch 'GPS' initiative," *Baptist Press*, June 13, 2008.
24. Willoughby, endnote 21.
25. Statistics compiled from annual reports of officer elections in *Baptist Press* and the 1996–2014 *SBC Annuals*.
26. "Proceedings of the SBC Annual Meeting, 157th Session, 169th Year, June 10–11, 2014: Items 33 and 39," 2014 *SBC Annual*, 68.
27. "Twenty-Two State/Regional Conventions have Elected Non-Anglos to serve as State Convention Presidents," a side-bar to David Roach, "Ethnic Participation in Convention Ministry: A Historical Perspective on the Election of Fred Luter," *SBC Life*, October 2012, www.SBCLife.net/Articles/2012/10/sla5.
28. *Ibid.*
29. "Nev. Baptists elect first black president," *Baptist Press*, November 21, 2014; and Lonnie Wilkey, "Ellis first black pres. of Tenn. Convention," *Baptist Press*, November 13, 2014.
30. "Article XXI, Social Service," *The Baptist Faith and Message*, 1925; and "Article XV, The Christian and the Social Order," *The Baptist Faith and Message*, 1963.
31. "Article XV, The Christian and the Social Order," *The Baptist Faith and Message*, 2000.
32. "Article III, Man, and Article VI, The Church," *The Baptist Faith and Message*, 2000.
33. Kevin Ezell, "Church plants: 5% gain in 2014," *Baptist Press*, March 17, 2015.
34. Analysis provided by Executive Committee staff from statistics compiled by the North American Mission Board's Center for Missional Research and Annual Church Profile reports from LifeWay Christian Resources, 1998 and 2013.
35. Anecdotal testimonies of members of the SBC Executive Committee Workgroup.
36. See Endnote 34.
37. Twentieth Anniversary Banquet Program, National African American Fellowship, SBC, Baltimore Convention Center, Baltimore, Maryland, June 9, 2014.
38. *The Journal of African American Southern Baptist History*, Vols. 1–6, June 2003 – June 2008.
39. See, for example, Karen Willoughby, "Black denominational network gives key award to Mohler," *Baptist Press*, June 15, 2004.
40. Karen Willoughby, "Denominational Servant's Network takes stock of year's milestones," *Baptist Press*, 17 June, 2003; and "Minutes," Black Southern Baptist Denominational Servant's Network, 3 August 2004.
41. Sid Smith, "Ten Years of Racial Progress in the SBC," *The Journal of African American Southern Baptist History*, vol. 1 (June 2003), 12–13.
42. *Ibid.*, 12–13.
43. *Ibid.*, 13.
44. Statistics derived from a review of the annual pictorial directories published by the Executive Committee, 1995–1996 through 2014–2015.
45. "Proceedings of the SBC Annual Meeting, 154th Session, 166th Year, June 14–15, 2011: Item 29," 2011 *SBC Annual*, 59–60.

46. "Review of Ethnic Churches and Church Leaders," an annual report created for the SBC Executive Committee Communications Workgroup (discussion only), for the February Executive Committee meeting for each of the following years: 2012, 2013, 2014, and 2015.
47. SBC President Background Orientation Materials, compiled by the SBC Executive Committee and provided to each newly-elected SBC president, section 1, paragraph C, "Participation and Inclusion," and paragraph D, "Diversity Encouragement and Reporting Requirements," language added Summer 2011.
48. "Proceedings of the SBC Annual Meeting, 155th Session, 167th Year, June 19–20, 2012: Item 10," 2012 *SBC Annual*, p. 58; "Proceedings of the SBC Annual Meeting, 156th Session, 168th Year, June 11–12, 2013: Item 9," 2013 *SBC Annual*, 58; Ronnie Floyd, "Our 2015 Committee on Committees of the Southern Baptist Convention," www.SBC.net/presidentspage/article.asp?id=102, posted 16 March 2015; and Ronnie Floyd, "Introducing our 2015 SBC Committee on Resolutions," www.SBC.net/presidentspage/article.asp?id=105, posted 30 March 2015.
49. "Committee on Order of Business Background and Orientation Materials," compiled by the SBC Executive Committee and provided to each year's elected Committee on Order of Business.
50. Committee on Nominations ,"SBC Recommendation and Information" form, compiled by the SBC Executive Committee and provided to each year's SBC Committee on Nominations, amended Summer 2011.
51. Committee on Committees, "Nominee for Service" form, compiled by the SBC Executive Committee and provided to each year's SBC Committee on Committees, amended Summer 2014.
52. Agenda of the SBC Executive Committee Communications Workgroup, February 17, 2015; February 18, 2014; February 19, 2013; and February 21, 2012.
53. David Roach, "Church bombing fueled their hearts' passion," *Baptist Press*, October 4, 2013.
54. David Roach, "Ethnic Participation in Convention Ministry: A Historical Perspective on the Election of Fred Luter," *SBC LIFE*, October 2012, www.SBCLife.net/articles/2012/10/sla5.
55. For representative stories, conduct appropriate searches at www.SBCLife.net and www.BPNews.net.
56. See www.SBC.net/forgedbyfaith/, www.SBC.net/pdf/MeetSouthernBaptists.pdf, and www.SBC.net/pdf/ACloserLook.pdf.
57 See *Hispanic Advisory Council* news reports: www.SBCLife.net/Articles/2011/10/sla5; www.SBCLife.net/Articles/2012/03/sla9, www.SBCLife.net/Articles/2013/05/sla14.asp; and www.SBCLife.net/Articles/2014/05/sla5; www. SBCLife.net/Articles/2012/03/sla9; *African American Council* news reports, http://www.SBCLife.net/Articles/2012/03/sla10; www.SBCLife.net/Articles/2012/06/sla8; www.SBCLife.net/Articles/2013/05/sla14.asp; http://www.SBCLife.net/Articles/2014/03/sla9.asp; and www.SBCLife.net/Articles/2014/09/sla14; *Asian Advisory Council* news reports: www.SBCLife.net/Articles/2013/03/sla15; http://www.SBCLife.net/Articles/2013/05/sla14.asp;http://www.SBCLife.net/Articles/2014/05/sla6.asp; and www.SBCLife.net/Articles/2015/05/sla12; and

Multi-Ethnic Advisory Council news reports: http://www.SBCLife.net/Articles/2014/05/sla7.asp and www.SBCLife.net/Articles/2015/05/sla9.

58. Roger S. Oldham, "Executive Committee Receives Input from Advisory Groups," *SBC Life*, May 2013, www.SBCLife.net/Articles/2013/05/sla14; and Rebecca Wolford, Southern Baptist Seminaries Respond to Changing Needs," *SBC LIFE*, June 2013, www.SBCLife.net/Articles/2013/06/sla8.
59. For a representative news story, see Andrew Walker, "CP Booth to Express Appreciation, Show Support, Highlight 'Many Faces' of SBC," *SBC Life*, June 2012, www.SBCLife.net/Articles/2012/06/sla7.
60. For a representative news story, see Joni B. Hannigan, "Panel: Diversity for the sake of Kingdom," *Baptist Press*, June 27, 2014.
61. "Diana Chandler joins Baptist Press staff," *Baptist Press*, March 26, 2012.
62. Diana Chandler, "Ken Weathersby named EC vice president," *Baptist Press*, March 18, 2013.
63. *SBC Annuals*, 1975–2014. Research conducted by Executive Committee staff.
64. Barbara Denman, "Ronnie Floyd wins Southern Baptist Convention presidency," *Baptist Press*, June 10, 2014.
65. Tom Strode, "ERLC summit: Reconciliation is Gospel imperative," *Baptist Press*, March 27, 2015.
66. K. Faith Morgan, "Ethnic summit seeks to reach diverse population," *Baptist Press*, May 20, 2015.
67. Quotation from Recommendation 3 of the *Final Report of the Great Commission Task Force of the Southern Baptist Convention*, "Proceedings of the SBC Annual Meeting, 153rd Session, 165th Year, June 15–16, 2010: Items 73–97," 2010 *SBC Annual*, 77–98.
68. "Executive Committee Ministry Report to the Southern Baptist Convention," Matters Referred by the Convention, "Item 14: Directing the Executive Committee to Study Greater SBC Involvement for Ethnic Churches and Leaders," 2011 *SBC Annual*, 138–142.

African Americans in the SBC

1. *Partners in Ministry*, Chan C. Garrett. Foreword: [1981], 1.
2. *Ibid.*, 2
3. Arthur B. Rutledge, *Mission to America* [Nashville: Broadman Press, 1969], 129
4. Garrett, 2
5. *An Orientation to the Southern Baptist Convention for Black Southern Baptists*. A joint publication of the Home Mission Board and the Baptist Sunday School Board, September 1984], 2
6. An excellent discussion of the early objections to the Christianizing of slaves and of the initial attempts to provide slaves with Christian instruction is found in Lester B. Scherer, *Slavery and the Churches in Early America, 1619–1819* (Grand Rapids: Wm. B. Eerdmans, 1975), 29–43, 63–101.

7. Author Mechal Sobel claims the first black Baptist church was founded in Virginia around 1758. See Mechal Sobel, *Travelin' On: The Slave Journey to an Afro-Baptist Faith* (Westport, Conn." Greenwood Press, 1979), pp. 102, 296. Other scholars continue to give primacy to the Silver Bluff Church, pending stronger evidence in support of the Bluestone Church.
8. A more detailed account of the life and work of Cary is provided in Leroy Fitts, *Lott Cary: First Black Missionary to Africa* (Valley Forge: Judson Press, 1978), pp 15–65. While Cary was the first black missionary to Africa, he was preceded by another black Baptist minister, David George, the resident pastor of Silver Bluff Baptist Church, after 1775. After the Revolutionary War, Cary had preached in Nova Scotia for ten years before going to Sierra Leone in 1792.
9. H. Shelton Smith, "In His Image, But..." *Racism in the Southern Religions*, 1780–1910 (Durham: Duke University Press, 1972), 47–55.
10. *Ibid*, pp. 114–27; and John Lee Eighmy, *Churches in Cultural Captivity: A History of the Social Attitudes of Southern Baptist* (Knoxville: The University of Tennessee Press, 1972), 10–16.
11. The existence of what has been called the "invisible church" can hardly be denied, but it is unlikely that it was organized along denominational lines. Rather, the invisible church was probably a denominational expression that covered the wide range of religious insights of the people who participated in the worship.
12. Fitts, 81–82; L. G. Jordan, *Up the Ladder in Foreign Missions* (Nashville: National Baptist Publishing Board, 1903; reprint ed., New York: Arno Press, 1980), 87,90; and Robert G. Torbet, *A History of the Baptists* (Valley Forge: Judson Press, 1950), 354–55.
13. An excellent study of how racial attitudes affected Southern Baptists and their relationship to blacks during the period is provided by Rufus B. Spain, *At Ease in Zion: A Social History of Southern Baptists*, 1865–1900 (Nashville: Vanderbilt University Press, 1961), 44–126.
14. "Growth of Black Southern Baptist Churches in the Inner City," Sid Smith. *Baptist History and Heritage*, July 1981, Vol. 16, No. 3. Published by the Historical Commission of the SBC and the auxiliary Southern Baptist Historical Society.
15. The Augusta Institute was moved to Atlanta and named Atlanta Baptist Seminary. It is now Morehouse College, a premier all-male HBCU.
16. Arthur B. Rutledge, *Mission to America: A Century and a Quarter of Southern Baptist Home Missions* (Nashville: Broadman Press, 1969), 133.
17. Rutledge, 133–134.
18. Rutledge, 134.
19. Rutledge, chapter 9.
20. See George D. Kelsey, *Social Ethics Among Southern Baptists, 1817–1969* (Metuchen, N.J.: The Scarecrow Press and the American Theological Library Association, 1973), 206–31.
21. Rutledge, 135–36.
22. May 23, 1968. *ibid*., 136.

23. Robert E. Wilson, "Establishing a Process at Sandtown Baptist Church, Atlanta, Georgia, to Mobilize Volunteers to Plant an African American Church in the Greater Atlanta Area", DMin Project, 29.
24. *African American Council Report*, June 2014.
25. *Partners in Ministry* [1981], 51-52.
26. *African American Taskforce Report*, African American Advisory Council, 2014

Asian Americans in the SBC

1. The ratio of Southern Baptist congregations to population in North America is 1 to 6,828.
2. *Documentation Center of Cambodia*. http://www.d.dccam.org/Projects/Maps/Mapping.htm (accessed February 12, 2017); *Yale University Genocide Studies Program: Cambodian Genocide Program*. http://gsp.yale.edu/case-studies/cambodian-genocide-program (accessed February 12, 2017).
3. Francois Ponchaud, *Cambodia: Year Zero* (New York: Holt, Rinehart and Winston, 1978); *The Killing Fields*, directed by Roland Joffe (Warner Bros, 1984).
4. "Chinese Baptists," *SBC Asian Advisory Council Report 2013–2015*. http://www.sbc.net/advisoryCouncilReports/asian.asp (accessed February 12, 2017), 16.
5. "Chinese Baptists," *SBC Asian Advisory Council Report 2013–2015*, 16.
6. Ibid., 17.
7. "The Spaniards as Colonial Masters," *Philippine History*. http://www.philippine-history.org/spanish-colonial-masters.htm (accessed February 16, 2017).
8. "2015 Philippine Statistical Yearbook," *Philippine Statistics Authority* (Quezon City, Philippines, 2015), 1–30.
9. Richard Deats, *Nationalism and Christianity in the Philippines* (Dallas: Southern Methodist University Press, 1967), 91–92.
10. Keith McNamara and Jeanne Batalova, "Filipino Immigrants in the United States," *Migration Policy Institute*, last modified July 21, 2015, http://www.migrationpolicy.org/article/filipino-immigrants-united-states (accessed February 17, 2017).
11. Yen Espiritu, *Filipino American Lives* (Philadelphia: Temple University Press, 1995), 22.
12. "Philippines Takes over China as Number One Source of Canadian Immigrants," *Canadian Visa Bureau*, last modified December 31, 2008, http://www.visabureau.com/canada/default.aspx (accessed February 16, 2017).
13. "National Household Survey (NHS) Profile: Canada 2011," *Statistics Canada*, last modified September 11, 2013, http://www12.statcan.gc.ca/nhs-enm/2011/dp-pd/prof/index.cfm?Lang=E (accessed February 16, 2017).
14. "Facts and figures 2011 — Immigration Overview: Permanent and Temporary Residents," *Government of Canada*, last modified October 16, 2012, http://www.cic.gc.ca/English/resources/statistics/facts2011/index.asp (accessed February 16, 2017).
15. "Hmong Baptists," *SBC Asian Advisory Council Report 2013–2015*, 43–46.

16. *History of the Hmong Baptist National Association*. http://www.hbna.org/history (accessed February 12, 2017).
17. *Hmong Baptist National Association*. http://www.hbna.org/ (accessed February 12, 2017).
18. "Japanese Church Planting Network," *SBC Asian Advisory Council Report 2013–2015*, 47–49.
19. "Korean Baptist Fellowship Report," *Asian Advisory Council Report 2013–2015*. 34–36.
20. Karen Willoughby, "Korean fellowship vote echoes SBC annual meeting," *Baptist Press*, last modified June 30, 2016, http://www.bpnews.net/47147/korean-fellowship-vote-echoes-sbc-annual-meeting (accessed February 12, 2017).
21. Ricky Hardison, "Korean Baptists celebrate missions; 450 commit to overseas service," *Baptist Press*, last modified May 29, 2003, http://www.bpnews.net/15990/korean-baptists-celebrate-missions-450-commit-to-overseas-service (accessed February 12, 2017).
22. *North American Immigration*. http://www.northamericanimmigration.org/179-laotian-immigration.html (accessed February 17, 2015).
23. Barbara Crossette, "Laotian Refugees Crown Thai Camp," *New York Times*, June 23, 1985, http://www.nytimes.com/1985/06/23/world/laotian-refugees-crowd-thai-camp.html (accessed 22 December 2014).
24. Toon Phapphayboun, "Laotian Americans," *The Face of Asian Pacific American: Numbers, Diversity, and Changes in the 21st Century*, edited by **Eric Lai and Dennis Arguelles** (San Francisco: AsianWeek, with UCLA's Asian American Studies Center Press, in cooperation with the Organization of Chinese Americans and the National Coalition for Asian Pacific American Community Development, 2003), 93–104.
25. *North American Immigration*. http://www.northamericanimmigration.org/179-laotian-immigration.html (accessed February 17, 2015).
26. Mark Pfeiter, "Hmong Americans," *The Face of Asian Pacific American: Numbers, Diversity, and Changes in the 21st Century*, edited by **Eric Lai and Dennis Arguelles** (San Francisco: AsianWeek, with UCLA's Asian American Studies Center Press, in cooperation with the Organization of Chinese Americans and the National Coalition for Asian Pacific American Community Development, 2003), 93–104.
27. *The Asian Population: 2010 Census Brief*. https://www.census.gov/prod/cen2010/briefs/c2010br-11.pdf (accessed February 17, 2015), 14.
28. Anh Do, Tran Phan, Eugene Garcia, "Camp Z30-D: The Survivors," *Dart Center for Journalism & Trauma*, March 1, 2002. http://dartcenter.org/content/camp-z30-d-survivors (accessed February 12, 2017).
29. Christian Phan, *Vietnamese Americans: Understanding Vietnamese People in the United States 1975–2010* (Maitland: Xulon Press, 2010), 24.
30. Shandon Phan, "Vietnamese Amerasians in America," *Asian Nation: Asian American History, Demographics, and Issues*. http://www.asian-nation.org/amerasians.shtml (accessed February 12, 2017).
31. Larry Berman, Jason Newman, "The Vietnam War and Its Impact," *Encyclopedia of the New American Nation*. http://www.americanforeignrelations.com/O-W/The-Vietnam-War-and-Its-Impact.html (accessed February 12, 2017).

32. Do Hien Duc, "The New Migrants from Asia: Vietnamese in the United States" *Organization of American Historians*. http://www.oah.org/pubs/magazine/asianamerican/do.html (accessed November 23, 2009).
33. Carl Bankston, "Vietnamese-American Catholicism: Transplanted and Flourishing," *US Catholic Historian* 18, no. 1 (2000): 36–53.
34. SBC national congregations' growth is 5 percent for the same period.

Hispanics in the SBC

1. See *World Book Encyclopedia* s.v. "Christopher Columbus" by Samuel Eliot Morison.
2. See *The World Book Encyclopedia*, s.v. "Juan de Oñate" by Richard A. Bartlett.
3. Harvard Encyclopedia, s.v. "Spanish," p. 953.
4. *Ibid.*
5. Pew Hispanic Center/Kaiser Family Foundation, 2002 National Survey of Latinos, December 2002, 19.
6. Some call this the 1.5 generation because they arrived as children, yet were not born in the host country.
7. Bobby Sena, "Diversity Among Hispanic Americans," in Daniel R. Sanchez, ed. *Hispanic Realities Impacting America*, Church Starting Network, 2006.
8. Source: Pew Hispanic Center, Roberto Suro and Jeffery S. Passel, *The Rise of the Second Generation*, October, 2003, 8.
9. Joshua Grijalva, *A History of Mexican Baptists in Texas 1881–1981: Comprising an Account of the Genesis, the Progress, and the Accomplishments of the People Called "Los Bautistas De Texas"* (Dallas, Tex.: Baptist General Convention of Texas, 1982), 121.
10. Some of these were Lloyd Corder and Gerald Palmer who worked for the Home Mission Board in the 1960's.
11. This list could include many others, however, those listed were among the pioneers who obtained a college education and went on to assume positions of leadership in Baptist work.
12. US Census Bureau cited in "Report, Hispanic Population Surging," *Dallas Morning News*, June 9, 2005, 13A.
13. Pew Hispanic Center population estimates and projections 2008.
14. D'Vera Cohn, "Hispanic population keeps gaining numbers," *Washington Post*, cited in *Fort Worth Star Telegram*, Thursday, June 9, 2005, 5A.
15. Based on Texas Data Center Series 2 Projections
16. Pew Research Center tabulations of 2000 Census and 2011 American community Survey
17. *Ibid.*
18. Pew Hispanic Center, Latino Settlement in the New Century, 2008.
19. Census Bureau, Counties classified by population change in Hispanic Population 2000–2010

20. D'vera Cohn, Washington Post, June 9, 2005.
21. Pew Research Center survey of Hispanics May 26–July 28, 2013.
22. *Ibid.*
23. *Ibid.*
24. *Ibid.*
25. Richie Stanley, Research Report, Hispanic Trends Population and Southern Baptist Congregations, Center for Missional Research, North American Mission Board, April, 2013.
26. A factor that needs to be taken into account is that this may be a matter of reporting. In other words, there may have been more Hispanic churches started than have been reported through official channels.
27. Richie Stanley, Research Report, Hispanic Trends Population and Southern Baptist Congregations, Center for Missional Research, North American Mission Board, April, 2013.
28. Richie Stanley, Research Report, Hispanic Trends Population and Southern Baptist Congregations, Center for Missional Research, North American Mission Board, April, 2013.
29. *Ibid.*
30. Pew Research Center Analysis of the Historical School Enrollment Time Series Time Table 4–5a
31. *Ibid.*
32. *Ibid.*
33. Pew Research Center, Tabulations of 2000 Census and 2011 American Community Survey.
34. See Pew Research Hispanic Center tabulations of 2011 American Community Survey.
35. Church Outreach: Methods of Reaching Hispanics, LifeWay Research for the North American Board, 2008.
36. *Ibid.*
37. Pew Hispanic Center, "Changing Faiths: Latinos and Transformation of American Religion." 2007
38. George Barna, Survey, 2013.
39. The Isaac Project is an example of this.
40. Resolution "On Immigration And The Gospel" adopted by the SBC June 14–15, 2011.
41. "1.7 Million Unauthorized Immigrant Youth May Benefit From New Deportation Rules," PEW Report, 2012.
42. Church Outreach: Methods of Reaching Hispanics, LifeWay Research for the North American Board, 2008.
43. *Gospel in the Rosary*, along with the Study Guide can be obtained through Amazon or by contacting Church Starting Network www.churchstarting.net

44. Daniel R. Sanchez and Rudolph Gonzalez, *Sharing The Good News With Roman Catholic Friends*, can be obtained through Amazon or by contacting Church Starting Network www.churchstarting.net
45. Information shared by Luis Lopez, staff member at LifeWay.
46. Miguel de la Torre, *Hispanic American Religious Cultures*, 366 –7
47. de la Torre, 366 –7
48. Pew Hispanic Center, "Changing Faiths: Latinos and Transformation of American Religion." 2009
49. Pew Hispanic Center, "Changing Faiths: Latinos and Transformation of American Religion." 2009
50. It is interesting to note that the secular world acknowledges the fact that cultural factors and values need to be taken into account in communicating with second, third, and fourth generation Hispanic Americans. While the television network Univision has attracted many Hispanics with the use of Spanish in its television programs. The leaders of this highly successful network have now started a new television network called "Fusion" which is done totally in English but done "from a Latino perspective." This rapidly increasing audience appreciates the fact that this network makes an effort to understand their cultural background in the preparation and presentation of their programs. There is much that we can learn from those who are being effective in communicating with second and third generation Hispanic Americans.
51. Pew Hispanic Center, "Changing Faiths: Latinos and Transformation of American Religion," 2007.
52. *Ibid*.
53. This was a quandary a Hispanic pastor faced with his own children. See Daniel Rodriguez, *op. cit.*, 68
54. This is not an argument against retaining cultural traits. This has its place. However, when the Hispanic church focuses only on retaining the culture, it runs the risk of losing the second and third generation.
55. These suggestions were given by speakers in the Leadership Network Conference held in McKinney, Texas, November 11, 2013. Some of the speakers were: 1) Rev. Wilfredo de Jesus, New Life Covenant, Chicago; 2) Steve Coronado, Solid Rock Church, Corpus Christi, Texas; 3) Roberto Tejada, Life Center Church, Tacoma, Washington; and 4) Jaime Loya, Valley International Christian Church, San Benito, Texas.
56. Wilfredo de Jesus suggests the following questions for a community survey: 1) Do you have second and third generation children?; 2) Do you prefer English of Spanish; 3) What is the heritage of your family; 4) What are some of the needs in your community?; 5) Don't ask, are you documented?
57. This was borne out in the surveys conducted by the Hispanic Advisory Council
58. The term "house church" is used here in a broad sense. It can include meetings in apartments, office buildings, conference rooms, etc.
59. This is a trend that is being observed in numerous states where there are concentrations of Hispanic persons.

60. Two dedicated servants of the Lord who have significant expertise on this subject are Lynn Godsey (214 562 1500 and Gloria Granados (469) 450 9068.

Native Americans in the SBC

1. Source: US Census Bureau, *2010 Census Redistricting Data, (Public Law 84–171) Summary File*, Table, 1
2. US Census Bureau
3. https://en.wikibooks.org/wiki/American_Indians_Today/Current_problems
4. Group labels named by Gary W Hawkins, National Church Planting Catalyst for the North American Mission Board
5. The Hughes Scale taken from *Perimeters of Light: Biblical Boundaries for the Emerging Church*, developed by Robert Hughes, professor of missions at Clear Creek Bible College in Pineville, Kentucky.
6. "Kill the Indian, and Save the Man," Capt. Richard H. Pratt on the Education of Native Americans
7. http://historymatters.gmu.edu/d/4929/
8. Born in 1850 in the industrial port city of Baltimore, Md., Armstrong, or "Miss Annie" as she was affectionately known, attended Seventh Church, which at the time met at Paca and Saratoga Streets (the current site of the Shrine of Saint Jude).
9. Missionary to the American Indians in New York, New Jersey, and eastern Pennsylvania. Born in Connecticut in 1718
10. Prepared by David Lytle, September, 2006, Southern Baptist Historical Library and Archives, Updated November, 2011
11. www.findagrave.com/cgi-bin/fg.cgi?page=gr&GRid=92432533
12. The Navajo Nation extends into the states of Utah, Arizona, and New Mexico, covering over 27,000 square miles of unparalleled beauty. Diné Bikéyah, or Navajoland, is larger than 10 of the 50 states in America.
13. In 1893, President Grover Cleveland appointed a commission, chaired by Henry L. Dawes, to negotiate land with the Cherokee, Creek, Choctaw, Chickasaw and Seminole tribes. *As a result of the negotiations, tribe members were entitled to an allotment of land, in return for abolishing their tribal governments and recognizing Federal laws.*
14. "Public Law 959". Indian Affairs: Laws and Treaties. Oklahoma State University Library. *Retrieved September 21, 2013.*
15. Bureau of Indian Affairs
16. In the United States, redlining is the practice of denying services, either directly or through selectively raising prices, to residents of certain areas based on the racial or ethnic composition of those areas.
17. Murrin, John; Johnson, Paul; McPherson, James; Fahs, Alice; Gerstle, Gary (2008). "Liberty, Equality, Power: Volume II: Since 1863, Enhanced Concise Edition". Cengage Learning. pp. 743–744. Retrieved December 25, 2014.

18. Source: 2012 American Community Survey (one- year estimates) Pew Research Center; Graphic by Jessica Schillinger

What the SBC Looked Like

1. "George Santayana said, …", www.brainyquote.com/quotes/quotes/g/georgesant101521.html
2. Douglas Beggs, Facts and Trends (Nashville: LifeWay Christian Resources May, 2001), 25.
3. Robert A. Baker. The Southern Baptist Convention and its People 1607-1972. Nashville. Broadman Press, 1974, 118-119.
4. Baker, 120.
5. Baker, 161.
6. Arthur B. Rutledge. Mission to America A Century and a Quarter of Southern Baptist Home Missions. Nashville. Broadman Press, 1969, 17.
7. Douglas Beggs. An Historical Analysis of Church Extension in the Southern Baptist Convention From 1845 to 2000,1–2.
8. Baker, 174–175.
9. Rutledge, 38–39.
10. Baker, 401.
11. Cecil Ray and Susan Ray, Cooperation: The Baptist Way to a Lost World (Nashville: Stewardship Commission, 1985), 1.
12. Beggs, 135.
13. Beggs, 129–130.
14. Beggs, 160.
15. Beggs, 130.
16. Beggs, 130–131.
17. Beggs, 141–142.
18. Beggs, 145.
19. Rutledge, 110–111.
20. Beggs, 147.
21. Beggs, 147–142.
22. Beggs, 147–148.
23. Arthur B. Rutledge and William G. Tanner. Mission to America: A History of Southern Baptist Home Missions. Nashville. Broadman Press, 1983, 267–269.
24. Beggs, 166.
25. Beggs, 166–167.
26. Oscar I. Romo. American Mosaic: Church Planting in Ethnic America. Nashville. Broadman Press, 1993, 12.
27. Beggs, 169–170.
28. Beggs, 169–171.

Synergy, Cooperation, and Autonomy

1. David S. Dockery, *Southern Baptist Consensus and Renewal: A Biblical, Historical, and Theological Proposal* (Nashville, TN: B&H Academic, 2008).
2. See, for example, W. A. Criswell's presidential address at the 1970 SBC annual meeting in Denver, Colorado, "Criswell Urges SBC: Hold Fast to Doctrine, Missions," *Baptist Press*, June 1, 1970, 1, http://media.sbhla.org.s3.amazonaws.com/3003,01-Jun-1970.pdf; Roy L. Honeycutt, "Southern Baptists: A Trusting People?," *Baptist Press*, February 14, 1995, 7–8, http://media.sbhla.org.s3.amazonaws.com/7925,14-Feb-1995.pdf; and Morris H. Chapman, "Axioms of a Cooperating Conservative," a paper presented at the "Baptist Identity Conference" (Jackson, TN, Union University, April 5, 2004), http://www.baptist2baptist.net/Issues/BaptistPolity/cooperatingconservative.asp.
3. "Criswell Urges SBC: Hold Fast to Doctrine, Missions," 1.
4. *Ibid.*
5. James L. Sullivan, *Rope of Sand with Strength of Steel* (Nashville, TN: Convention Press, 1974).
6. By definition, "The Cooperative Program is Southern Baptists' unified plan of giving through which cooperating Southern Baptist churches give a percentage of their undesignated receipts in support of their respective state convention and the Southern Baptist Convention missions and ministries." See "Proceedings," Item #27, *Southern Baptist Convention Annual* (Nashville, TN: Executive Committee of the Southern Baptist Convention, 2007), 60, and http://www.sbc.net/cp/default.asp.
7. Chapman, "Axioms."
8. *Ibid.*
9. "Proceedings," Items #112–19, *Southern Baptist Convention Annual* (Nashville, TN: Executive Committee of the Southern Baptist Convention, 2000), 76.
10. "Proceedings," Items #73–97, *Southern Baptist Convention Annual* (Nashville, TN: Executive Committee of the Southern Baptist Convention, 2010), 77–97.
11. This common phrase is woven throughout Southern Baptist documents and opinion pieces. For a recent illustration, see Randy Davis, "'Getting' the Cooperative Program," *SBC LIFE*, vol. 25, no. 2, Winter 2016, 15.
12. "Preamble and Constitution of the Southern Baptist Convention," *Proceedings of the Southern Baptist Convention* (Richmond, VA: H. K. Ellyson, Printer, 1845), 3.
13. Article II of the original Constitution stated: "It shall be the design of this Convention to promote Foreign and Domestic Missions, and other important objects connected with the Redeemer's kingdom, and to combine for this purpose, such portions of the Baptist denomination in the United States, as may desire a general organization for Christian benevolence, which shall fully respect the independence and equal rights of the Churches." See endnote 12 above, 1845 *Proceedings of the SBC*, 3.
14. "Bylaws," *Proceedings of the Twenty-Sixth Session of the Southern Baptist Convention* (Cincinnati, OH: Elm Street Printing Company, 1881), 6; cf. "Proceedings," Item #53, 17 of the same 1881 SBC Annual.

15. Frank William White, "Sunday school enrollment growth shows largest increase since 1976," *Baptist Press*, February 11, 1992, 4–5, http://media.sbhla.org.s3.amazonaws.com/7390,11-Feb-1992.pdf.
16. Quotation from the preamble of "Penetrating The Lostness: Embracing a Vision for a Great Commission Resurgence among Southern Baptists," the final report of the Great Commission Task Force of the Southern Baptist Convention, "Proceedings," Item #73, *Southern Baptist Convention Annual* (Nashville, TN: Executive Committee of the Southern Baptist Convention, 2010), 77.
17. "Proceedings," Item #73, "Recommendation One," *Southern Baptist Convention Annual* (Nashville, TN: Executive Committee of the Southern Baptist Convention, 2010), 87; see also http://www.sbc.net/aboutus/missionvision.asp.
18. William L. Lumpkin, *Baptist Confessions of Faith*, second revised edition, ed. Bill J. Leonard (Valley Forge, PA: Judson Press, 2011), 376–78.
19. John L. Dagg, *Manual of Theology* (N.p., SC: The Southern Baptist Publication Society, 1857; rpt., Harrison, Harrisonburg, Virginia, 1990); and *Manual of Church Order*, (N.p., SC: The Southern Baptist Publication Society, 1858; rpt., Harrison, Harrisonburg, Virginia, 1990).
20. "Proceedings," Item #16, *Proceedings of the Twenty-Fourth Session of the Southern Baptist Convention* (Atlanta: Jas. P. Harrison & Co., 1879), 14–15.
21. "Proceedings," Item #53, *Annual of the Southern Baptist Convention* (Nashville, TN: Marshall and Bruce, 1925), 70–76.
22. "Proceedings," Items #112–122, *Annual of the Southern Baptist Convention* (Nashville, TN: SBC Executive Committee, 1963), 63.
23. "10. SBC Referral: Requesting Study of *The Baptist Faith and Message*," Background Material for the September 19–20, 2016, SBC Executive Committee meeting (Nashville, TN: SBC Executive Committee), 126–40, http://www.sbcec.org/documents/ECBookSep2016.pdf (password protected).
24. *Ibid*.
25. For a comparison of the wording of "Article I. The Scriptures," from the three editions of *The Baptist Faith and Message* (1925, 1963, and 2000), see the side-by-side "Comparison of 1925, 1963 and 2000 Baptist Faith and Message," posted at http://www.sbc.net/bfm2000/bfmcomparison.asp.
26. A letter from chairman of the 2000 *Baptist Faith and Message* committee that outlined the goals of the committee and the recommended changes it made to this current edition of this Convention-adopted statement of faith is posted at http://www.sbc.net/bfm2000/bfmchairman.asp.
27. Jason K. Allen ably illustrated this in his chapter, "A Never-Changing Witness in an Ever-Changing World: The Enduring Southern Baptist Mandate," in *The SBC and the 21st Century*, ed. Jason K. Allen (Nashville, TN: B&H Academic, 2016), 3–4.
28. Rob Phillips, "SBC baptisms lowest since 87," *Baptist Press*, April 23, 2008, http://www.bpnews.net/27890/sbc-baptisms-lowest-since-87.
29. *Ibid*.

30. *Ibid.*
31. Carol Pipes, "ACP: more churches reported; baptisms decline," *Baptist Press*, June 7, 2016, http://www.bpnews.net/46989/acp-more-churches-reported-baptisms-decline.
32. A cursory reading of numerous analytical articles in *Baptist Press*, state Baptist papers, and numerous Southern Baptist blogs revealed that trust among and between pastors, associational leaders, state convention leaders, and SBC leaders had sagged to a low ebb.
33. See Southeastern Baptist Theological Seminary President Danny Akin's "Twelve Axioms for a Great Commission Resurgence," reported by Jason Hall, "Seminary head calls for great commission resurgence, streamlining denomination," Baptist Press, April 16, 2009, http://www.bpnews.net/30282/seminary-head-calls-for-great-commission-resurgence-streamlining-denomination; 2009 SBC President John Hunt's Ten-point Declaration for a Great Commission Resurgence, listed in "SBC president's declaration calls for a 'great commission resurgence,'" *Baptist Press*, April 28, 2009, http://www.bpnews.net/30387/sbc-presidents-declaration-calls-for-a-great-commission-resurgence; and James A. Smith Sr., "GCR: Akin discusses its history, intent," *Baptist Press*, May 5, 2009, http://www.bpnews.net/30430/gcr-akin-discusses-its-history-intent.
34. The SBC Committee on Order of Business recommended that the SBC president rule out of order one-third of the thirty-one motions introduced by messengers from the floor at the 2009 SBC annual meeting, noting that several "reflected harshly on particular individuals," Keith Hinson, "Motions: GCR task force endorse," *Baptist Press*, June 25, 2009, http://www.bpnews.net/30774/motions-gcr-task-force-endorsed.
35. "SBC natl, state leaders sign unity pledge, *Baptist Press*, June 13, 2015 http://www.bpnews.net/35533/sbc-natl-state-leaders-sign-unity-pledge.
36. *Ibid.*
37. Mark Kelly, "Unity, cooperation pledge tops EC agenda," *Baptist Press*, June 14, 2011, http://www.bpnews.net/35539/unity-cooperation-pledge-tops-ec-agenda.
38. For the full statement of "Affirmation of Cooperation and Unity," see "Proceedings," Item #29, *Southern Baptist Convention Annual* (Nashville, TN: Executive Committee of the Southern Baptist Convention, 2011), 59–60.
39. For a history of the Calvinism Advisory group, see http://www.sbclife.net/Articles/2013/06/sla1. To read the final report and see the individual comments of each member, see http://www.sbclife.net/Articles/2013/06/sla5.
40. The appointment, meetings, and reports of these advisory groups have been chronicled in *SBC LIFE*, the official news journal of the SBC Executive Committee, and can be researched at http://www.sbclife.net.
41. "Penetrating The Lostness," the final report of the Great Commission Task Force of the Southern Baptist Convention, "Proceedings," Item #73, "Challenges to All Southern Baptist Churches" section, *Southern Baptist Convention Annual* (Nashville, TN: Executive Committee of the Southern Baptist Convention, 2010), 89.
42. *Ibid.*
43. See endnotes 12 and 14 above, 1845 *Proceedings of the SBC*, 3.

44. "Constitution," *Southern Baptist Convention Annual*, (Nashville, TN: Executive Committee of the Southern Baptist Convention, 2016), 7.
45. See especially chapter 3, "Toward a Theology of Cooperation," in Chad Owen Brand and David Hankins, *One Sacred Effort: The Cooperative Program of Southern Baptists* (Nashville, TN: Broadman and Holman Publishers, 2005), 53–77.
46. *Ibid.*, 66–67.
47. *Ibid.*, 67–68.
48. Carol Pipes, "ACP."
49. Statistical research developed by the SBC Executive Committee staff during the Fall of 2016 from the 2015 Annual Church Profile report, research from the North American Mission Board's Center for Missional Research based on the 2014 ACP report, and New Orleans Baptist Theological Seminary's Caskey Center for Church Excellence based on the 2013 ACP report.
50. *Ibid.*
51. *Ibid.*
52. *Ibid.*
53. Frank S. Page, president of the SBC Executive Committee, made this point in "The Cooperative Program and the Future of Collaborative Ministry," in *The SBC and the 21st Century*, ed. Jason K. Allen (Nashville, TN: B&H Academic, 2016), 14–16.
54. Elmer Towns, *Is the Day of the Denomination Dead?* (Nashville, TN, Thomas Nelson, 1973).
55. "Ministry Reports to the SBC," *Annual of the Southern Baptist Convention* (Nashville, TN: SBC Executive Committee, 2016), "Seminary Comparative Data," 198.
56. *Ibid.*, "North American Mission Board," 197.
57. Mike Ebert, "Class of 2015 church plants impacting communities," *Baptist Press*, May 12, 2016, http://www.bpnews.net/46846/class-of-2015-church-plants-impacting-communities.
58. Julie McGowan, "Trustees: IMB celebrates balanced budget," *Baptist Press*, November 11, 2016, http://www.bpnews.net/47882/trustees-imb-celebrates-balanced-budget; and McGowan, "50 new missionaries appointed by IMB," *Baptist Press*, November 14, 2016, http://www.bpnews.net/47886/50-new-missionaries-appointed-by-imb.
59. *The Southern Baptist Convention: A Closer Look* (Nashville, TN: SBC Executive Committee, 2016), 5, http://www.sbc.net/pdf/acloserlook.pdf.

Contributors

Candi Finch, PhD serves as assistant professor of theology in women's studies and occupies the Dorothy Kelley Patterson Chair of Women's Studies at Southwestern Baptist Theological Seminary. She graduated with her B.A. in Communication from the University of South Florida and with her MDiv in Women's Studies and her PhD in Systematic Theology from SWBTS. Candi has contributed to several books for women and youth, including the *Women's Evangelical Commentary on the New Testament and Old Testament* and also the *Impact Bible*, as well as serving as editor for the Pentateuch and Pauline Epistle sections for *The Study Bible for Women*. She has contributed a chapter on the wives of Adoniram Judson to the book *Adoniram Judson: A Bicentennial Appreciation of the Pioneer American Missionary* and a chapter on the impact of feminism on the home and family to *The Christian Homemaker's Handbook*.

Ray Gilder has rendered denomination service at the associational, state, and national levels. He served as executive director of Bivocational and Small Church Leadership Network (2007–2016), chairman of the SBC Executive Committee's Bivocational and Smaller Church Advisory Council, and as a member of the SBC Executive Committee's Convention Advancement Advisory Council. He has been a conference leader, trainer, and denominational/vocational mentor, and has published numerous articles and books focusing on the life, functions, and challenges for those ministering in bivocational and smaller church settings. He graduated from Memphis Baptist College with his undergraduate degree and attended Mid-America Baptist Theological Seminary and Luther Rice Seminary. He and his wife Diane have three children.

Gary Hawkins is a Creek/Cherokee Native American residing in Jenks, Oklahoma, with his wife Paula. They are the parents of three adult children and seven grandchildren. He was ordained into the Gospel ministry in 1980 and has pastored in Muscogee Creek, Oklahoma; Blackfeet, Montana; Central Tribes of Oklahoma; and the Northern Pueblos of New Mexico. He became a church planting missionary in 2002, and was jointly employed by the Baptist Convention of Oklahoma and the North American Mission Board for almost ten years as a multi-cultural church planting missionary whose primary focus group was the Native People of eastern Oklahoma. He is also the first executive director of FoNAC, Fellowship of Native Americans, a faith-based 501(c)(3) that works in partnership with NAMB. Presently, he is planting an inter-tribal church, Native Stone Baptist, focusing on the Native population of Tulsa, Oklahoma, and the surrounding areas.

Rhonda H. Kelley, PhD, is an adjunct professor of women's ministry at New Orleans Baptist Theological Seminary where her husband Chuck Kelley is president and professor of evangelism. She is a speaker and author who has written Bible study resources for women with B&H Publishing Group (*The Study Bible for Women, Old and New Testament Commentaries, The Devotional for Women*) as well as Bible study books for LifeWay (Life Lessons from Women of the Bible). She has written *Talking is a Gift: Communication Skills for Women* with B&H Academics and served as chair for SBC Executive Committee Women's Advisory Council. Building on her undergraduate and master's degrees in speech and audiology from Baylor University, Kelley earned the PhD in special education and speech pathology from the University of New Orleans. She also holds the basic and advanced certificates in women's ministry from New Orleans Baptist Theological Seminary. Rhonda has been director of the women's enrichment ministry at First Baptist Church in New Orleans since 1991 and is a past president of the SBC Ministers' Wives (2009–2010).

Contributors

Paul Kim, DMin, retired after thirty years of service as pastor of Berkland (now Antioch) Baptist Church, Boston, in Cambridge, Massachusetts, and is the Asian Relations Consultant with the SBC Executive Committee. He received his Master of Divinity and Doctor of Ministry degrees from Southwestern and Golden Gate Baptist Theological seminaries and has served in various leadership positions in the SBC, including ten years as a trustee of the International Mission Board. He has traveled to seventy-one countries as an IMB trustee, church planter, and missionary. With more than twenty churches planted and growing worldwide, he is considered an expert in team-based church planting and long-term growth strategy. He is also a former police chaplain, veteran, and an author.

Minh Ha Nguyen, ThM, is research manager in global research at the International Mission Board. He obtained his Bachelor of Theology degree at the École Biblique et Missionaire Emmaüs in St-Légier (Switzerland), his Master of Divinity degree at the Columbia International University in Columbia, South Carolina, and his Master of Theology degree at Southeastern Baptist Theological Seminary, where he is completing his Doctor of Philosophy in applied theology. Minh Ha is the founder of the International Community Church, a multi-ethnic network of house churches in Richmond, Virginia. The network meets monthly for worship celebration, gathering migrant believers from Cambodia, Nepal, Iran, China, Middle East, Russia, Ghana, Nigeria, and Vietnam. In recent years, the network has helped start sister-networks in Boston, Dallas, and Fredericksburg, Virginia. Minh Ha serves on the board of the V3 Church Planting Movement of the Baptist General Association of Virginia, the Convention Advancement Advisory Council of the Executive Committee, SBC, and the A2CP2, an Asian American network seeking to mobilize Asian American Southern Baptists to engage in church planting and international missions. Minh Ha is married to Corinne, his wife of twenty-five years, and together they have two young daughters.

Frank S. Page, PhD, was elected president and chief executive officer of the Southern Baptist Convention Executive Committee in October 2010 and served until March 2018. He was president of the Southern Baptist Convention (2006–2008), and served as vice president of evangelism for the North American Mission Board of the Southern Baptist Convention (2009–2010). He was a member of the SBC's Great Commission Task Force (2009–2010) and a director of Baptist Global Response (2008–2010). He received the Master of Divinity degree and earned his Doctor of Philosophy degree in Christian ethics from Southwestern Baptist Theological Seminary. He is the author of several books, has written articles for various publications, and was the lead writer for the Advanced Continuing Witness Training material. He is married to Dayle, and from their union three daughters were born.

Roger S. (Sing) Oldham, ThD, is vice president for Convention Communications and Relations, SBC Executive Committee. He served as pastor of First Baptist Church in Martin, Tennessee, for twenty-one years (1986–2007). He earned the Master of Divinity degree and the Doctor of Theology degree in systematic theology from Mid-America Baptist Theological Seminary. He has been an adjunct instructor in the Doctor of Ministry program at Mid-America Seminary and was an adjunct instructor at Mid-Continent Baptist Bible College in Mayfield, Kentucky; the University of Tennessee at Martin, and Union University (Hendersonville, Tennessee, campus). He and his wife Debbie have three adult daughters and six grandchildren.

Daniel R. Sanchez, PhD, is a professor of missions at Southwestern Baptist Theological Seminary, here he also was director of the Scarborough Institute of Church Planting and Growth, associate dean of the Roy Fish School of Evangelism and Missions, and director of the Hispanic Theological Studies Program. He earned a Doctor of Philosophy degree from the Oxford Centre for Mission Studies, Oxford, England, a Doctor of Ministry degree from Fuller Theological Seminary, and a Master of Divinity degree from Southwestern Baptist Theological

Seminary. His ministry experience includes service as a missionary in the Republic of Panama, as a church planter, and in other state and national denominational positions. He and his wife, Carmen, have three adult children.

Bobby Sena, DMin, serves as the Executive Committee's Hispanic Relations Consultant, SBC Executive Committee. He is also serving as the director of the Hispanic Doctor of Ministry program at Midwestern Baptist Theological Seminary in Kansas City, Missouri. For more than fifty years, Bobby has served in a variety of roles in the Southern Baptist Convention. He has been a pastor of small and large Hispanic churches in Texas and Georgia, a church planting missionary in New Mexico, national multi-ethnic evangelism consultant for the Home Mission Board, Hispanic evangelism associate in the Baptist General Convention of Texas, and national Hispanic missionary at North American Mission Board. He holds a Master's degree from Southwestern Baptist Theological Seminary and a Doctor of Ministry from Golden Gate Baptist Theological Seminary. He and his wife, Priscilla, have been married for almost five decades. He is a fourth-generation Hispanic born in the United States and a second-generation Southern Baptist.

Richard "Richie" Stanley is team leader at the North American Mission Board's Center for Missional Research in Alpharetta, Georgia. He is an author who holds a Master of Divinity degree from Southeastern Baptist Theological Seminary and a Master of Science in Statistics from the University of Kentucky.

Mark Tolbert, DMin, is a professor of preaching and pastoral ministry at New Orleans Baptist Theological Seminary, and founding director of the Caskey Center for Church Excellence. He has held numerous denominational ministry positions and has been pastor or interim pastor of several Southern Baptist churches. His denominational service includes: Executive Committee Convention Advancement Advisory Council (2015 –); vice chair, EC Bivocational and Smaller Church Advisory Council (2014 –2016); and trustee, Annuity Board of the Southern Baptist Convention (now GuideStone Financial Resources), 1994–1996.

Kenneth Weathersby, DMin, is vice president for convention advancement with the Southern Baptist Convention Executive Committee, the first African American to hold an EC vice presidential position. He previously served as presidential ambassador for ethnic church relations with the North American Mission Board, and has held a series of trail-blazing positions with various SBC entities and state convention ministries. He has planted and pastored churches in Alabama, Ohio, and Baton Rouge, Louisiana, where he started and led Douglas Avenue Baptist Church from 1989–1993. He holds a Master of Divinity degree from The Southern Baptist Theological Seminary and a Doctor of Ministry degree from Reformed Theological Seminary. He and his wife, Belva, have two adult children.

Rodney Webb, DMin, served in numerous capacities for thirty-five years with the Home Mission Board/North American Mission Board of the SBC. He began his career as a missionary with the Deaf in the northeastern United States, and went on to serve as language missions director for the Mississippi Baptist Convention, director of language church starting department at HMB, and manager of the Anglo Church Planting Unit at NAMB. He holds a Doctor of Ministry/Missiology degree from Trinity Evangelical Divinity School, and a Master of Divinity degree from Southwestern Baptist Theological Seminary. Dr. Webb was interim pastor of several churches through the years and in retirement served as director of missions and evangelism for the Wyoming Southern Baptist Convention.

Robert E. Wilson Sr, DMin, serves as adjunct faculty at the Marietta, Georgia, campus of New Orleans Baptist Theological Seminary/Leavell College. His ministry service within the Southern Baptist Convention spans more than three decades, including denominational staff, church planter strategist and pastor. He holds his master's degree and the Doctor of Ministry degree from The Southern Baptist Theological Seminary. He has been married to Alice Marie for nearly five decades. They have eight children, twenty-four grandchildren, and five great grandchildren.

Peter Yanes Jr is a church planting catalyst at the North American Mission Board and an ethnic church strategist with the Baptist Resource Network in Greater Philadelphia. He is president of the Filipino Southern Baptist Fellowship of North America, Inc. Peter studied at Baptist Bible College and Seminary and has a Bachelor's degree in Theology Upon completion of his theological and pastoral training, he served at his home church, Grace Baptist Church of Pangasinan, as an associate pastor, and later as senior pastor. While there, he obtained his Master of Pastoral Ministries degree at the Golden State School of Theology (Philippine Extension). In April 1998, he migrated to the United States, where he ministered as a church planter and pastor. He earned a Master of Divinity degree at Cairn University. Peter has been married to Irene for 22 years, and they have two adult children.

Lennox Zamore is senior pastor at Ebenezer Memorial Baptist Church in St. Thomas, Virgin Islands, and director of the Ebenezer Counseling Center. He holds a Master's degree in Clinical Psychology from the University of the District of Columbia. He has a diverse background of professional and ministry experience. Rev. Zamore is a seasoned pastor with sixteen years of experience in congregational and association leadership. He is an effective Christian counselor, serving on the SBC Executive Committee Mental Health Advisory Group, and is a faith-based software developer, a gifted preacher/teacher, a writer and author, an award-winning public sector administrator, and a musician and recording artist.

Index

A

Abbot Baptist Church 202
Abyssinian Baptist Church 55
Adult Vocational Training Program 152
African American 28, 29, 30, 31, 32, 36, 38, 39, 40, 41, 42, 46, 54, 55, 65, 66, 67, 68, 69, 70, 71, 72, 73, 74, 75, 76, 77, 78, 79, 80, 81, 82, 140, 150, 231
African American Church Planting Unit 69, 70
African American Fellowship 41, 69, 70, 75, 79
African American History Month 31
Alabama Baptist State Board of Missions 203
Alaska Native 144, 153
Alexander, Lyman 68
Amerasian Homecoming Act 111
Amerasians 111, 118, 233
American Baptist Anti-Slavery Convention 58
American Baptist Publication Society 60
American Baptist Theological Seminary 62
American-born Chinese 92
American Free Mission Society 58
American Indian 144, 150, 153
American Jews 164
American Muslim 168
Anderson, Jimmy 150
Anglo 8, 26, 27, 28, 29, 39, 40, 41, 43, 45, 53, 123, 125, 126, 138, 160, 185, 196, 197, 199, 201, 215, 224, 226, 248
Annie Armstrong 76, 79, 80, 149, 195
Annual Church Profile 41, 91, 116, 203, 221, 226, 228, 242
Annual Meeting 10, 51, 87, 119, 207, 226, 227, 228, 230
Annuity Board 70, 103, 248
Antioch Church 20, 22, 25
Antoine, Ira, Jr 202
Apache 150
Arab American 168
Asian 45

Asian Advisory Council 84, 116, 117, 229, 232
Asian-Americans 83
Asians 26, 27, 29, 84, 101, 115
Associational Missions Division 198
Assyrian Catholic 168
Augusta, Georgia 58, 59, 186, 219

B

Bailey, J.W. 60
Baptist Church Manual 220
Baptist Faith and Message 40, 219, 221, 228, 240
Baptist Foreign Mission Convention 59
Baptist Press 48
Baptist Sunday School Board 67, 68, 172, 218, 230
Barrow, David 57
Beachum, Andy 10
Beachum, Vernon E. Jr 202
Beall, Noble Y. 62
Begaye, Russell 151
Beggs, Douglas 191
Bellamy, Guy 63
Belvin, B. Frank 150
Berry, Debra 70
BF&M, *See Baptist Faith and Message*
biblical mandate 16, 20, 74, 93
Big Cities Program 192
Bingham, Lincoln 67
Biswas, Paul 202
Bivo 205, 206, 208, 211, 212, 243
bivocational 194, 196, 202, 206, 208, 209, 210, 211, 212, 223, 243
Bivocational and Small Church Leadership Network 209
Bivocational and Smaller Membership Church Advisory Council 205
Bivo/Small Church Advisory Council 212
Black Baptist convention 55
black Baptists 56, 57, 58, 59, 60, 61

Black Church Development Section 67, 68
Black Church Extension Division 66, 68, 69, 198
Black Church Leadership Week 42, 73, 75
Black Church Relations 66, 67, 68, 81
Black Southern Baptist Denominational Servants Network 41
Board of Domestic and Indian Missions 60
Board of Domestic Missions 58
boat people 110
Bold Mission Thrust 194
Boyce, James P. 221
Brabson, Fredrick Sr 202
Brainerd, David 149
Brand, Chad Owen 223
Brewer, Paul 71
Brisbane, Herbert 69
Broadman-Holman 177
Brotherhood 98, 102, 103
Browder, Kathryn 67
Brown, Austin 67
BSCLN 202
Buddhist 94, 106

C

California African American Ministries Division 68
California Southern Baptist Convention 55, 67, 68, 69
Calvary Chapel 203
Cambodia 83, 85, 86, 87, 88, 104, 107, 117, 118, 232, 245
Cambodian 85, 86, 87, 88, 89, 107, 110, 116, 232
Cambodian Southern Baptist Fellowship 87
Canada 40, 91, 95, 96, 100, 105, 106, 116, 117, 159, 196, 199, 232
Canadian Convention of Southern Baptists 91
Caribbean 70, 122, 163, 164
Cary, Lott 57, 230
Caskey Center for Church Excellence 202, 203, 209
Caucasian 185, 196, 199
Census Bureau 31, 34, 100, 101, 108, 116, 118, 120, 122, 226, 234, 237
Central America 122
Central Baptist Church 202
Central-Eastern Africans 170, 171, 172, 173, 174, 179, 180, 181, 184
Chaldean Catholic 168
Champion Forrest en Español 140
Chandler, Diana 45
Chaplains Commission 67
Chapman, Morris H. 218

Chile 34
China 80, 83, 89, 90, 91, 95, 97, 101, 104, 105, 107, 110, 117, 232, 245
Chinese 28, 39, 45, 83, 89, 90, 91, 92, 93, 94, 96, 97, 108, 110, 116, 149, 190, 232, 233
Chinese Baptist Fellowship 91
Choctaw 150, 151, 152, 237
Christian Life Commission.
    See Ethics and Religious Liberty Commission
Church 19
Church Loans Division 198
church planting 40, 41, 47, 48, 70, 75, 76, 87, 88, 91, 99, 100, 107, 115, 123, 126, 127, 128, 137, 138, 139, 140, 143, 150, 152, 196, 198, 200, 201, 212, 222, 244, 245, 247, 249
Civil Rights Movement 64
Civil War 58, 59, 60
Clark, Bobby 202
Cloud, Olivia M. 10, 68
Collegiate Week 73
Colley, W.W. 59
Committee on Order of Business 37, 44, 51, 52, 229, 241
Communist Party 86, 89, 111
Community Baptist Church 63
Community Foundation for Southern Arizona 10
Convention Advancement Advisory Council 9, 183, 217
Cooperative Program 44, 45, 47, 49, 76, 91, 103, 164, 188, 192, 195, 204, 205, 216, 218, 222, 224, 239, 242
Cornelius, David 68
Cortéz, Hernán 120
Costa Rica 34
Cotton, Roy 69
Council of Korean Southern Baptist Churches 102, 103
Cox, Michael 68
Creek 150, 151, 152, 237, 244
Crescent Bay Association 68
Criswell, W. A. 218
Croston, Mark 71
Cubans 120, 121, 122, 125, 126
Culp, Jim 67
Curtis, Jeffrey 70
Custalow, Mark 147, 148, 151

D

Dagg, John L. 220
Daily Bulletin 48
Daniels, Alvin Charles 66
Dargan, E. C. 220
Davis, Phillip 69
Davis, Victor 68
Day, Bill 203
Deaf 45, 160, 162, 190, 215, 248
De La Cruz, Ivery 67
Kim, Dennis Manpoong 39
Department of Black Church Relations 66
Department of Cooperative Ministries with National Baptists 65
Department of Work with National Baptists 64
Dexter Avenue King Memorial Baptist Church 69
Diehl, William 191
Dispersal Policy on Refugees 112
diversity 8, 24, 37, 38, 43, 44, 45, 46, 47, 48, 51, 52, 55, 123, 143, 190, 224
Division of Chaplaincy 198
Domestic and Indian Mission Board of the Southern Baptists 150
Domestic Board of Missions 150
Domestic Mission Board 55, 60, 150, 187
Donahoe, Gordon 202

E

East End Baptist Church 71
Ellis, Ken 71
El Salvador 34
Emmanuel Baptist Church 203
ERLC. *See* Ethics and Religious Liberty Commission
ESL 129, 133, 141, 168
Ethics and Religious Liberty Commission 38
ethnic groups 7, 23, 27, 37, 40, 43, 49, 88, 90, 93, 103, 122, 125, 144, 163, 214, 215, 216, 226
Ethnic Leadership Development Program 126
Ethnic Study Committee Report 43
Evangelio en el Rosario 134
Executive Committee Convention Advancement 10
Ezell, Kevin 40, 228

F

Fain, Maurice 190
Falls, Emerson 151
Farmer, Verlene 67
Filipino Americans 94, 95, 96, 108
Filipino Church Planting Network of North America 96
Filipinos 28, 39, 94, 95, 96, 101
Finch, Candi 184
First Baptist Church, Chataignier 202
First Baptist Church Dallas 218
First Baptist Church, Gordonsville 202
First Baptist Church of Greenville 67
First Great Awakening 56
First Nations People 150
Florida Baptist State Convention 69
Foreign Mission Board 59, 67, 68, 187, 197
Fountain, Leroy 70
Franklin Avenue Baptist Church 39, 71
Frost, Gary 36, 39, 69
Fuller, Richard 221
Furman, Richard 57

G

Gainey, Leroy 68
Galusha, Elon 58
Garrett, Chan 55
Gateway Seminary of the SBC 173
GED 129, 133, 141, 154
George Barna Institute 132
Galphin, George 56
Liele, George 57
Georgia Baptist Convention 70
Gilder, Ray 53, 202
Glass, Victor 64
Glorieta Baptist Church 151
Golden Gate Baptist Theological Seminary 63, 68, 247
Gospel in the Rosary 134, 235
Great Awakening 205
Great Commission 3, 16, 17, 18, 19, 20, 21, 22, 23, 24, 25, 38, 41, 49, 93, 94, 98, 115, 131, 135, 139, 203, 205, 214, 219, 220, 222, 223, 225, 230, 240, 241, 246
Greater Friendship Baptist Church 63
Greek Orthodox 168
Grijalva, Joshua 126, 234
Grinstead, S.E. 63
Guangdong 90
Guatemala 34
Guidestone Financial Services 70

Index

H

Hankins, David 223
Hawkins, Gary 9, 53, 244
HBNA 98, 99
HeartCall 179
Heath, Kenny 202
Hernandez, Rudy 126
Hindu 94
Hispanic 9, 10, 26, 27, 28, 29, 32, 33, 34, 35, 38, 39, 45, 53, 120, 121, 122, 123, 124, 125, 126, 127, 128, 130, 131, 132, 133, 134, 135, 136, 137, 138, 139, 140, 141, 142, 143, 154, 226, 229, 234, 235, 236, 246, 247
Hispanic Advisory Council 9, 131, 132, 134, 135, 229, 236
Hispanic Heritage Month 34
HMB 62, 64, 65, 67, 68, 69, 70, 192, 193, 194, 196, 198, 248
Hmong 83, 97, 98, 99, 116, 118, 232, 233
Hmong Baptist Fellowship 98
Hmong Baptist National Association 98, 116, 232
Holmes, Albert 69
Home Mission Board *see also* HMB 40, 59, 60, 62, 63, 64, 65, 66, 81, 82, 98, 102, 103, 124, 125, 126, 149, 150, 151, 187, 188, 190, 192, 193, 194, 195, 197, 230, 234, 247, 248
Home Mission Society 58
Honduras 34
Hong Kong, 89, 110
Hopkins, Hal 202
Howell, R. B. C. 221
Hunt, Johnny 39

I

Iglesia Bautista La Cosecha 203
Iglesia Cristiana Bautista 203
IMB 68, 79, 80, 96, 102, 104, 114, 115, 116, 142, 157, 181, 209, 225, 242, 245
immigrants 83, 84, 85, 89, 90, 92, 94, 95, 96, 101, 102, 108, 111, 112, 113, 114, 118, 122, 149, 167, 168, 197, 232
immigration 8, 83, 89, 95, 96, 101, 112, 117, 121, 127, 132, 166, 167, 233
Indian Nations Baptist Church 203
Indian Relocation Act of 1956 152
Indochina Migration and Refugee Assistance Act 106
Indo-China War 104
Indonesia 90, 110

International Mission Board *See also* IMB 42, 68, 71, 80, 115, 173, 209, 222, 225, 245

J

Jackson, Andrew 152
James, Betty Sue 10
Japan 83, 100
Japanese 39, 99, 100, 101, 116, 232
Japanese Americans 39
Japanese Church Planting Network 99, 116, 232
JCPN 99, 100, 101
Jefferson, Keith 71
Jeffray, Robert Alexander 113
Jerusalem Church 20, 20
Jeter, J. B. 220
Johnson, William B. 220
Jones, Stephen R. 202

K

Kelley, Rhonda 184
Kelly, Tom 55, 68
Kentucky Baptist Convention 67
Ketchens, Victor 69
Khmer 85, 86, 88, 117, 119
Killing Fields 85
Kim, Paul 9, 13
King, Jerome 70
Kiowa 150
Knight, Walker 64
Korea 83, 101
Korean 39, 45, 46, 101, 102, 103, 104, 117, 118, 119, 140, 232, 233
Korean Baptist Overseas Mission Board 102

L

Lampkin, Adrian Jr 190
Land, Richard 38
Lao 98, 104, 105, 106, 107
Laos 83, 97, 104, 107
Laotian 104, 105, 106, 107, 117, 118, 233
Latin America 122
Latin American countries 34
Latinos 136, 234, 235, 236
Leavell Center for Church Health 203
Lee, Richard 70
Leland, John 57
Liberia 57
Liele, George 56

LifeWay 70, 71, 116, 131, 133, 135, 173, 177, 179, 226, 228, 235
Lighthouse Baptist Church 202
Long Beach Harbor Association 68
Losch, Pusey 202
Luckel, Henry 202
Luter, Fred 39, 45, 71, 227, 228, 229

M

Malaysia 90, 110
mandate 7, 16, 17, 18, 20, 25, 74, 93
Manly, Basil Jr. 220
Manly, Basil Sr 220
Martin, Jaye 179
Maryland State Mission Board 62
Mason-Dixon line 196
Matson, T. B. 64
Mayflower 83
McAlpine, William H. 59
McCall, Emmanuel 64, 66, 71, 81
McCall, E. W. 70
McIntosh, Ledtkey (Lit) 151
McIntosh, William H. 60
McNairy, Chris 70
McPherson, Willie 67, 68
Mega Focus Cities 68
Mell, P. H. 221
Messianic 164, 165
Metropolitan New York Association 69
Mexico 34
Mickels, Walter 71
Midwestern Baptist Theological Seminary 173
Ministry-Based Evangelism 132, 155
Minnesota/Wisconsin Baptist Convention 69
Mission Pathways 81
Mitchell, Dennis 69
Mitchell, Gary 202
Mohler, R. Albert Jr. 41
Mojica, Mike 126
Monmouth Baptist Church 191
Mountain View Community Church 202
Moon, Lottie 76, 79, 80
multi-ethnic 28
Multi-Housing Church Planting 70
multi-racial 28
Muslim 94, 168
Muslims 150, 151, 160, 168

N

NAMB 40, 41, 45, 46, 69, 70, 71, 79, 80, 91, 92, 93, 96, 100, 103, 104, 107, 115, 140, 142, 151, 157, 164, 181, 208, 209, 210, 211, 225, 227, 244, 248
National Baptist Convention, U.S.A. 61
National Baptists 64, 65
Native Americans 29, 58, 144, 146, 147, 148, 150, 151, 152, 153, 154, 155, 156, 157, 158, 165, 166, 185, 236, 237, 244, Native American 29, 58, 144, 146, 147, 148, 150, 151, 152, 153, 154, 155, 156, 157, 158, 165, 166, 185, 236, 237, 244
Navajo 151, 237
Ndonga, Robert 71
New American Nation 111, 117, 233
New Covenant Baptist Church 202
New Hampshire Confession of Faith 220
New Hope 177
New Orleans Baptist Association 70
New Orleans Baptist Theological Seminary 173, 203
Nguyen, Minh Ha 9, 53, 83, 84, 245
Nicaragua 34
non-Anglo 8, 27, 39, 40, 41, 43, 45, 160, 224
Non-Native or tribal people 147
North American Mission Board 10, 40, 42, 45, 69, 80, 96, 100, 115, 116, 149, 150, 151, 173, 179, 208, 225, 228, 235, 237, 242, 244, 246, 247, 248, 249

O

Offutt, Garland 63
Oldham, Roger S. (Sing) 10, 11, 171, 218
Oñate, Juan de 120

P

Page, Frank S. 3, 9, 13, 43, 45, 171, 222, 242, 246
Palmer, Wait 56
Paredes, Carlos 126
Patterson, Paige 38
Paul, Kim 10, 37, 53, 83, 245
people group 8, 19, 106, 144, 146, 158, 165, 197, 215
People's Republic of China 89, 101, 110
Perez, Joel 203
Perkins, Bill 68
Pew Research Center 127, 168, 234, 235
Philadelphia Baptist Church 203
Philippines 83, 90, 94, 95, 96, 110, 117, 232
Pigg, Michael 203
Pilgrims 54, 83
Pollard, Robert T. 60
Pol Pot 85, 86

Pow Wows 146
Pratt, Richard H. 148, 237
Precept 177
Prestonwood en Español 140
Public Law 959 152, 237
Puerto Ricans 120, 121

Q

Quassey 54

R

race relations 58, 66
Race Relations Sunday 64, 66, 67
racial reconciliation 3
Racial Reconciliation Resolution 42
Racial Reconciliation Task Force 38, 39, 227
Ray, Cecil 188
Ray, Susan 188
recommendations, Convention, SBC 3, 36, 37, 38, 43, 51, 114, 129, 131, 140, 142, 165, 166, 215, 222
Reconstruction 59
Redwood Empire Association 68
resettlement 8, 86, 87, 105, 106, 112, 113, 125, 126, 197
resolution 7, 36, 38, 39, 58, 132, 189, 210
Resolution on Racial Reconciliation 12
Revolutionary War 56, 231
Rice, Luther 57, 244
Richmond African Baptist Missionary Society 57
Rising Star Baptist Church 39, 69
Roman Catholics 168
Romo, Oscar 8, 125, 126, 197
Russian 166, 167, 168

S

Sabians 168
Sac and Fox 151
Sanchez, Daniel 9, 15, 16, 53, 120
SBC Executive Committee 10, 48, 172
SBC Implementation Task Force 38
SBC Inter-Agency Council 38, 227
SBC LIFE 38, 48
sbc.net 179, 183, 184
SBC President's Notebook 43, 51
SBC seminaries 38, 99, 103, 142, 225
SBMF. *See also* Southern Baptist Messianic Fellowship
sbwomen@sbc.net 183

Second Great Awakening 56
Seminary Extension 142
Seminole 150, 152, 237
Sena, Bobby 9, 10, 37, 53, 83, 123
Send City 72, 75
Send North America 91, 140
Shadow Mountain en Español 140
Sharpe, Henry 56
Sharp, Mary Jo 179
Sierra Leone 57
Silver Bluff 56, 230
Simmons, Willie 67
Simpson, Samuel 66
Sin, Jeremy 100
slavery 36, 54, 55, 57, 58, 60, 163, 186, 187
slaves 54, 56, 58, 163, 186, 230
Smith, Chip 203
Smith, Joshua 70
Smith, Roland 62, 64
Smith, Shannon 203
Smith, Sid 42, 55, 66, 67, 68, 69, 228, 231
South Carolina Baptists 187
Southeastern Baptist Theological Seminary 173
Southern Baptist African American History Project 41
Southern Baptist Conservatives of Virginia 151
Southern Baptist Messianic Fellowship 164
Southern Baptist Pastor's Conference 52
Southwestern Baptist Theological Seminary 173
Spain 122
Spanish Americans 120, 121
Springfield Baptist Church 60
Springfield Church 67
Stanley, Richard 9, 15, 26, 225
Sullivan, James L. 218, 219, 239
Sunday school 60, 98, 141, 240
Sunday School Board 60, 67, 82, 218, 230

T

Tafoya, A. Scott 203
Teague, Collin, 57
Thailand 86, 90, 97, 99, 104, 105, 107, 110
The *Journal of Black Southern Baptist History* 41
The Southern Baptist Theological Seminary 41, 63, 66, 173, 221, 248, 249
Thurman, Michael 69
Tolbert, Mark 202, 203
Tomas Rivera Policy Institute 127
Towns, Elmer 225
Triennial Convention 57, 58

Tsoi, Simon 39
Turnipseed, Arvella 64
20/20 Vision 96

U

Union University 45
unreached 19
US Immigration and Naturalization Services 108
US Virgin Islands 70

V

Vacation Bible School 135, 155, 190
Valentine, Foy 64
Vang, Joshua 97
Vang, Tong Zong 98
VBS 177
Vernon, William T. 66
Vietnam 83, 84, 90, 97, 98, 104, 105, 107, 108, 109, 110, 111, 112, 113, 114, 116, 117, 197, 233, 245
Vietnamese 28, 84, 86, 101, 107, 108, 109, 110, 111, 112, 113, 114, 117, 118, 126, 197, 233
Vietnamese Communist government 109, 110
Villarreal, Elizondo Marcos 203
Virginia Foreign Mission Society 58
Virginia Sugg Furrow Foundation 10

W

Warfield, Steven 68
Weatherby, Ken 45, 70, 171, 184, 202
Webb, Rodney 9, 53, 171, 185, 248
Weeks, A.E.L. 62
Wells, Elgia (Jay) 68
Western Baptist Association 202
Wilborn, James A., Jr 67
Wilson, Robert 9, 53, 68
Woman's Missionary Union/WMU 66, 70, 98, 102, 103, 173, 177, 181, 195, 222
Women's Leadership Forum 176
women's ministry 174
Women's Ministry Advisory Council 171
Woodman, Cliff 203

Y

Yanes, Peter 9, 53, 83, 84, 249
Yazidis 168
Young, Joe 203

Z

Zamore, Lennox 9

www.ingramcontent.com/pod-product-compliance
Lightning Source LLC
Chambersburg PA
CBHW071358160426
42811CB00111B/2239/J